MENCKEN DOESN'T LIVE HERE ANYMORE

Mencken Doesn't Live Here Anymore

Tales of Baltimore In The 1980s

By Dan Rodricks

A collection of his columns edited
by Dr. Judith Dobler
assistant professor of writing
and media, Loyola College in Maryland

Sunspot Books
GALILEO PRESS • BALTIMORE • 1989

Copyright © 1989 by Dan Rodricks

Published by Galileo Press Ltd.
7215 York Road, Baltimore, Maryland, 21212

Sunspot Books is the non-fiction imprint of The Galileo Press

Cover Photo: Jed Kirschbaum
Cover Design: David McElroy, Silver Shoe Graphics

LIBRARY OF CONGRESS CATALOGING-IN-PUBLICATION DATA
Rodricks, Dan, 1954 -
Mencken doesn't live here anymore: tales of Baltimore in the
1980s / by Dan Rodricks; edited by Judith Dobler. p. cm.

ISBN 0-913123-27-7: $18.95

1. Baltimore (Md.) -- Social life and customs.
I. Dobler, Judith, 1944- II. Title F189.B15R63 1989
975.2'6043--dc20   89-21900
CIP

ACKNOWLEDGEMENTS

All of the pieces in this book were previously published in The Baltimore Sun and are reprinted here with permission of The Sun

Special thanks to the Loyola College Word Processing Center (Nancy Marshall, Marion Wielgosz, Melia Peisinger and Carla Bundick) and editorial assistants: Jennifer Meyer, Nini Sarmiento, Ann O'Grady, Christine Canale, Stacey Tiedge and Kathi Klaus.

Production of this book would not have been possible without the support of Dr. David Roswell, Dean of the College of Arts and Sciences at Loyola College in Maryland.

The overall support of The Maryland State Council on the Arts and our annual donors underwrites the operations of The Galileo Press Ltd., a tax-exempt non-profit corporation organized under the laws of the state of Maryland.

To Joseph A. Rodricks

and

Rose M. Rodricks (the former Rose Popolo)

who lit the candles for me

"The Baltimore of today is not innocent."

"The indubitable charm of the old town . . . Stay there long enough and it will infallibly descend upon you and consume you, and you will remain a Baltimorean, in spirit if not in bodily presence, to the end of your days."

"What fool would be in New York tonight, dodging the taxicabs, blinded by the whiskey signs, robbed by the waiters? Who would leave Baltimore, once Baltimore has taken him to her arms?"

-- H.L. Mencken, 1913

FOREWORDS

On my first day as a police reporter for the Baltimore *Evening Sun* in 1946, an old hand from the opposition *News-Post* decided to start me off right. At seven o'clock in the morning, we went to a bar in East Baltimore somewhere -- was it Henrietta Street, or maybe Boston Street? -- and he offered a toast to my new career.

"This is called Gin and It," he said. "We have it every morning here to start the day." It was a small glass of gin with a few drops of Angostura Bitters in it. I had to drink it and I almost got sick at my stomach.

From there, I went to the Western District Police station to start the working day. On entering the dark, grimy building, I was about to approach the desk sergeant and tell him, "I'm the new man from the Sunpapers." This, I was told, would open any door. But the desk sergeant was otherwise engaged. A girl was sitting in his lap. She patted his cheek, smiled, and said, "Okay Sarge, what's new in the old Western District this morning?" I was in trouble. Sex was superior to Sunpapers in the Western District.

I was beginning my life in the newspaper business and in the world Dan Rodricks knows so well -- Baltimore of the side streets. In the months that followed, I had access to the city -- from Guilford to Brooklyn, Dundalk to Catonsville, Greene Street to the Green Spring Valley -- as only a newspaper reporter does. I found laughs in unexpected places. Like Police Court.

Judge Walter Dewees of the Northwestern District had a chronic case he didn't know exactly what to do with. He was a middle-aged alcoholic, a soft, wispy, quiet man who lived with his mother. Every few months, he would go on a binge severe enough that he ended up in court. His Honor would lecture him, plead with him, but finally send him to jail for a spell, hoping that shock treatment might help.

He had almost forgotten the man until a week before Christmas, when he received a poem in the mail, written from

City Jail. It was a plea to be released to spend Christmas with his mother, and forty years later, the opening line still rings in my mind.

"A wonderful judge is Walter Dewees, Northwestern District, thank you, please..." It wasn't Shakespeare, but it got the job done. He went home for Christmas and was back in court by New Year's.

I found sadness surrounded by luxury when my city Editor Edwin P. Young Jr. sent me to a lovely home in Guilford. "Lady's husband's been missing for six months," he said. "I have an idea he wants to be missing. Ask the lady for a picture, say we'd like to help find him."

I asked her, through the small opening she left when she opened the door. "I have no picture," she said. "And I have nothing to say." Her face seemed to say that Ed Young was right.

I learned about the real world of the slums. An idealistic young man from the Housing Department took me to a slum home. He showed me the bites on the children from the rats that crawled into their beds at night. He showed me the gap under the battered front door where the rats made their entrance. Then he nailed a thick board across the empty space. The next day, he brought me back to show me the hole the rats had gnawed in the board to make their usual nightly foray into one man's castle. I learned more about my city in the few months I was a police reporter than in all the time since.

Dan Rodricks has, by choice, spent his career in side-street Baltimore. His writing evokes the smell of crab cakes, the slur of the language called Bawlmerese, the silent screams of the homeless, and most of all, the warm feeling that Baltimore gives a person as it envelops him in its casual, underplayed life style.

Dan leads us through Baltimore by telling us of the midget lying asleep in the bar near Mencken's house, the "Mayor" of the neighborhood called Pigtown playing cards with his pals.

The real mayor of Baltimore -- Rodricks calls him Willie Don Schaefer -- christening the National Aquarium by jumping in the seal pool in an old-fashioned bathing suit and a straw hat, playing with his rubber duck. He takes us to many bars and a few funerals, to early morning on West Pratt Street near Pulaski, and to the birth of a foal at Sagamore Farm on a frosty, moonlit October night.

In this book, we join an old-fashioned throwback of a ballplayer named Dempsey on the greatest day of his life, when he became the World Series Most Valuable Player, and a little boy named Jason on his happiest day, when the Fort McHenry American Legion Post gave him the wheelchair he had longed for.

Margaret and I have long remembered a Baltimore grand dame introducing a friend of ours from Greenwich, Connecticut, to everyone at an Elkridge Club wedding reception as "Mr. Yudain . . . from out of town." Provincial? Insular? Indeed. To the true Baltimorean, there is only Baltimore and "out of town."

But Dan Rodricks has found what I found when I moved here at age thirteen, and what Margaret and I found when we came home again after a thirty-year sabbatical in the New York-Connecticut area.

Baltimore is not a pretender. It is itself, Formstone fronts, painted screens, and all. It is also Stuart Janney, Jr., gentleman sportsman. He was four-time winner of the Maryland Hunt Cup as a rider, Princeton Phi Beta Kappa, Harvard Law, owner of Ruffian and the 1988 favorite for the Kentucky Derby, Private Times.

At the age of eighty-one, a few months before his death, he agreed to a lengthy television interview, probably his first. At the end of the session, as a lady associate director was leaving, he said, "Please excuse me for not rising, but things like this tire me out these days." A Baltimore gentleman is a gentleman to the end.

And if Harbor Place should last a thousand years, and the re-making of Baltimore should continue forever, there still will be oyster roasts and bull roasts and Highlandtown and Pigtown and Bawlmer accents and -- yes, the Bachelor's Cotillion and the Worthington Valley, too.

Dan Rodricks knows all this and tells us about it in this excellent book.

He really knows us.

And imagine.

He came here from out of town.

-Jim McKay

NOW, MY TURN

A wise man, lost in history, once said, "The more things change, the more they remain the same." Dan Rodricks' collection of columns, which have appeared in *The Evening Sun*, verified this truth. Dan Rodricks is currently a columnist for *The Evening Sun*, writing about what is happening today. Jim and I were reporters, hanging out in the city room of that paper forty years ago, and we knew all these people of whom Rodricks is writing. We met them in dirty bars and on dirty street corners and we wrote their stories.

We took a long sabbatical in New York and Connecticut and we are now back home where we belong. While we were away, the city changed. It grew a new face. Old buildings came down and new buildings rose from the ashes. The Beltway is a ribbon of traffic around the city, a glittering necklace of lights by night, and the Bay Bridge is a triumphant arch over the Chesapeake. And, of course, there is the miracle of Pratt Street and the Inner Harbor, and the renovation of the crumbling, old slum houses into handsome townhouses of the 1800s.

But Dan Rodricks is not writing about the Inner Harbor and the renovated houses. He is writing about the town that hasn't changed much. He is not much concerned with the building and the shops and the restaurants. He by-passes the Symphony and the theatre and the museums and galleries. He looks for his stories among the ordinary people who pass through this quick life with no particular distinction, no special accomplishment, with a minimum of joy and a high quotient of pain. He is the chronicler of Every Man.

There is a little of H. L. Mencken in Rodricks, and a bit of O. Henry and Damon Runyon. But mostly it is pure Rodricks, writing with warmth and kindness and extraordinary understanding about the losers. He does not stray too far uptown. He strolls the back alleys, the police courts, the shabby places. He is drawn to the nondescript and he observes them with extraordinary vision and a wry humor, and always, with sympathy. He listens and he hears all the sounds, the sighs, the whimpers and the whines, the little cries, and the occasional laughter, sometimes gentle, sometimes raucous.

In our time of excessive hype and peculiar values, when the dropping of names, however manufactured, is the parlor game to play, and celebrities come and go like flash fires, Rodricks goes his own and different way. He covers the nobodies. In their lives he finds meaning and goodness and courage, even hope. He carefully pulls away the onion skin until he gets to the heart. That's all this book is about -- the heart of the matter.

Jim and I are very proud to be a small part of it.

-Margaret McManus

AUTHOR'S NOTE

Henry Mencken never left the town and, though the Baltimore he described so affectionately in verbose essay is long lost to the ages, I can understand why the man kept 1524 Hollins as a home address for all but four years of his life. The other four, the Mencken matrimonial years, were spent at 704 Cathedral. The sage went to New York City one week every month to edit *The American Mercury*, but he hated New York. A man of his talents, reputation, and eccentricities could have been a smash at the Algonquin Club, could have travelled fast and giddily with the literati of his time, but he chose to sweat it out in tank top in his Baltimore backyard. Mencken preferred the style and quality of life here and championed it in his travels.

I do much the same now. I enjoy the opportunity to talk Baltimore up when in the company of quick-lipped friends from Boston and New York. They warned me years ago that, by taking a job at *The Evening Sun* -- Mencken's newspaper -- I was signing on for a hitch in a backwater. "A couple of years there and you'll be dying for New York, any place with a heartbeat," said a chum who believed the world spun around Madison Avenue and that the only baseball team worth a damn wore pinstripes. Fred Allen once said, "Anything outside of New York City is Bridgeport." That kind of attitude still prevails in the media, in arts and entertainment. But there are those of us who came of age in an increasingly mobile society, who found life beyond the George Washington Bridge, and I don't mean Jersey.

I was born in Brockton, Massachusetts, which was Rocky Marciano's hometown. I attended college in Bridgeport, which was P. T. Barnum's haunt. I ended up in Baltimore, which Mencken loved and could never leave. After thirteen years here, I know why Mencken had such a hard time packing his bags. Though the city I adopted in 1976 was vastly different from the one Mencken adored -- I think Henry would have a hard time adjusting to the Baltimore of today -- I came swiftly to love it. As you'll see from my "Epistle to Tourists" the city still has enough charm to offset all its drawbacks. I like Baltimore for its lack of pretension, for its determination not to emulate New York in any way. (I used to wish we had New York-quality pizza but even in that department Baltimore has made impressive gains.)

So I am a lucky man. I have the best job in the world. As a wise man said, writing a newspaper column is like making love to a nymphomaniac -- as soon as you finish you have to start all over again. But in Baltimore, there's always plenty of material to start all over again with. Early reporting chores at *The Evening Sun* accorded me a chance to learn the city fast. Within just a few days, I knew that while it might be pronounced Droodle, it's spelled Druid Hill. I learned the street names, the names of cops and firefighters. A family in Little Italy, the Mannettas, adopted me as a second son. Mencken was right: "Who would leave Baltimore, once Baltimore has taken him to her arms?"

Before he died in 1988, I had numerous chances to thank Philip Heisler, *The Evening Sun's* late managing editor, for the opportunity to become a columnist, even though I was only twenty-four at the time, terribly unsure of myself, and tempted to test the waters in a larger city. Once Heisler gave me the column, I tried to keep faith with my upbringing as a reporter. Always, to me, the story was the thing; the cutting edge I needed to make the column complete as an article of informed opinion would come later, with time. So I used the telephone and I took to the streets. I learned something new about the city every day. It was, and remains, a joyous job. And I feel lucky to have had this assignment in Baltimore during a time when the city shed its tattered old overcoat for a new suit. I feel lucky to have witnessed the entertaining mayoralty of William Donald Schaefer, the brief tenure of Du Burns, and the rise of Kurt Schmoke.

Mostly I feel lucky to have worked with people who became dear friends, who helped me and supported me through the day-to-day grind of producing a column. Mike Wentzel, always offering a lead; Mike Wheatley, the editor who provided the most help in developing the column, in giving it voice; Carl

Schoettler, the best writer I know and the man whose fine hands put a luster on some otherwise dull tomes. Allow me to add more names to the list of people to whom I am indebted for editorial guidance, inspiration, and comradeship: George Hanst, Frank Roylance, Bob Byrnes, Michael Hill, Dave McElroy, Dave Cohn, Wayne Hardin, Elaine Nichols, Sue Reid, the Sunpapers librarians, Mac Finney, Wally Reid, Jim Bready, Jed Kirschbaum, Mike Shultz, Kathy Klein, Mike Kane, Fred Rasmussen, John Scholz, Ernie Imhoff, the late Nick Yengich, the late Dave Woods, Paul Mindus, Neil Grauer, Joan Jacobson, Linell Smith, Norman Wilson, Sharon Dickman, Bob Keller, Jeff Valentine, Karin Barry, Alan Doelp, Stephanie Shapiro, Scott Duncan, Mike Bowler, Mike Lane, Patrick Gilbert, Tom James, Lee Baylin. I thank Jack Lemmon, who succeeded Phil Heisler as managing editor, and Jim Day and Dan Donahue, Vince Bagli, Rudy Miller, Ken Brown, Phil Dypsky, John Cooke, Milton Bates, people of conscience like Sister Patty, Ralph Moore, Lois Hess, Brendan Walsh, and Willa Bickham. All these people -- and many others -- have helped keep me in the game for the last ten years. I would also like to thank Andy Ciofalo and Judith Dobler Ciofalo for their support, encouragement and hard work in assembling this book.

Most of all, I thank my wife Lillian Donnard, who stuck with me through some periods of utter darkness that threatened to incapacitate me as a writer. I am a lucky man, in more ways than I wish to share right now. This little gig started on a cold Monday, January 8, 1979. I really never thought I could last this long. Only my wife and my friends -- and all the people of Baltimore who have touched my life -- could have made it possible. To them, I say thank you.

Dan Rodricks
Baltimore, July 1989

CONTENTS

Forewords (by Jim McKay and Margaret McManus)... v
Author's Note x

THE CITY

A Epistle To Tourists 2
Snow: Baltimore's Best Excuse 8
Willie Don Turns Sixty. 10
Harborplace Opens 13
A Gourmet Slice Of Life -- Cheap. 15
Baltimore Under Glass 18
Welcome, Mr. Schmoke 20
The Angel Of Reservoir Hill 22
Code F 26
Fireman In The Water! 29
Classic Street, Baltimore. 34
Baltimore, When The Light Is Perfect 36
A Sign Of The City 38

CRIME AND PUNISHMENT

The Pigeon. 42
Gold Street 45
They Like Soap Operas 48
Pardon, But Your Slip-up Shows 50
The Southern Went Dark 53
All Dolled Up 57
No Demonstrations For David Gordon. 59
In Which A Comma Counts 62
Mr. Levitt In Handcuffs At Last. 64
Televised Justice 66

GOOD SPORTS

Bobby Bags The Elephant 70
Rick Dempsey's Greatest Day. 72
The Last Kiss 75
Balls 77
Foul Ball 80
The Legend As Legacy. 82
Bush Hog Builds Character 84
More to Fishin' Than Catchin' 87
Native Flesh And Blood 89

THE NEIGHBORHOOD

The Ripe Stuff 94
Inventive Look At Future Past 96
O Ye Great Urban Homesteader 99
The Good Doctor. 101
Pigtown Will Shine Tonight. 104
The Korean Down The Street. 107
Kindness Still A Feast Of Life 110
White Marble Steps 112
The Clock Stopped 115

SOCIAL STUDIES

Mr. President, Get A Job 120
State Of The Union 122
The Story Of Frank 125
Dollars And Cents 128
Our Daily Bread 130
A Wish For Charlie 133
Couple Dollars, Old Friend. 135
They Tried To Save Margaret. 137

The Vicar Died With AIDS 141
Every Creature Born 144

AT HOME

Swept Away 148
Greenhouse Affect 150
Pit Bulls They're Not 153
Garlic Earns Bouquets. 155
Joey -- Born Again 157
Screwdriver Will Do, In A Pinch 159
Maryland's Best Kept Secret 162

HISTORY LESSONS

Search For The Pride 166
Hometown Boy. 169
Home From Beirut 172
Reagan's Tribute To Beirut Dead 176
Colonel Shred 178
Requiem For A Survivor. 181
Nations Under Stone 183

SIGNIFICANT OTHERS

Little Sun Man. 188
Soft Shoes 190
Turkey Joe's Was Some Joint. 193
Blue Baby. 196
The Old Boyfriend 198
Ida And Grace 201
Billy Boy. 203
The Piano Man. 205

A Lively Smile To Stand On 208
The Beauty of Hilda. 210
Gift From A Stranger 213

CHRISTMAS CAROLS

A Christmas Wish Or Two 218
Christmas Rose. 220
Light For Sergio 223
Little Eddie's Big Night 225
A Chair For Jason 228
The Man Who Had Everything 230

ENDPAPER

Postface (by Alexander Clunas) 233

THE CITY

In which we note the behavior of powerful men, the transformation of a city, the rise of the sun, and the simple events in the life and times of good old Baltimore.

AN EPISTLE TO TOURISTS

While there is always a chance of getting mugged in good old Baltimore -- as there is such a chance, I suppose, in any American city -- there is a much better chance that a visitor to this burg might find himself invited to dinner by a dentist. This happened to me a few years ago, and I hold the experience up as evidence of the kind of hospitality that endears Baltimore to new arrivals.

Afflicted with a swollen mouth, I was referred to an East Baltimore tooth doc named Charlie. Charlie agreed to fix me up after hours. When he had sufficiently lessened the pain, Charlie suggested I try out my chops on dinner at Haussner's, the art museum/restaurant where every dish on the long, long menu is practically guaranteed to be fresh and hearty -- from the pigs knuckles to the crab imperial. Charlie knew all the waitresses. "They come to me," he said. "They have a great dental plan here."

So there I was, having suffered miserably with a tooth ache all day, being treated to sour beef, dumplings, creamed spinach, and fried eggplant by a dentist. The only condition of Charlie's hospitality was that I avoid ordering anything causing cavities. Thus, I passed up the strawberry cheesecake. But who could complain? When was the last time a dentist worked overtime, then treated you to dinner?

I suppose this kind of thing could happen to anyone anywhere. But I dare say it's the sort of thing more likely to happen in Baltimore.

Certainly the town has problems: quarter-only parking meters, sleazy car-towing services, decrepit housing, drugs, crime, industrial pollution, slow cab service, and largely mediocre pizza. But, having spent too much time in places like Brockton, Massachusetts, and Bridgeport, Connecticut, let me tell you: Baltimore is A'Kay. The city doesn't beat you up every day. It scores high on the folksy charm meter. The people are pleasant and friendly, and they talk funny. The town is peculiar, weird, eclectic, intimate, obstinate, a bit bohemian, and sometimes even cosmopolitan. Small town, big city. Home of John Waters and William Donald Schaefer. Oz On The Chesapeake.

Baltimore has many secrets. Harborplace is not one of them. Neither is Little Italy. Every visitor gets advice to go to these places, and I guess that's all right. But if you really want to inhale authentic Baltimore atmosphere, get the hell away from downtown. Go for crabs at Gunning's in Brooklyn or Bud's on Lombard Street. Expect the waitresses to be friendly but business-like, the meal to be beautifully sloppy. Go with a veteran crab-picker who can show you the procedure, watch carefully, and repeat. You'll notice that while the waitress provides a wooden mallet, a real Baltimore crab-picker makes limited use of this tool. Don't get carried away with the mallet; it's not necessary. The crab is already dead and if you make too much noise, everyone in the crab house will know you're from out of town. And do not ask to have your crabs washed off; we eat them with plenty of seasoning here. Baltimore is hospitable, but it's also stuck in its ways.

Pick a neighborhood bar for an after-dinner drink. The more modest the exterior, the better the atmosphere inside. I never take visitors to trendy new joints. Recently, we stopped at a place on Hanover Street, Johnny's Old-Time Rock N' Roll, where the Orioles game was on television and the barmaid was perfectly glum. Drink the beer straight from the can. If you go to Silk's in Canton, make sure you get there well before midnight because that's when the joint closes and, even if your drink is still fresh, the lady of the house will kick you out. Baltimore is hospitable, but it's also stuck in its ways.

If you are fortunate enough to make the right connections for a ticket to a bullroast, you will have gained passage to a uniquely Baltimore happening, staged annually by civic, fraternal, and political mobs in church halls or catering establishments. These events are sometimes called oyster roasts or bull-and-oyster roasts, names the newcomer will find confusing. Let me assure you that, whatever is stated on the ticket, in Baltimore you will never be asked to dine on "roasted arsters." Chesapeake oysters, when available, are served raw, on the half shell, though there is a chance you will find oyster fritters at a bull roast. You will find plenty of grilled beef, usually cooked over large steel pits outside the rear door of the hall.

Baltimoreans take cardboard plates with them to fetch the beef from the outdoor buffet, and I have seen men with impressive stomachs lined up for oysters with three or four of these plates in their hands. Point of etiquette: it is wise to tip the shucker handsomely (and purposely associate your tip with your face) the first time around, rather than try to wrestle dollar bills from your pocket while juggling plates of oysters. Second, third, and fourth helpings are encouraged at bullroasts. There is usually music and dancing, but the main point of Baltimore bullroasting is the consumption of food and the enjoyment of conversation.

John Waters has already declared Baltimore the "hairdo capitol of the world." And there is no better way to understand what Waters was getting at than by attending a Baltimore bullroast, preferably one during an election year anywhere east of Patterson Park. You will see hair as you have not seen hair since 1962, and I guarantee that you will readily appreciate what is meant by the expression "Bullroast-Class Curls," for some of them are so large you will become convinced that the women who sport them used coffee cans to shape them.

My favorite Friday lunch is the perogi, that East European ravioli made fresh by the ladies of St. Michael's Catholic Ukrainian Church on Wolfe Street. You can get the perogis to go, they're not expensive, and they will definitely stick with you for the rest of the day. Plus, proceeds from perogi sales go to the building fund for a new church.

You want steamed shrimp? Go to the John Stevens in Fells Point, a great place to absorb atmosphere. The last time I was there, a goofy poet read me some of his new poems. Almost any place in Fells Point offers a good time; it's really hard to go wrong there, though my Yuppie brother once encountered a Saturday night fist fight in one of the bars. Baltimore is hospitable, but we don't take no guff from nobody, hon.

The idea that Baltimore was a slow little backwater proved to be myth. I had only been here a few months when some wayward angel crashed his airplane in Memorial Stadium after a Colts game. The Colts may be gone now but their last years here provided great theater with Bob Irsay, the kooky owner, as lead clown. For great dinner conversation, just mention his name among locals. You will hear Irsay's name bandied about with scorn. From virtually the first day the man gained control of Baltimore's Grand Ole Team he was out of control.

The Colts dynasty tottered and Irsay alienated Baltimore football fans, which, given their almost maniacal loyalty, was an impressive achievement. And he held the city hostage, refusing to sign a long-term lease for Memorial Stadium, flying about the country to be courted by other cities, until finally in 1984, he had the Colts' equipment packed in moving vans and shipped to Indianapolis in the middle of a snowy night.

Just a couple of months earlier, Irsay had denied he was intending to move the team -- and denied he was lying when he denied he was intending to move the team. "I'm a good Catholic," he told us. "Don Schaefer is my friend."

Don Schaefer actually would have liked to punch Irsay's lights out. As mayor of Baltimore, he considered losing the Colts a profound tragedy. Has there ever been a public official who took such public matters, matters beyond his control, so personally? Schaefer was so bent out of whack after the Colts left town that a gang of his lackeys in City Hall decided he needed to be cheered up, and this needed to be done in a big way, for the Schaefer ego was as large as it was fragile.

The city, it was alleged, was suffering from a case of municipal depression after the Colts left. This was malarkey. The Colts had been a rotten team for years. The fans hated Irsay. When he left, there was far more sighing than weeping. But Schaefer, peculiar man that he is, brooded. Some Schaefer sycophant in City Hall got the idea for Pink Positive Day. A play on Think Positive, get it? There would be a day so named, featuring a city-wide, come-on-get-happy festival in the streets. People were encouraged to wear pink. Public works crews painted sidewalk curbs pink. Local TV anchors wore pink carnations.

I recommended that city mounted police feed their horses pink straw so they could leave little pink plops on city boulevards. Schaefer, the pouting child, came out of his brood. Pink Positive Day gave him a chance to mug for the cameras and carry on, as is his way. He is a strange bird, this one: politically keen, intimidating, temperamental, spiteful, unpredictable.

He was mayor when Baltimore rose from the ashes, and so he gets credit for the glorious things that have happened to downtown Baltimore in the 1980s. Never have I seen a pol so chauvinistic about the palatinate he governed, and never one so simultaneously bold and insecure about it. Baltimore was Schaefer's town. This was all the bachelor mayor had ever known or cared about. He defended it. He boosted it relentlessly. The way he carried on in public -- in striped Victorian tanker and straw boater, swimming with a rubber duckie in the seal pool the day the National Aquarium opened here in 1981 -- who will ever forget it? The man could be so deeply incensed one moment, so silly the next. Whatever it takes. Whatever it takes. Mr. Mayor, we'd like you to dress up in this turkey suit. Whatever it takes. Mr. Mayor, we'd like you to dress up like a big turtle. Whatever it takes.

His hero was Richard Daley, and, knowing this, I used to wonder what The Boss would have made of a guy who kissed rubber duckies in public. But this buffoonish man got things done. No denying it. There's been a lot of concrete poured in Baltimore in the last ten years. The meek skyline I first saw when I came to Baltimore in 1976 is lost from memory now. Schaefer gave this city a kick in the pants; it's been on a roll ever since. After fifteen years as mayor, he finally went on to become governor, taking his imperial ego with him. The day he left for Annapolis, he stepped inside a large gift box. The box was sealed and hoisted onto a boat with a crane. The box was marked, "Baltimore's Gift to Maryland." I'm glad Big Don is still around. In New York, columnist Jimmy Breslin had Hugh Carey, whom he called Society Carey, "a dream character in dancing pumps." After ten years of columns, I still have Don Schaefer, whom I call Don Donaldo, Lord Governor, a dream character in clown shoes.

And there's the rest of the cast of characters, some now sadly absent who, for better or worse, gave this town its reputation for the peculiar: Spiro Agnew, Mary Avara, Edith The Egg Lady, Eddie The Chicken Man, Charlie The Lamp Man, Foto Lewis, Rudy *The Sun* Lies Man, Mr. Diz, Jeffrey Levitt, Abe Sherman (go to his newsstand on Park Avenue; you can still feel Abe's grumbling presence).

Never a dull moment in this town. Just when things slow down, some politician gets indicted. Or the governor has a fit in public. Or some schnook attempts the crime of the century. A few years ago, two guys tried to rob a bank by tying one end of a chain to a night deposit box, the other to the bumper of their car. When they hit the gas, the bumper broke off. The yahoos fled the scene, leaving the bumper -- and the license tag -- behind. Baltimore may not be New York, but there's always something strange in the wind.

And while the town is big on honky-tonk, it has class, too. If you don't want Old Bay and crab mustard all over your fingers and necktie, you can always go to places like the Belvedere Hotel or the Prime Rib, the Brass Elephant or Marconi's. If you can find the front door, Martick's isn't a bad place for a delightful dinner, either. Another nice, unpretentious place is Henninger's Ale House on Bank Street. You can have your palm read at the Palmer House, too. And then there's Frankie Bova, reading tarot cards daily and giving thoroughly optimistic predictions at Pizza Palazzo on North Howard.

I could go on, but I won't because no tourist deserves to know too many of Baltimore's secrets. You've got to stay and work the town, which is what I did. You've got to have enough sense to know that Harborplace, while nice, ain't Baltimore. So, as Moe used to tell Larry and Curly: "Spppprrrreeeeaaaadddd out!" Check out the side streets; they are many and colorful, and the seedier they are the greater the potential for discovery. Watch for muggers. But also watch for that folksy charm I'm talking about; it'll grab you long before any mugger does.

April 14, 1988

SNOW: BALTIMORE'S BEST EXCUSE

The breathless radio announcer with the all-points-bulletin voice said Overeaters Anonymous was cancelled. I bet that announcement brought happy sighs to rush hour last night. If there's anything good to be said about an approaching Killer Snowstorm, it's that some happy fatties get a night to indulge their human desires. Bless their hearts.

Everyone thinks it's the fear of being snowbound that sends snowanoid Baltimoreans to grocery stores to stock up on chicken noodle soup, bagels, and Doritos. But I think it has more to do with organized dieters preparing for a night off from organized guilt. What other explanation for Overeaters Anonymous being so swift to cancel its meeting yesterday? Another myth has it that school kids are the only living things that look forward to snow cancellations. But snow cancellations delight plump adults who hate diet therapy, expectant mothers sick of prenatal clinics, pets sick of pet-grooming classes, board members bored with board meetings, and just about anyone who'd rather be home doing nearly nothing anyway.

Snow hysteria -- and all the cancellations it causes -- is good for anyone who ever joined anything they didn't want to join in the first place. It's life's best excuse for getting back, as Billy Clyde Puckett says, to life its ownself: eating and sleeping, eating and drinking, baking bread and making love. Most important of all, snow hysteria is a comfort to those of us who possess a chilling fear of getting into a slip-sliding road accident on the way to something we'd rather not go to.

Take Overeaters Anonymous, for instance. Now that's a private thing, just what it says: anonymous. No one wants to run the risk of their private activities ending up on Metro Traffic Control. No one wants it getting out that they cracked up the car in a desperate attempt to get to a binge-eater therapy session. "Oh, Charlie," suddenly sympathetic friends say the next day, "we didn't know." People, after all, are very conscious of how things look -- especially if they have a fear of imminent danger or even death. Take clean underwear, for example. The wearing of it has less to do with personal hygiene that it does with saving face, so to speak, in an emergency ward.

Somewhere out there is a chap who always keeps a copy of *The Brothers Karamazov* by his bedside on the chance the good Lord doesn't let him make it through the night. Of course, he never reads *The Brothers Karamazov*. But he figures it'll be a nice detail for someone to include in a eulogy: "Charlie was such a well-read man, intimate with the great writings. Why, the night before he died, he was reading Dostoevsky." No one wants it said he went to the great beyond after thumbing through the January issue of *Hustler*.

I think the same psychology applies to all the things people do when weather permits -- and all the things that get cancelled when it doesn't. We know that, deep down, our friends aren't going to be very sympathetic about a car that gets totaled on the way to aerobics. Of course, this is just a theory. But so far, it's the best explanation I've come up with for snow hysteria, something I've been trying to figure out since moving to Maryland from Massachusetts nine years ago.

Baltimoreans react hysterically to the threat -- indeed, the rumor! -- of snow. It's as if arms control talks broke off and some Russian Boomers were on their way to Hunt Valley Mall. The radio announcers and TV weatherpersons turn on their Emergency Broadcast System voices. And life gets cancelled.

Yesterday, the meeting of the Anne Arundel County Literacy Council was cancelled. So were gatherings of Compassionate Friends, the Howard County Board of Education, the Reisterstown Civil Air Patrol, Baltimore County Police Community Relations, Child Birthing at Union Memorial Hospital, Retired Firefighters, the National Organization for Women. There were so many Nights of Games -- even one at a monastery, according to the radio -- being put down that I'd need a three-part series to mention them all.

Thing is, I doubt the public at large was too broken up about all that. Give a guy a chance to put off until tomorrow something he'd rather not do tonight, and he'll jump at the offer. What? No chair-caning class tonight? Gee, that's too bad.

So I think I've finally found the reason why Baltimoreans, more than any other group of living things in the northeastern United States, allow themselves to become victims of snow hysteria. It's a big act to get out of doing everything they do but would rather not do.

When you think about it, the scheme is quite ingenious, mass psychology that works for the common man's good. We've been trying for years to find a way out of aerobics and diet workshops and PTA meetings. And here it is, simple as nature, as life its ownself: snow from the sky. And the snow doesn't even have to fall for the scheme to work! Baltimoreans, I applaud you.

January 11, 1985

WILLIE DON TURNS SIXTY

The cab driver and the English language had not yet reached an understanding, so he kept leaning over the front seat, spewing cigarette smoke and yelling: "Bah-Hee Zerk? You say Bah-Hee Zerk? Not know this place, please!"

"Barre Circle," I said. "Baaaaarrrrrreeeee."

The cabby didn't know Barre Circle because he hadn't taken many fares there. On that cloudy winter day in 1976, Barre Circle was a deserted slum. So we drove around and around. After fifteen minutes, the driver announced that he didn't like the scenery, which was of vacant buildings, chain link fencing, and graffiti. Finally, the cabby spotted West Barre Street. And there was William Donald Schaefer, in a topcoat, sort of waddling along, in the company of two of his devoted disciples: Robert C. Embry Jr., then city housing commissioner, and

Roger Windsor, from the city's homeownership development office.

Someone had placed a portable podium in the middle of the street. And now William Donald Schaefer, the mayor of a city climbing out of its worst days, strutted behind this podium, looked up and out, and started his song. His eyes went into orbit, focused on a distant planet. Snow whipped his face. He punched the air with his fist.

"This is a great day for the city of Baltimore," he said, as if addressing multitudes. Actually, I was the only pencil-pusher there. Walter McCardell, a *Sun* photographer, was there. So were Ed Smith and Jim Mustard, a cameraman-reporter team from Channel 11. Dick Davis, information officer for the housing department, might have been there. But that's all. Didn't matter to the mayor. William Donald Schaefer looked up and over my head, over the glass eye of the TV camera, over the shambles of this deserted street and proclaimed February 3, 1976, "a great day for the city of Baltimore."

That day, William Donald Schaefer announced that 125 houses would be auctioned off for a dollar each in the city's infant homesteading program. "Instead of tearing everything down," the mayor said, "we have moved toward preservation." Notice the use of the "we" in the declaration. William Donald Schaefer's old sweetheart -- the city -- moved toward preservation, renaissance, and renovation and all those other things that have become cliches since he started his mayoral road show ten years ago today. Today also happens to be his sixtieth birthday.

When he pumped the city from his platform, reporters and editorial writers snickered and grew quickly bored. But Schaefer sang the jingle for so long, people started to learn the lyrics. They saw his name on signs and park benches and trash cans and sanitation trucks. Every announcement, be it about solid waste or shopsteading, was "a great day for the city of Baltimore," brought to you by William Donald Schaefer, mayor.

And if the press didn't believe every word, didn't jump to join the chorus, Schaefer would spew shrapnel. His scarlet-forehead temper is legend. In 1977, after *The Sun* printed an important series of stories which linked Baltimore's relatively high cancer rate to heavy industry, Schaefer marched into a press conference with the clipped-out articles in hand.

"We're in a life and death struggle with cities in the Sun Belt," he said. "Can you imagine what they're going to do with this? We're trying to bring industry in . . . and I can just see the reaction of people when they're looking for places to go. They are going to think this is a cancerous area." Another time, Schaefer summoned the press to the lobby of Penn Station to announce a major renovation plan. "This is a great day for the city of Baltimore," he said.

That was almost six years ago, and the Penn Station renovations have progressed at a considerably slower pace than other projects. But who's counting? After a couple thousand choruses of "Great Days For The City Of Baltimore," the crowd must be feeling pretty good. The host, after all, knew how to enliven the joint. And now a lot of people believe. They know the lyrics. The mayor of Baltimore can jump into a pool at the National Aquarium with a rubber duckie, and no one blinks.

I still hear a lot of well-founded moaning out there. But the fellow has shown vision, and you can't deny a good public relations man his successes. Bring up Schaefer's name in conversation with ten people from the right part of town, and seven or eight will talk about him as if he were a popular, though somewhat eccentric uncle -- the one who remembers all birthdays and can fix a leaky roof. As of this date, he hasn't become a snob; at least he doesn't show it. If all the accolades and national attention went to his head, they stopped just below his jowls. He still inspects cracks in sidewalks, still lives in his boyhood home, still whines like a cranky baby, still works late and worries a lot. All are signs of health.

One Saturday night, I was cracking crabs at Bud's and looked up to see this chunky middle-aged man in a suit. He was standing by the juke box waiting for his ladyfriend, Hilda Mae Snoops, to emerge from a restroom. And that's all he was doing, just standing there, and no one paid much attention. I waved hello, and he waved back. I was tempted to ask how he was doing but remembered I already knew the answer. No matter how William Donald Schaefer was doing, "This is a great day for the city of Baltimore." And if I begged to differ, he'd probably have looked up and over my head, out to his imaginary multitudes, to start another chorus.

November 2, 1981

HARBORPLACE OPENS

And now look! ... Look at the castle by the water. Look at the pleasure dome called Harborplace. Look at the big, beautiful, fast-money dazzle. Look at the House of Rouse. Merchants, stained glass, wicker chairs, gourmet goat stew, kites galore, everything for the palate, and much, much more. Look at the people swarming to the feet of their temptress-queen. Look at the Renaissance Mayor, coming into the harbor with his fleet. Look. Just look.

A few blocks and a million miles from Harborplace, in a small kingdom void of fine cuisine and fashionable shops, Winky Rich and Junior June pass the time with make-believe royalty. They play with kings and queens, black and white. They straddle a bench and ponder a chess board, a well-used chess board. It's the thinking man's game, the only thing that keeps Winky going in the summer. Fingers leave chin and grab the opponent's bishop. Fingers leave chin and dispatch a knight. Check. It goes on for hours. The day is pleasant and chess is a fine way to keep the mind in gear.

The sky is sweet over West Baltimore. A soft breeze stirs the weeds in the cracks in the sidewalk at North Gilmor and Fayette. Cars go by. Old men sit on stoops and talk to themselves. Old women waddle along with shopping bags full of rags. Up the block, at West Lexington, a city summer crew makes a new crosswalk on a street that needs much more. They don't use paint here. They use long strips of some kind of white vinyl adhesive. Then they lay the strips down and press them against the street. Afterward, they throw the scraps on the sidewalk.

And now look! . . . Look at the vacant houses behind the chain-link fence, with the cracked paint, with the trash and the boarded-up windows and the old man leaning on his cane and picking something off the sidewalk. Look at the alley with the pile of garbage, with the malnourished scavenger dog and the kids playing with rusty Tonka Toys on the curb. Just look.

Junior June owns the used-furniture shop across the street. His chess rival is Winky Rich and he's good, real good. When you've been out of work for a year, there is plenty of time to practice.

"No jobs," Winky says. "Most of my friends are out of work. Harborplace is a real good thing for the city but it's not the only thing that needs to be done. There are no jobs. No work. You have to find, like a popular business, to attract workers so that people can find jobs and build up the industry again. Only then," he adds, "can people go down to that nice place and spend their money. But I'm not going. I got no money to spend." Then Winky squints a little, crosses his arms and says, "I just don't care anymore. I just put up with it, and go from one day to the next."

The voice of frustration comes up out of the streets all the time, not just now, on the eve of Baltimore's great adventure at the Inner Harbor. Last August, when Jimmy Carter came to East Lanvale street, the people on the sidewalk said they needed jobs. They spoke of the need for housing, better schools, and more.

And now we come to Harborplace, and those needs are still with us. Unlike the snow that brought out the looters in 1979, they won't go away. The Bureau of Labor Statistics claims more than half of inner-city blacks between sixteen and nineteen were unemployed last year. Baltimore is one of the nation's biggest welfare cities, with payments going to more than 148,200 city residents each month, while still more receive social services. There are more than twenty thousand families waiting for public housing. And the people who throw these numbers around say all of this, all of this desperate talk, has nothing to do with today's main event. "Half of the people in Baltimore," says a worker at a housing assistance agency, "have nothing in common with Harborplace."

Tonight, Baltimore clears away some of its trash, creates an immense launching pad, and throws rockets at the moon. Spirits are high and it takes a wayward soldier to find too much fault with the experiment of Harborplace. It is indeed a marvelous adventure. But there are people who have gone way overboard. They want to make James Rouse a hero and have us believe that Harborplace will save the city. Today is the day, in the words of one establishmentarian, "when Baltimore truly passes over an invisible line into a new era."

New eras are seldom noticed at North Gilmor and Fayette. So this kind of sentiment gets lost on men like Winky Rich, Junior June, and their friends who are out of work and cling to a rope of quiet desperation. So when the rockets shoot toward the moon, Winky Rich and Junior June will probably play chess. Harborplace may be great; it just has nothing to do with them.

July 20, 1980

A GOURMET SLICE OF LIFE -- CHEAP

I am walking this marvelous stretch of West Pratt Street, from Payson to Pulaski, and it is alive. It is *right raw*. It is filled to the brim, bustling, sweaty, and swollen with the results of decades of human habitation. Sometimes, it looks as though an earthquake rattled all the rowhouses of West Baltimore and all the tables, chairs, hair-dryers, fat boys, ceramic cats, and grandmothers landed on this block. Stand there, stick your hand out in any direction, and you are in touch with life, with the intimate, obstinate old Baltimore the Rouse Company left behind.

Morning breaks with a cascade of events. Four guys wait on steps for another guy to arrive with a bottle; they smell of booze and too many days in the sun. A fat lady with no front teeth comes bounding across Pratt; she's wearing a T-shirt, pushing a soda bottle through her pucker, walking and yelling at her daughter the whole time. A kid comes crying out of the Rite Aid because mama didn't buy her anything. A woman sprays cleaning fluid on a storefront window. Lovers lean against a van and kiss. There's a guy in the street, looking west and yelling, "Wa-a-a-a-lter!" What a mad, mad world this is.

It's a shopper's paradise, too. Harborplace, about twenty blocks east, has nothing over this place. Ruth Cooper was on the sidewalk yesterday selling silver skull earrings and old paperbacks for twenty-five cents. Among these books were *Fell's Guide to Mobile Home Living, Holistic Running, The Lunatic Fringe,* and Truffaut's *The 400 Blows.* Ruth had a problem recently. She was gabbing on the sidewalk and some young man sneaked through the front door and up to the second floor of her house. Ruth figures the guy was up there four, maybe five hours before she discovered him -- and she only discovered him when he came out the front door with her purse. He couldn't use the rear door because it was blocked by a stove.

There are stoves all over this part of town, some of them abandoned, some of them for sale. Refrigerators, too. In fact, there's a refrigerator on the sidewalk in front of Barry's Appliance right now. They're asking a hundred dollars for it.

You can buy anything here, from fresh fish to dead men's sport coats. There are thrift stores: Veterans Warehouse, Volunteers of America, Value Village. There's a fish market that used to be someone's garage. The Discount Outlet has a magnificent window display: laminated portraits of Hulk Hogan, Jesse "The Body" Ventura, unicorns, and saints. Offered for sale are Hulk Hogan pillows ($3.99), two-pound bags of Mountain Mist polyester stuffing, and some of the largest and most exquisite ceramic pigs in this city that adores ceramics and rather likes pigs. Across the street, there's a nameless little shop with old Star Wars figurines for sale ($1.50 each) along with ceramic unicorns (there is a lot of unicorn worship in this part of town), owls, horses, puppies, and a minibust of Jesus. How all this stuff ends up for sale on West Pratt Street is a mystery. It is my theory that while we sleep, the earth roars and quakes and all bric-a-brac falls out of buildings and lands here, and someone puts a price tag on it.

The door to Lucky 3 Groomer Dog Grooming & Pet Care opens. A guy with Popeye arms, thick eyeglasses, and a beard walks out. He's wearing a T-shirt, blue bell-bottoms, and cowboy boots. His petite gray poodle has just been groomed. The poodle looks stunning. Its owner looks like he could use a makeover.

Apple peddlers arrived here in the morning. They come every fall. They come in from Western Maryland or West Virginia to sell fresh apples, red and yellow Delicious, out of the back of a station wagon or pickup. I talk to two of them. They are from West Virginia; neither wants his name in the newspaper. "I'm a Christian man," one of them explains. "I've never been in jail and never had my name in the newspaper."

They drove up from Martinsburg with fresh apples picked the day before. "Got 'em from my ex-brother-in-law's place," the other one says. "Bohemians pick 'em." They were getting a dollar a bag, twenty-five cents apiece on the street yesterday.

"See, I got sugar," the other one says. "I sell apples to keep busy 'cause I got high sugar." I buy two bags of apples from the guy with high sugar. I buy four paperbacks from Ruth Cooper. I buy a dead man's sport coat from the Veterans Warehouse. Whole thing costs $7.10, with no charge for the color and pageantry of Pratt Street.

What does $7.10 get you in Harborplace?

October 10, 1986

BALTIMORE UNDER GLASS

Two men -- one with a gun, the other with approximately two hundred dollars owed to the gunman -- came sprinting down North Fulton Avenue. Shots rang out. It was the middle of a summer day in the city of Baltimore.

"It was last year," said the man everyone calls Kimmy. "Soon as they got to this corner, the first guy, he jump into my store." The store is an old grocery, packed -- *packed* -- with retail-goods, at West Lexington and Fulton. Columns of cereal boxes nearly touch the ceiling. Winter hats, gloves, umbrellas, and scarves hang from criss-crossed clothesline over a pyramid of groceries in the middle of the floor. Yesterday, three old women were in the place carefully checking the price of buns and applesauce. The clerk, Kimmy's wife, worked behind thick, smudged glass covered with earrings and other trinkets.

"My cousin was working behind the glass that day," Kimmy explained, a cigarette burning between fingers of his right hand. "The one guy come in the store and he stands over there. The gunman, he didn't come into the store but he shoot into the store." One of the shots wounded the guy who owed money. "I was three hours cleaning up after the police," Kimmy said. Another bullet ricocheted off the small revolving window on the side of the glass cashier booth. It hit a girl in the arm. The girl was shopping at the time. This is one of the stories Kimmy told when asked about life as a small-business man in West Baltimore. He's been a small-business man in West Baltimore for fifteen years.

"One time a guy comes in and holds gun to my wife's face," he said. "That was ten year ago. She'd only been here two weeks from Korea. She started crying. I put in all the bulletproof glass then. I got a gun." The gun, a black revolver, hangs in a holster against a vest under Kimmy's winter jacket. There's a beeper in a pocket in the vest.

Kimmy is a busy guy. Spirited. Energetic. Funny. Tough. He works seven a.m. til nine p.m. He owns the grocery as well as the deli one block north. Events in this deli last Monday night go on the list of crime experiences in Kimmy's fifteen years as a small-businessman in West Baltimore.

"The one who was standing here, he'd just ordered cheese steak," said Johnny, full name Ki Young Yoon. He is brother-in-law to Kimmy. He manages the deli. He stood in the deli's small waiting room yesterday morning, just a few steps off Fulton Avenue. "The one here," he added, pointing to a spot directly in front of the cashier's revolving window, "he just yell through glass, 'More cheese, please! More cheese, please!' And they shoot him, right here, just like that. . . . And this one, standing next to, he got shot. He died too."

There were four young men in the deli at five minutes before eleven Monday night. Johnny was behind the counter, behind the glass, facing them. "There was another in corner," Johnny said. "And one more boy in front of him." Someone holding a nine millimeter pistol walked in on them all. The one who ordered the cheese steak sub was shot in the head. He was twenty-three years old, the thirty-sixth homicide victim in Baltimore in the first fifty-eight days of 1989. The kid next to him died early Wednesday morning. He was fourteen, the city's thirty-seventh homicide. The two others in the room were wounded. Bullets left round, nickel-size dents in the plexiglas that separates the waiting room from the kitchen. In two spots, bullets pierced the glass. One of them winged Johnny's left side and left a scratch.

"One other time, guy come in here," Johnny said, "must have been two year ago. There were five people in here. He hold up gun, then he shoot. Then they got into fight and they run out." Another shooting, another story. Johnny and Kimmy do business in West Baltimore and, from time to time, the other business of West Baltimore -- drugs and all related crime -- bangs into their lives. Johnny and his wife work behind the glass all day, then they go upstairs to sleep with their nine-month-old son. Next day they're behind the glass again. If Washington is a "city under siege," Baltimore is at least a city under glass, which creates a kind of siege of its own.

"Nobody shoot in Korea," Johnny explained. "You don't know my country, eh? Nobody shoot. Nobody have gun. Not my people."

"I call police about gangs on the corner," Kimmy said. "The old people, after three or four o'clock, they can't come out." And Kimmy and his extended family stay behind the glass.

March 3, 1989

WELCOME, MR. SCHMOKE

On the day he was elected mayor of Baltimore, a day filled with great promise, it was decided for Kurt L. Schmoke that his first order of business should be the location of suitable domicile for the woman called Mrs. Hutchins. This consensus was reached in a street corner caucus at Broadway and Eager by people who, from their windows, seldom see the strong stoop to help the weak.

It was dusk when Mrs. Hutchins, evicted from her apartment last Thursday, walked into the alley behind 1002 Broadway to show where she had spent recent nights. Trash two feet deep was packed against the wall of the building and this line of garbage continued around a corner and into a rear yard. Here is where Mrs. Hutchins, a young woman with a pleasant face, said she had tried to sleep.

"On those steps," Mrs. Hutchins said, and she pointed to a dislodged concrete stoop in the middle of the yard. Her furniture had been put in the alley. The police told her not to sleep on the steps. After they left, she sat in one of her chairs in the alley until the sun came up. She wore a heavy tan coat and a wool scarf. She had missed two rent payments, and her landlord moved a new tenant into her apartment as soon as he had moved Mrs. Hutchins out.

"Two hundred dollars," Mrs. Hutchins said her rent was, and her monthly welfare check is only $170. If she was supposed to receive an additional subsidy from her government, it apparently did not come in time to please the landlord. How, with $170 a month, she managed to make any payments at all -- and why, knowing of her income limits, the landlord agreed to take her as a tenant in the first place -- remain questions without answers today. But this much is true: On election day, Mrs. Hutchins was on the street and her furniture was in an alley. And this is typical of how a person becomes homeless in the city Kurt Schmoke now inherits.

The weak cry out for the help of the strong, and that was the song of Broadway on Election Day. "Jobs," said Gerald Carter, who was sitting on steps across the street.

"Tell him jobs," answered Leroy Scott, seated next to him. "Decent jobs. And tell him decent homes for black people. *Not* just black people. People who need. They set that woman out over there, put her stuff in the alley. It was terrible."

"It's ridiculous what they pay for these rat-infested homes," Carter went on. "Most of them should be condemned. They get $190, $195 for some of them; most of them are $200 and $250, roof's fallin' in. They get twenty dollars for the deposit on the key to go look at a house. That's right. Twenty dollars just to go look at the house; they don't even *go* with you to show you the house. You should see some of these homes."

"And the schools," said Scott, who became angry at the mention of the name of Baltimore's last elected mayor. "Schaefer's only concern was building up that Inner Harbor to bring in the tourists. Look at all the money went in that harbor and look at the schools. Kids carryin' guns in the schools, half the time schools got no heat in the winter. Do you know something? I been to that harbor four times in my life; it's done nothing for me that I know of. Tell Schmoke to get on these landlords and get these houses done up."

Carter stood and pointed to the work gloves in his hip pocket. "I do day work. That's the best I can get."

Still, with all these groans, it was election day and Baltimore was finally electing a black mayor. "Yeah, I'm happy to see it," Carter added. "Schmoke knows a little more about what it is."

"He's got to know more than Schaefer did," said Scott, and if that was one angry man's indictment of the previous order, it also was an assertion of faith in the new one.

"I don't care what color he is," said Carter. "Green, black, white. . . . What's he gonna do for me? We'll wait and see on that."

Schmoke has energy and brains, but also considerable sensitivity to the problems that groan like faults in the earth just below the new concrete of this resurgent metropolis. Everyone knew those problems were there, knew all along, but put off facing them. Schmoke knows the cycle: shabby housing, shabby schools, shabby lives for people who deserve better.

Fortunately, Baltimore is a city of considerable momentum, a city on a roll. The Schaefer years left Schmoke with much to build on -- but also much to build up. Substandard schools, deplorable housing, a lack of jobs in the inner city, children with guns, women without homes -- all of these things are now handed over to Kurt Schmoke. They make a dark inheritance. They make an exquisite challenge.

November 4, 1987

THE ANGEL OF RESERVOIR HILL

By seven o'clock, the pews of First Emmanuel Baptist Church were swelling with people in winter coats and sweaters. Many more stood three-deep in the side aisles and, for the better part of an hour, still more walked in twos up the main aisle to the little casket bearing the body of La-Tonya Wallace.

The mayor of Baltimore found an opening and walked quickly to a seat at the front of the church.

An organist played quietly as the choir assembled in the chancel behind him. On the white wall above the choir was a cross bearing seven red lights. As they came to view the body, the mourners, many of them children, turned away quickly, some with quiet sobs, others with heavy grief. The City Council president took a seat near the mayor.

A United States senator came into the church. The principal and teachers from La-Tonya's school, Eutaw-Marshburn Elementary, filled at least one pew. A detective who had spent another day hunting La-Tonya's killer viewed the body, said something to the family, then found standing room to the far right of the sanctuary. The temperature inside the church rose quickly. White-gloved ushers passed out cardboard fans and small paper booklets with La-Tonya's face on the cover.

Starting just after dusk, people came in groups from the rowhouses and apartment buildings of Reservoir Hill, across Park Avenue, to the small brick church where La-Tonya was a Sunday school student. The last time she was in this church alive -- Sunday, January 31, just two days before she was strangled and stabbed -- La-Tonya was called upon to read a psalm.

"She didn't know which one to read," Rita Lyle, her Sunday school teacher, said. "I gave her the Twenty-third Psalm . . . The Lord is my Shepherd. And La-Tonya read that in the main church."

Last night, at La-Tonya's funeral, a preacher with a heavy voice read that psalm. As he did this, you tried to imagine a child speaking those same, familiar words. You tried to imagine what this child was like, for everyone who knew her made it clear: If you never met La-Tonya Wallace, you missed a chance to smile, a chance for fresh hope. "If there was any child who was going to get out of this neighborhood and do something with her life, she was one of them," said the Reverend Eugene Belcher, pastor of First Emmanuel.

La-Tonya was a good student in a city where too many students drop out of school. She was bright, asked a lot of questions, got involved, had a hungry mind, liked the library, took part in Sunday school projects. Just last week, she helped with the Black History Month display on the bulletin board in the church basement. "And as we walked home from church that Sunday," said Rita Lyle, "she promised me she was going to make Sunday school every Sunday."

Now the church was packed. The viewing ended. The casket was closed. The Reverend Aggie Brown asked the mayor of Baltimore to speak. Kurt Schmoke rose from his seat and stepped softly to the center pulpit, just above the casket. He had never looked so pained in public. He cleared his throat. When words came from his mouth, they were quiet and broken.

"Mrs. Holley," he said, looking down to La-Tonya's mother, Natalie Holley. "To the family and friends . . ." The mayor stopped and cleared his throat.

"I . . . ah," he started again. "This is a terrible tragedy . . . not only for your family . . . but for the entire city . . ."

And the voice broke again. Right here, right now, the weight of an entire city shifted to the young mayor's shoulders and there was beauty in his honesty, his humanity, and his humility. Kurt Schmoke was committing his heart to Baltimore -- to its children, to its future -- with a soft, broken speech over a little casket. This child had given tired school teachers hope, and that aspect of the tragedy seemed to reach Schmoke somewhere deep inside. And what the mayor felt, the people in the church felt.

"La-Tonya," he started again, "was Baltimore's child."

"Yes," the people answered him. "Amen . . . Yes."

"I had the privilege, just a few weeks ago, to visit La-Tonya's school. . . . I don't know if I touched her. . . ." Schmoke's voice broke again, and for a moment you could see him among school kids, reaching for their small hands in a classroom. "But it's obvious she touched many lives. . . . And God touched her life. . . . Now she is home." There was silence as the mayor returned to his seat.

Now Mary Pat Clarke, the City Council president, came to the pulpit and confessed to tears, like everyone else, for this little girl who died so violently. "She sounded like such a wonderful go-getter," Clarke said, and there was in her words and her voice a trembling sadness for all the pain a city suffers on the way to the future. Clarke asked for prayers for La-Tonya's friends, that "those who were children with her might grow up to live in a better world." The people answered her passionately.

Barbara Mikulski, the United States senator, went to the pulpit and confessed anger, like everyone else, over the death of this little girl. Anger over "all the things -- the poverty, the ignorance, the greed -- that kills little girls." God had called up another angel, Mikulski said, "an angel named La-Tonya . . . the angel of Reservoir Hill . . . an angel to us all."

And then the assembly broke into full applause. It was a stunning moment in the life of this city -- three of its most important leaders exposing their deepest feelings over the casket of a little girl. It is difficult to recall a time when a tragedy -- and the city has experienced many -- affected so many so profoundly, and compelled politicians to public tears. The more you heard about La-Tonya Wallace -- and how she touched so many people -- the more you ached.

Her principal, Louise Smith, asked all teachers, students, and parents of Eutaw-Marshburn Elementary to stand as she spoke from the pulpit. La-Tonya, she said, had been a teacher. "She taught us how to be happy; she was one of the happiest children I've ever known. . . . She taught us how to smile. . . . She taught us how to love. . . . She taught us how to dream a dream. . . ."

And she was just eleven years old.

Another hour of song and prayer, and the service was finished, and the people filed out of the church and onto Park Avenue, which was dark and cold. Twenty men and women held floral bouquets and formed a line on the sidewalk. Then pallbearers carried the little casket down the stairs to the hearse. The avenue was very crowded, very quiet. The mayor waved politely to some people and walked silently up the street to his car.

February 10, 1988

CODE F

In that moment after his men had beaten the fire and one of his lieutenants went into the house, Mike Caplan, the thirty-eight-year-old battalion chief, waited for the message on the radio. He had been fearing the worst ever since he awoke in the station and saw the hour. "Any time I have a dwelling fire at four in the morning, I know I have a life problem," Caplan said.

It was only a matter of minutes between the time Lieutenant Thomas Poe, of 22 Truck, went to the second floor of the rowhouse on Park Heights Avenue and his radio message came back to Caplan, who was on the sidewalk.

"Request your presence on the second floor, Chief," the voice said. There was a certain tired defeat in the voice, and Caplan knew the only reason he'd be called to the second floor: fire had killed again in Baltimore.

"Okay, I'll be right up."

Caplan walked into the living room, where the fire had started and eaten walls clean to the brick. The sofa, where a cigarette had smoldered early in the morning, was nothing but a charred frame and black springs now. Caplan walked up the stairs, a light in his hand. The first floor was dark and hot; the second floor was even hotter. Caplan met Poe at the top of the stairs.

"We got fatalities," Poe said.

"How many?"

Poe said either four or five.

Caplan radioed fire communications: "Be advised that I have a Code F times four, minimum." This meant there were at least four deaths at 4147 Park Heights Avenue. At headquarters, acting Deputy Chief Joseph Spadaro prepared to make a run out to the house.

On the second floor, it was now Caplan and his hand light and the dark bedrooms. He walked past Poe to the rear room at the top of the stairs. The door to the room had been cracked open about two feet. When Caplan pressed his hand against the door, he felt pressure from the inside. He poked his head and the hand with the light through the opening. On the floor by the door was a woman, her body on its side. She was wearing a dress. There was a man on the floor next to her. He was on his knees. His body was hunched over, and his head touched the floor.

Caplan spent only a few seconds making a mental note of this scene. Then he turned and walked down the hall, past still firefighters with trances on their faces. He walked through the next doorway, flashed his light, and saw the bodies of two children on the floor by the bed in the center of the room. He did not spend a lot of time there either. His tour had one more stop.

The three windows in the front bedroom had been raised. Someone had opened them, more than likely the young girl on the floor. Caplan found her when he walked around the side of the bed in the room. He also found two smaller children, one in diapers. The children had stopped here, probably because the fire had shot through the front windows on the first floor, leaped around the porch roof and up to the windows of their bedroom. "Children are the worst part," Caplan said later in the day. "They don't have anything to do with this. They're just there when it happens."

When he came back into the hallway, Caplan remembers that his men were standing around, just staring into the darkness. There was a long, tedious pause until he said something that started the men moving again. He remembers taking one last look through the second floor and shaking his head and allowing himself a moment with the tragedy and futility of a Baltimore rowhouse fire. Then he went back outside.

All activity around the house stopped now, as firefighters made way for investigators. The men who had fought this fire went out to the street and took off their helmets and sat down on the curbs. The younger men kept staring at the house. Spadaro, who fourteen years ago first inspired Mike Caplan to become a Baltimore City firefighter, arrived. Caplan met him out front.

"What do you have, Mike?" Spadaro asked.

"Seven fatalities."

Caplan remembers seeing a strained look of disbelief on his superior's face, just before Spadaro went into the house. "You go into something like that," Spadaro said, "and no matter how many times you do it, you never get used to it, you never do." Soon the fire chief, Pete O'Connor, was on the scene and he took command.

In four days, seventeen people had died in Baltimore rowhouse fires. And at headquarters, they know this too well. They know they've tried to educate people. They've tried to put smoke detectors in houses. Yesterday morning, a fire official was on the phone and he said: "What the *hell* can we do? It's carelessness. It's just *carelessness*. It makes you feel like tucking it all in and going home." And there is nothing more to say; there never is. Later in the morning, Mike Caplan went home to his apartment, showered, and made french toast for breakfast. In the afternoon, he and his men went back to the station on Reisterstown Road.

May 19, 1982

FIREMAN IN THE WATER!

Don Schafer had a nice fat plate of steamed jumbo shrimp and thick grilled steak lined up for dinner, succulent leftovers from a family cookout, just the kind of meal a Baltimore firefighter loves. It was a few minutes after five o'clock Sunday evening, May 18. Schafer, fresh on his shift, slid the plate of shrimp and steak into the microwave at the firehouse on Patterson Park Avenue, home of 24 Engine. He was primed for dinner. He raised his finger to push the button on the oven.

Then the call came. Big fire in Fells Point. Bottom of Broadway. Sixteen-hundred block Thames Street. The old Terminal Warehouse. Shrimp and steak would have to wait. Schafer left his dinner in the oven. He pulled on his boots and turnout coat and stepped into the jump seat of the truck. The truck headed for Thames Street.

The fire was out of control and roaring like thunder. The old pier was seventy yards long, its planking very dry, and its pilings saturated with creosote. The fire had started on the far end of the pier. It already had eaten several yards of wood. It was now gobbling a large shed and rolling toward a warehouse that fronted on Thames Street. On the other side of Thames Street were buildings in which people live and drink. Clouds of smoke climbed several hundred yards into the sky and the wind pushed it north until it darkened and fouled city streets a half-mile away.

Schafer and ten other firefighters grabbed a hose and carried it along a catwalk on the northern edge of the pier. They fired water at the blaze, hoping to keep it from spreading deeper into the shed or into the six-story warehouse. So powerful was the fire that Schafer and his buddies needed air masks to breathe. The smoke was so thick Schafer could not see the firefighter in front of him. There was nothing but heat and a curtain of gray.

Schafer held his stretch of hose and took tiny steps toward the fire. He could see nothing. Moments later, the guns of a fireboat in the harbor opened up and a long, powerful stream of water hit the fire from the far end of the pier. When this happened, the fire heaved toward Schafer and the other men from 24 Engine. It pushed them back toward Thames Street. "It rushed toward us," Schafer says. "The smoke was so thick I couldn't see the guys who were working with me. At that point, you feel like you're alone. You know other guys are holding the hose, but you can't see them. I knew I was somewhere near the edge of the pier, but I couldn't see it."

There was a ferocious gush of heat and smoke. Someone yelled, "Get outta here!"

Schafer felt the hose drop. He squatted, turned, and started to crawl away from the fire. He reached for the hose on the pier, hoping to follow it back out to Thames Street. There was no railing on the pier. Schafer knew he was somewhere near the edge. His right foot slipped. He flipped sideways into the air. He spun upside down. He lost his helmet. He flipped right side up. His boots hit the water first. "This all happened so fast I had no idea what was happening to me. I flipped completely over. Did a one-and-a-half. I went into the water and started sinking immediately."

Schafer's turnout coat weighed ten pounds. His blue air bottle weighed thirty-five pounds; it was strapped over his shoulders and buckled around his waist. Water gushed into his boots, which were pulled to mid-thigh.

In the water, as on the pier in the midst of smoke, Schafer could see nothing. "It was pitch black down there. I was hyperventilating. I was panicking. I tried to move my arms to swim. I was so heavy I didn't dare stop moving my arms. I must have gone down about fifteen feet. I was kicking frantically. My right boot came off. What's funny is, I had been thinking about getting thicker socks. I had been wearing thin socks and they made my boots loose and I was getting blisters on my feet. I wanted to get thicker socks to make the boots fit better." But he hadn't a chance to do that.

And now, in the harbor, alone in the blackness, the air from his bottle keeping him alive, the mask tight against his face, Don Schafer was lucky for thin socks. He kicked again. And again. The left boot started to slip. "It took me another ten or fifteen seconds to get it completely off. As soon as I felt the boot slip off, I felt myself going up."

Schafer is twenty-seven years old. He is a third-generation Baltimore City firefighter. He weighs a hundred sixty tight pounds. He and his father, who just celebrated thirty years with the department, lift weights. They both have muscular arms. It was the muscles in his arms that brought Don Schafer to the surface again.

"As soon as my head popped out, I ripped off the mask. It's a positive pressure mask. A good thing, too. Because it kept the air coming the whole time and kept the water out. It's not like the old masks we had. With the old masks, you had to suck for air. With these new ones, you feel better because the air is always there." When Schafer came to the surface, he was still in darkness, still in smoke. The pier was still burning wildly.

The Plexiglas plate of his air mask had separated from the regulator, which is the mechanism that brings air from the bottle on his back. Schafer wanted to release the thirty-five-pound air tank. But the moment he tried this, he started to sink again. "I didn't dare stop swimming after that. I guess I was five feet from the pier. I tried to make it over to a piling. I couldn't see . . . I swam toward the pier. I made it to the piling. I grabbed it and held it with my legs and arms. I still have a mark on my legs where I held the piling."

Now Schafer was sopping wet, still weighed down by turnout coat and air bottle, clinging to a pier that was old and dry and burning like hell above him. He had almost drowned. Now he was in position to either suffocate or burn.

"I looked under the pier and I saw this board between the pilings. It was a piece of wood connecting the pilings. Horizontal. I thought maybe I could get to that and straddle myself over it." He was out of breath, out of energy. He didn't have the strength to cling to the piling anymore. So Schafer used one last rush of energy to leap toward that wide board. The board ran between pilings along the surface of the water.

"I leaped and didn't really make it. But I still had my gloves on and one of them snagged the board. So I was able to sort of pull myself over using the glove." He got to the board and flopped over it. He felt his heart throbbing in his throat. He removed the air bottle from his back and placed it on the board with him. Then he removed his coat. He draped that over the board, too. He could see the fire eating the pier about ten feet above him.

"I don't know why, maybe it was because of a lack of oxygen, but I couldn't feel my hands or my feet. I thought I was going to die."

The heat bore down on him now. In a matter of minutes, his blue uniform shirt and blond hair dried. When the heat grew more intense, Schafer dropped his face in the water. This whole time he was semi-conscious, exhausted, terrified. Schafer remembers having a word or two with God. "I really thought that was it. The fire was directly over my head now. I was under that pier, I guess, four or five minutes."

Schafer thought about dropping off the board and floating out into the harbor where rescuers could see him. But he gave up on that idea, fearing that he would drown. He had no strength left. The smoke was still very thick. But apparently Schafer's blue shirt could be seen by people who had come to watch the fire from another pier. Police Agent David Datsko, who was on the next pier, called for the Police Department's rescue boat. There was so much panic and action on the pier above him, so much smoke and confusion, that Schafer's buddies from 24 Engine still hadn't missed him.

"I kept sticking my face in the water to cool it off. This police boat came out and made a couple of passes by the pier. The smoke was so thick they couldn't see me. And, I was yelling like crazy. I was yelling everything. I was talking to Him. I was saying, 'God, please, I don't want to die yet.' I was drying out real quick. I could feel the heat on my back."

Schafer saw the twenty-five-foot police boat pass him. The men in it couldn't see him. At that moment, Schafer saw bubbles in the water under the pier. His air bottle was still working. The bubbles came from the regulator, which was dangling in the water. Schafer grabbed it, held it to his mouth, sucked some air. His face was burning. He dropped it in the water again. He raised it from the water. An orange life ring hit him on the shoulder.

The men in the police boat -- Sergeant George Kirchenbauer and Officers Bill Geiger and John Bunker -- had heard Schafer's cries for help. One of them threw the life ring at the sound coming from the thick smoke. The sound was the guide to Schafer's position under the pier.

"We went in and out from the pier three times. We went directly into the smoke," says Geiger. "It was so hot we were afraid of the gasoline on the boat blowing up. We had to keep backing away. We heard him screaming. We yelled to him, 'Keep screaming, keep talking, we'll find you.'"

"Sergeant Kirchenbauer threw the life ring. I don't know how [Schafer] lived through this. When we got him, there was fire all around him -- on top of him, behind him, on all sides. He looked like charcoal when we brought him outta there." Schafer grabbed the life ring. The police boat towed him fifteen feet from the pier. Schafer had nothing left. The ring started slipping away. Geiger jumped in the water and grabbed him by the belt and hoisted him to the boat.

"When they grabbed me and got me in the boat, I heard all these people cheering," Schafer says, "like someone had just scored a touchdown." It was the crowd on the next pier, applauding the rescue. In the boat, Schafer worried that other firefighters might have fallen into the water; they hadn't. Then he looked back to the pier and the huge fire and, through the torn curtain of smoke, he managed a glimpse at his turnout coat. It was still draped over the board under the pier.

It was burning.

June 4, 1986

CLASSIC STREET, BALTIMORE

The border between the two worlds is a foggy veil. There is no fence. You hold out your hand to find the way from one to the other. You think you're in one world, but you're really in another. You dip into one, then stumble into the next. In Baltimore, two cities in one, it's easy to do.

On Charles Street, the Classic Address of Baltimore, you can buy a piece of chocolate mousse cake for $2.75 . . . or you can walk across the street and make a contribution to the old lady on the bench. And you can wonder about her. Wonder, in particular, if she's the woman we used to call Raggedy Ann. Is she the woman from the old Armistead Hotel? Was she among the old folks delivered to the street?

Could be.

But you're not sure. Something has happened to her since the hotel fell to a wrecker's ball. Her face is dark gray now. Her left cheek looks as if it were dragged across a bed of rocks. Her bruised arms are wrapped around her body. There's a chrome walker on the sidewalk in front of her. She is mumbling and looking up Classic Street. It is seven a.m. on a Saturday. One world dawns, another yawns. The troubled are up and about while the rest of us sleep off the good night.

Walk down this street, walk down any street in dear old Mobtown, and you step from one world to another. Just a couple blocks from the old woman of the decaying dawn, there is the new hotel with a doorman in white gloves and every room with a doorbell. Very nice . . . for $145 a night. The lobby floor is marble. The ceiling is adorned with a large chandelier. It is a place for the du Ponts while they're in town for the Preakness. It is a place for Yuppie pleasure.

On Franklin Street, the line for the soup kitchen forms outside the parking lot the businessmen use for lunch hour. They get out of their cars, don their gray plaid suit coats, and walk down to Tio Pepe's. They keep their backs to the ragged men in line at the soup kitchen. The ragged men in line at the soup kitchen keep their backs to the businessmen.

People were stunned to see the street man named David way out on Loch Raven Boulevard, near Taylor Avenue in Towson. He camped on the big lawn near the grove of trees by the fire station. He was there most of the summer. He carried plastic jugs and cardboard boxes and pieces of paper. He took notes. He wrote things. He listened to "Sanford & Son" on one of those radios with a TV wave. Everyone was surprised to find him there. Like the leopard of Kilimanjaro, no one has yet explained what David was seeking at that altitude.

Or what he was doing in the other world.

Your world looks rather pleasant without David in it. Your world is simple and solid and steady without the shadow of David. David makes us think too much, doesn't he? But, for thinking men and thinking women, there is no such thing as thinking too much. Consider the elders of the little shul on Park Heights Avenue. There they were, gathered on a pleasant Saturday morning in summer, thinking, discussing the holy books with a scholar, when a woman of the street walked in . . . when the ragged stepchild took a chair at the table.

"The kids call her bag lady," one of the elders said.

The men seldom have food at the shul. But there were some cookies. They gave the woman the cookies. "All our teachings say we must help," the elder said. "So what do you do? You help the little that you can." One of the men took her home and fed her and sent her on her way.

The woman showed up at the shul again another week. She discussed a passage from Isaiah with the men. "I would call her lucid," the elder said. "She answered questions. I guess she was in her thirties. That's what was pathetic about it. So young. She was pitifully dressed. She said she had come from Ohio, that her parents were alcoholic. . . . We haven't seen her since. . . . But I'm left wondering: how does this come about? What can we do about it? We discussed how in a country this rich -- thank the good Creator -- a country this rich, how this can go on. Here she was, brought right to our door."

One world knocking on another. Better the awkwardness and the discomfort it brings, better the thought it stirs...better that than the tower of ignorance . . . better that, say I, than the penthouse suite.

September 11, 1985

BALTIMORE, WHEN THE LIGHT IS PERFECT

Somewhere in the afternoon -- I'm not sure if it was when the fat man threw the cigar wrapper in the street or when the girl yelled at the guy in the truck -- the first light of October turned Baltimore, the whole city, into a thing of beauty. Each of its citizens, each of its trees, every square yard of its concrete appeared clean, fresh, real, and ready for the canvas.

I bet artists like Charlie Newton, John Kefover, maybe Tony DeSales, Gordie Marsh, or Joe Sheppard would like a couple of manic days sketching the hell out of Baltimore when it looks this good. And then they could close their pads and hustle back to the studio, the visions still fresh as the crack of day, and put it down -- put it all down -- and, most important, try to capture the sense of crisp but mellow light October brings.

October light is a very special light. It softens this tough, old city around the edges. It takes the harsh summer squint out of eyes. It seems to purify the air. It is this wonderful light that burns little moments into memory -- burns them in so deep that, no matter how many years go by, no matter how many new visions cover the old ones, the old ones are always there, always brilliant. It would be a shame to waste the first light of October.

So, if you had the day and the talent, what would you paint? Give me ten little portraits of the city, ten testaments to what life was like here in the first week of October, 1987.

If I were the one with the brush, I'd start with the fat man. He was beautiful. About fifty years old. Big thick neck with a baseball cap. He wore an orange T-shirt that said "Solid Waste" in big letters and "Bureau Of" in small letters. The back of the shirt said, "Trashball 87." He opened the door of his pickup truck on South Broadway. Before getting into the truck, he peeled the cellophane wrapper off a pack of cigars, stuck a cigar in his mouth, then threw the wrapper in the street. So much for Trashball 87. I'd call this painting "Job Security."

These don't have to be large cityscapes. Too many artists waste their talent painting the Inner Harbor. I'd like to see some artist sketch Baltimore the way Daumier sketched Paris: moments from the street, landlords showing apartments, an unhappy man visiting an in-law on a holiday, men swimming in the Seine, easy and ordinary stuff.

Give me a study of the girl I saw screaming at a guy in a truck. They were stopped at a light on Eastern Avenue in the afternoon. They were engaged in amorous violence. She was giving him an earful, and the October light was there in the truck with them. The guy looked besieged. I'd paint her hair flying, her mouth open, and him with eyes trained down on his hands. It was not a happy moment, but it happened. It was there in the street in the first week of October, 1987. I'd call it "Eastern Avenue Heartburn."

I'd paint the four people who were sitting at the counter in the Broadway Market, sipping coffee and reading newspapers in the light from the market windows. Out in the street was a guy with a camera. He was taking a picture of a sign in the window, but actually it appeared he was taking a picture of the people at the counter.

I'd paint the Highlandtown kid on the skateboard. I saw him on Ellwood Avenue. He would make an exquisite portrait of "Street Kid, 1987." He wore a denim jacket, T-shirt, shorts, and high-tops. Wind blowing in his face, he looked like an adolescent Al Pacino, had some wild glint in his eye.

I'd paint Mugs' place in Little Italy, with Mugs or his brother frying sausage behind the counter, and October light coming through the front door.

There were three stately elderly women waiting with shopping carts in the parcel pickup drive at the Giant on York Road. They looked quite beautiful in the October light. I wish Charlie Newton had a chance to put them on canvas.

Charlie, by the way, is one of the premier painters of the Baltimore scene. He would have liked what I found in Fells Point. Mr. Cappy and his buddy, Jerry, were outside their Old World Antiques store on South Broadway. Cappy sat in a big, soft chair he was hoping to sell; he smoked a cigarette. Jerry was examining an old guitar. Then, he raised it to his chest. He strummed on it hard. Then he sang "La Bamba." It was a great little moment. I would not have wanted to be any place else at the time. You see? It lasted only two minutes, but years from now I will remember the scene and the song on the old guitar in front of Cappy's antiques store. And I will remember that, at that particular moment, the light was perfect.

October 2, 1987

A SIGN OF THE CITY

On seeing a midget, very late at night, asleep, with his head on the bar of a West Baltimore tavern . . .

Just when summer seems a sweaty beast smothering the city and about to choke it, you walk into dens where the demons drink and are reminded that, in its every corner, Baltimore has soul. It has heart. It has a pulse. It has color in its cheeks. It remains, wheezing and coughing in the dead air, very much alive.

New York boasts itself the city that never sleeps. On seeing the midget, mouth agape and head on the bar of the saloon near H. L. Mencken's house, you feel that there is nothing here, aside from theater, pizza, and cab service, that is inferior. Had he been awake at the time, I would have purchased the little man a drink in his honor. I would have liked to thank him for his exquisite repose, there in the blue hour, in the great yawn of summer -- and just when I was entertaining thoughts of departure.

For the sleeping midget is, for me, the sleeping giant of intimate, obstinate Baltimore that stands firm, in dingy blue jeans, against the flash floods of change. He is the last man you would ever consider calling a Yuppie. I doubt that he's been to Harborplace more than once. That was no quiche stain on his T-shirt. It was probably Skoal.

And so, in a time when you no longer know what to expect -- fifty-cent drafts or three dollar bottled imports -- when you walk into a neighborhood bar, the sleeping midget is a monument to the firm muscles of old, familiar Baltimore. He is not an anachronism. He is, like ceramic dolls in rowhouse windows, the best of Baltimore on display. His mere existence, in the flickering, gray glow of an overhead television set, makes it difficult for the frustrated to leave this vale and to say they are leaving for "something better."

Of course, the city's promotion priests would never include a snapshot of the midget in their tourist brochures. He never-once appears in that sweet, new TV commercial touting Maryland as a beautiful place to visit. None of the television stations features him in their promotions or high-glitz show openings. And that is sad, for the sleeping midget, even with his mouth open and only snores coming out, has something to say. And he would say volumes more than that sweet, new TV commercial, which looks pretty much like all the other come-visit-us spots around the country. He would not say, "Maryland, you're beautiful." He would say, "It's okay to sleep in our taverns." And then the world would have a complete picture.

I know people who are angered by this. They believe in property values. They have invested in the city in the last decade or so, buying into old rowhouses as well as the James Rouse line that cities are fun again. They do not like to know of midgets sleeping in dirty old bars. That is not the proper image of a city on the make. They see these romanticized vignettes of city life as aberrations witnessed and reported by voyeurs. "You don't have to live with the smell," they say. And that's where they are wrong.

By intent, much of life in this state centers on Baltimore today. Maryland's best press clippings are datelined in this city. Our governor reigns in Annapolis because of his wonderworks in Baltimore. The city is full of conventioneers.

People who live in surrounding counties spend more time in Baltimore than ever before. New townhouses and condos sell quickly along the waterfront. Though it is today a poorer, smaller city, Baltimore remains the centerpiece of Maryland. Everyone has some piece of the action.

So we *do* have to live with the smell. There is good and bad here, and the judgments are completely subjective. But there's a fact we must live with: This is not some re-invented city of clean, new brick and happy endings. It has gone through transitions, but none so dramatic that its personality has permanently changed. You can dress Baltimore in a tuxedo, but it will still be happier at a bull roast than in a ballroom.

I keep hearing men complain about people who oppose two new sports stadiums, and the complaints stem from the attitude that Baltimore is overcrowded with hicks who, deep down, fear success and really want to live in 1954. What these complainers don't understand is that no matter what kind of new clothes we put on Baltimore, underneath always will be a comfortable, familiar -- and probably stained -- T-shirt. There will be people who stayed with Baltimore through the bad times, or came for the good times, because it was different and peculiar, a big town with small-town charm. And because we care about our little people, and we let them sleep wherever, whenever they need.

July 20, 1987

CRIME AND PUNISHMENT

I visit the scenes of crimes. I watch people pick through their shattered lives. I find a great many stories in courtrooms. When The Baltimore Sun, *morning and evening, decided to stop sending reporters routinely to the district courts, I found the beat uncovered and mine for the asking. So I make the rounds of the districts. Or I go uptown, to the big solemn courtrooms, where all the problems of people living in cities seem to spill out and end up on the record. These stories are often sad, sometimes funny, mostly tragic, and infuriating. It's all there.*

THE PIGEON

At noon, several hours after his arrest, the little boy went out to play with the pigeon. He ran into the filthy alley behind his mother's $207-a-month rowhouse on Booth Street, a dreary place in southwest Baltimore where poor people and their children share the sidewalks with drug dealers. The little boy grabbed the little pigeon and crumpled it in his hands as if the bird were a wad of black-and-white paper. Then the boy threw open his hands. The pigeon's wings unfurled, flapped, and made that familiar smacking sound. The bird flew limply, just above the concrete, into a cage beneath the rickety rear porch of the house.

This bird may have been a pet, but its little master, eight years old, was brutalizing it. It seemed to be a game: Crumple the bird, squeeze the bird until it almost dies, then release it. The bird never flies very far, either; it scurries back to the tenuous safety of a cage. Hear the life story of this little boy, and maybe you understand why his hands are full of torture, why he'd grab and squeeze a little bird like that. For most of his life, he has been on the receiving end of the long, slow brutality that grabs and squeezes little boys in this city.

This particular eight-year-old became an overnight legend. Wednesday night, he was arrested. Police say they found fourteen bags of cocaine in his black sweat suit. A cop saw him late at night with an older man -- the uncle of a six-year-old playmate -- selling dope on a street corner. He had been handcuffed, processed, lectured, then released into the custody of his mother. Just before noon yesterday, the mother, a thin woman twenty-eight years old, came to the door on Booth Street. She was barefoot and dressed in red pajama pants and a gray Boston Marathon T-shirt. The living room of the shabby rowhouse was dark, the shades drawn. A boy in jeans slept under a blanket on the couch. This was the woman's twelve-year-old son.

Her eight-year-old, the pigeon-keeper and accused drug

holder, came down the stairs when he was called. He was about four feet tall and thin, with knobby elbows and knobby knees. He wore a stretched Max Headroom T-shirt, black shorts, blue Adidas with silvery blue tongues, and no laces. He sat on a coffee table missing its glass top. He thrust his little hands into the pockets of the shorts.

"The police brought him here in the handcuffs," his mother said. "See, they know him. They known him a long while. I've been telling them about these big boys giving him drugs. It seems they're waiting for one of my children to get killed before they do something."

"Have you been in trouble before?" I asked the boy.

"I got caught stealing," he mumbled.

"We lived in the Fayette Street building, the projects," his mother said. "And we had trouble over there with this child molester, this doctor who came up from Washington and molested children. He molested *him*." And she pointed to the twelve-year-old on the couch.

"When was this?"

"A few years ago, when we were in the Fayette housing. There were a lot of kids molested. This man was taking kids out and stuff and buying them stuff. . . . I moved out of there. But see, I was supposed to get Section 8 housing so I could move somewhere decent." She paused a moment, then added, "He seen a drug dealer get shot."

"*Who* saw this?" I asked.

She pointed to the eight-year-old on the coffee table.

"He saw a shooting?"

"David Ruffin. He was dealing drugs. They shot him."

"You saw David get shot?" I asked.

"We was going downtown," the eight-year-old said. "We just come out of the Lexington Street building." David Ruffin, twenty-four, was shot to death August 24, 1985, near the projects in the seven hundred block of West Lexington Street.

So this little boy in the Max Headroom T-shirt was five years old when he witnessed his first murder.

"David used to buy him a lot of clothes," the mother said, and there was the implication that, even at the age of five, her son might have been holding dope for dealers. This is not unusual in Baltimore. Appalling, yes. But not unusual. We live in a city where children get fifty cents a day to hold guns for cocaine dealers. "His father was killed," the mother said now.

"His father?"

"He was shot, too. It was drugs." She gave a name. The police have this name in a file. A man by this name was shot to death in a drug-related homicide in 1982. His death didn't even make the papers.

"His father was killed because of drugs. What do you tell him about all this?" I asked.

"I told him. I told him, 'They're gonna catch you holding drugs.'. . . I had a court order, from a judge down the courthouse, to take him through the penitentiary, for a tour in there, so he could see. We went last month. The guards talked to him. . . . It didn't do any good. Now I got to move. There's a court order from Child Protective Service. They say I got to move my children out of here or they're gonna snatch them away from me. But I'm supposed to get Section 8, and if those people at Social Service would find me someplace decent, I would move."

She gets $418 a month from the government. She shares the house with her twin sister, who works as a security guard. "I thought it would be better when we moved out of the projects. But it's worser over here. All these older guys know him [the eight-year-old]. Walkin' down the street, they see him, they say, 'Hey . . .' like they know him. They threaten him. They say he's got to be with them. They're gonna buy him clothes and give him money."

"Did you get money?" I asked the eight-year-old. He nodded.

"How much? You told the police you were getting a hundred fifty dollars a day."

"I spent it. I buy a lot of stuff."

A carnival was in town, on Edmondson Avenue. "The carnival's been here two weeks and he played the carnival all two weeks," the mother said. The mother got up and walked through the small kitchen to the rickety rear porch with its dreary view of the filthy alley. "This is where the police arrested him," she said. "Under the porch here." Below us, the little boy ran across the spot where the cops had grabbed him the night before. He grabbed the pigeon, squeezed it, and threw it into the air. The bird flapped its wings and struggled back to the cage under the porch.

May 20, 1988

GOLD STREET

The old woman threw up the sash of the second-floor window above the sidewalk where the fire department had just washed away the blood of a man named Rodney Edward Young. The sidewalk dried fast in the warm sun of the first day of autumn in the city of Baltimore. The old woman said she'd be right down. She lived in the first house on the north side of the six hundred block of Gold Street, near Pennsylvania Avenue. A few hours earlier, Rodney Edward Young, twenty-five, and another man named Zachary Roach, twenty-four, had been shot to death at her front door.

Crime lab technicians had chalked white circles all over the steps. After the bullets hit him, Rodney Edward Young lurched off the stoop and fell face down on the sidewalk. He was then shot numerous times in the head. The police used yellow chalk to outline his body. His head had landed next to a lid from a Kentucky Fried Chicken cole slaw container. The alley next to the spot where he died is filthy, loaded with trash, and dozens of yellow-jackets buzzed there. The store on the corner was locked and boarded up.

Now, the old woman opened the front door, a small bird of a woman, in a green bathrobe and stocking feet. Her name was Sarah Woods, seventy-five years old. She said she had lived in this rundown house on Gold Street for four years. She had been sleeping at the time of the murders. "It woke me up," she said. "Bang! Bang! Bang!" At 6:15 a.m. if she had been standing by her door, Sarah Woods would certainly have been hit with a bullet for many were fired by the person or persons who wanted this Rodney Edward Young dead.

The police figure these bullets were fired from a semi-automatic weapon. This type of weapon, of course, does not just fire bullets; it sprays them. The bullets sprayed at Young went through him and left four holes, grouped like a constellation of death, in the frame and door, over a graffiti inscription: "Tony a.k.a. Sniffy big time." One of the bullets went through the door and into a sheet of brown paneling on the left wall of the vestibule inside Woods' house. "The police took all this off," Sarah Woods said, pointing to the sheet of brown paneling, pried loose from the wall of the vestibule. "I guess they took it off so they could get to the bullet in the wall."

Sarah Woods said she wasn't surprised that two young men had been sitting on her front step. "I tell them to get away from there, but after I go to bed, they come back and sit there. I call the police and they come and run 'em off, but they come back after a little while. They're out there all the time." She said she didn't know the men who were shot. "I heard the shots and I come down here and look out. I seen him lying there on the pavement full of blood." She was talking about Young. Roach ran about twenty-five yards from the steps and collapsed in the middle of Gold Street. The fire department did not do such a good job hosing away his blood.

"They're shooting out there all the time," she added. "They're always crazy, shooting. If I get money, five hundred, probably six hundred dollars, I'm gonna move out of here. I'm sorry I ever moved here.... You can't stop them drugs. Them people get drugs, you can't stop 'em. You mess with 'em, they'll kill you."

Out on the street, Western District Patrolman C. L. Mahoney was putting a guy with a shopping bag in a paddy wagon. "Caught him breaking into a truck up the street," Mahoney said. "Routine." The police say this neighborhood is known for drugs. A man was shot on Gold Street on the other side of Pennsylvania just a couple of weeks ago. "Years and years ago, we had a homicide in the vestibule here," Mahoney said. "You're talking about ten years ago."

The woman who lives next door to Sarah Woods is Marie Wilkerson. "It was daybreak when it happened," she said. "The shots woke me up. I was scared to death. I jumped up and went to the window. When I heard those shots, I got away from the window. I didn't know these boys. I didn't want to see."

Marie Wilkerson is eighty years old, lives alone, and spends most of her time being scared to death. Mahoney knows her. She calls the police a lot. Lots of poor old people live scared to death in these poor old houses. "I don't sit on the front steps," she said as she stood in her doorway, her hand on the screen door so she could close it fast if she had to. "This is as far as I get."

Up the street younger people -- two men, two women, a child in diapers -- sat on steps taking in the sun, right across from where Zachary Roach had fallen. They said they knew neither Young nor Roach. A woman wearing gold chains around her neck and curlers in her hair walked up to look at the bullet holes in Sarah Woods' front door. She was impressed. She said, "I'm glad the children and stuff weren't out here."

September 24, 1986

THEY LIKE SOAP OPERAS

They crept along the broken pavement of East Baltimore Street, three young men with steel under their belts and the life of Robert Perrear in their hands.

They went to a bar near Shot Tower Park, a couple of blocks from police headquarters. The bar shares a street with Klein The Tailor, a real estate company, and the old Bolero Bar. There's a couple of newly spruced buildings safely fenced within the city's Shopsteading Program. That's about it. The rest of the block is junk.

The three young men wore dark, heavy clothes against the cold. The police say they arrived just after nine p.m.

The other morning, in the paper, the name came at me. It had a familiar tone, it had character, it had something . . . and after a few minutes I knew it was the kid from Fayette Street. Robert Perrear was a tall, slender black man, twenty-four years old.

Last May, he walked behind a wheelchair, pushing a bum named Roy through an alcoholic fog. Roy was a white man, busted flat in Baltimore. His wife had left him and he'd been injured during an epileptic seizure. He'd also been kicked out of his apartment. So there he was, on the street crying out for help from the basement of the city. Roy's wheelchair tipped over a couple times and only Robert Perrear was there to help. He was a good kid. Other people laughed when the wheelchair tipped over.

At 9:10 p.m. they came into the saloon, Charley's Place. They wore orange ski masks that turned their faces into jack-o-lanterns.

There were four customers at the bar. One was Robert Perrear. Another was asleep, his face against the wood. There was a barmaid, Teresa Keene, and upstairs was the owner, Jasper "Charley" Anderson.

Up in the corner, a television made the bar glow blue. The television puts life into Charley's Place. In the afternoon, everybody watches "The Young and The Restless." They come in and drink beer out of cans and watch the television. At night, they do it some more.

Robert had different jobs. Sometimes he worked, sometimes he didn't. He said something once about having worked on the Baltimore subway. His mother says he worked on trucks, too. "Never bother nobody," she says. "I think he said something about the man in the wheelchair last year. And there was this blind man he helped. He used to see if the blind man needed to go downtown, and Robert would help him go downtown."

He didn't finish high school. He roamed a little, drank a little. He had three sisters and four brothers. He lived with one of the sisters for a time. Then, last Monday night, he got caught in a routine act of terror that kills young men in the basement of the city. It happens about two hundred times a year.

The three pieces of steel began to move. The masked men brought the guns out front and the steel gleamed in the light from the TV. They had two revolvers, and a very ugly sawed-off shotgun.

The guns came out and the three men announced the holdup.

Robert Perrear was on a stool. The one with the shotgun hit him and knocked him to the floor. He fell against one of the cigarette machines and the jukebox. The one with the shotgun stood over him.

A handgun struck another customer and he fell to the floor. The room shifted. One of the robbers jumped behind the bar with the barmaid, and his hand went in the cash register. The sleeping customer at the bar remained still.

Robert lived with his mother on the west side. And for a while, he stayed with his sister on the east. The sister was the first kin to find out about Robert. A friend read the story in the paper over the phone Tuesday morning. Mildred called her brother and the brother called the mother.

The quick hand came out of the cash register with seventy-seven dollars.

Robert was still on the floor, and the TV glowed.

Then, almost casually, the one with the shotgun dropped his arm.

The arm aimed the gun at the floor.

And the gun stared at Robert Perrear's face on the floor.

And then Robert Perrear's name went into the paper.

The three young men with the jack-o-lantern faces regrouped in front of the bar and ran into the street.

There was no struggle, no warning, no reason. The ski masks would have kept anyone from making an identification. The police are working on it. A detective named Ozacsewski says it was the worst he's seen. Tuesday, Robert Perrear's brothers went to a funeral home on West North Avenue. They told their mother not to go. Yesterday, at Charley's Place, three men and a woman watched soap operas. They said they were hooked on them.

February 14, 1980

PARDON, BUT YOUR SLIP-UP SHOWS

When a character in a George Higgins crime novel was asked what he needed for a bank job, he replied, "A guy, a guy, a guy, a guy . . . and a car."

The other morning in Anne Arundel County, it was a guy, a guy, a chain, and a car. The guys pulled into a bank lot, tied one end of the chain to the night deposit box, the other end to the bumper of the car, figuring, you know, out comes the box. So they pulled away and -- wouldn't you know it? -- the bumper came off. Sensing trouble the guys fled the scene, leaving the bumper -- and the license plate. The cops liked very much that the guys left the license plate. This story will go down as one of the great moments in crime comedy. Reports of the misadventure were greeted in law offices and station houses yesterday with laughter and cackles.

Since crime is a dreary subject, the moments of comic relief must be cherished -- but only when the crooks help the cops. Like last month, when a burglar tried to get a cash refund for a ninety-three dollar pair of shoes he had swiped from the Bolton Hill home of State Senator Julian Lapides. To do this, the burglar left his name and address with a salesman at the downtown Hamburger's store. The police found this information helpful; they made an arrest. Lapides, blessed with a sense of humor, has been telling this story all over Baltimore. At the Unity Democratic Club the other night, he said, "I brought the house down with it."

There was the time an ace holdup man went into a Baltimore bank and slipped a cash-demand note to a teller -- a move that would have been a Willie Sutton classic had the robber not signed his real name to the note. Another time a bank robber decided there would be no handwriting on his note because, see, the cops have these handwriting experts nowdays. So the robber typed the note. Only one problem: He used stationery from his place of employment.

In Baltimore County last year, the police encountered a very gifted stickup man who thought he could hold up a 7-Eleven with a single bullet. To do this, he put the bullet between his teeth, went into the convenience store, and mumbled, "Give me all your money or I'll blow your head off."

The store clerk looked at this Mork version of the criminal element and said, "Get outta here!" Police charged Mork with attempted armed robbery. Prosecutors later dropped the case.

Then there was the conscientious bank teller who insisted that a robber give her a receipt for the loot. The robber obliged with name, address, and phone number. And there were the bandits who took two cans of spray paint into a bank and smothered the lens on each security camera with said paint. Very bright, except they left the cans -- along with fingerprints -- behind. This, of course, aided the police in their investigation.

Once three robbers masterminded a brilliant city bank robbery. They made all necessary plans, used a stolen car for the getaway. When they reached a prescribed escape point, they ditched the stolen car, got into their own, and drove off. Just one minor, itsy-bitsy hitch: The robbers left their plans, written on yellow legal-size paper, in the stolen car, with names and addresses of all participants. The city robbery squad liked this touch.

A few years ago, a crook decided he'd dig a tunnel into the manager's office of a city department store. The thief was very diligent, worked very hard. But in his haste, he must have lost track of time. He busted into the manager's office during store hours. Recalled prosecutor Dana Levitz: "They were all sitting there when he came in."

Several years ago, two brothers -- both very short and skinny -- decided they wanted to rob a jewelry store on Light Street. So they waited until the store closed, climbed to the roof, and climbed down the chimney. One of the brothers made it into the store but tripped a silent alarm. This alerted the cops, who arrested the burglar and put him in City Jail. When police asked for the whereabouts of his brother/partner, the burglar refused to talk. At the time, he was unaware that his brother had gotten himself stuck in the chimney. The first brother's loyalty to the code of silence kept the second brother in the chimney for four days. When the police finally knocked a hole in a second-floor wall to free him, the second brother was ecstatic.

One time, a crook broke into a city rowhouse and demanded that the lady of the house hand over cash. The lady was out of cash. "Would you take a check?" she asked. The robber agreed. So she wrote a check and the robber took off. Days later the police were very happy when the robber tried to cash said check.

At St. Paul and North a few years ago, a young entrepreneur waltzed up to two big guys and asked if they wanted to buy a television set. Not only were the two men interested in the TV, but they wanted to see what other appliances the salesman had to offer. So the salesman obliged and opened the trunk of his car to display what amounted to a small branch of Radio Shack. The two guys were so impressed, they decided to give the salesman some personal background on their lives. They showed the salesman little cards that indicated the two men worked for the federal government -- specifically, the Federal Bureau of Investigation. Upon seeing this, the salesman was impressed. He said, "Oh, my." He then put his hands on the car roof.

Then there was the story, now legend, of the chap who stole a car, said car having a telephone on the dashboard. The owner of the car decided, what the heck, to place a call to the car. The slick thief answered. The two men agreed on a place and a time at which the thief would return the car for a two hundred fifty dollar ransom. The thief met his appointment. So did the cops. The thief, it should be noted, did all this without the benefit of a college education.

June 18, 1982

THE SOUTHERN WENT DARK

Somewhere near the top of the docket, the bouncer from Hammerjack's approached the bench to tell the judge about the malicious destruction of a barroom mirror. The bouncer was mumbling. It was doubtful the courtroom microphones could pick up his voice.

"This is the last day of Southern District Court," said Marshall Shure, the veteran prosecutor who prosecutes from a barroom stool a cop got him years ago. "Speak up. You're going down in history. . . . Now, state your name."

"Nine-One-Sixty-Five."

"How about your *name*?" Shure grumped. How about getting this guy some coffee? This is history happening here. We are closing a courtroom forever. This is it. No more dingy walls and cramped seating and lousy lighting and dirty ceilings. We are moving on to a new location with new scenery for old dramas. Somebody shake this guy up so he states his name and not his date of birth. This is *posterity* we're talking here. Let's get it *right*.

Matters pertaining to Hammerjack's have frequently come before the judges of the Southern District. But here on the last day in this grand old fortress on Ostend Street, Judge James J. Welsh expresses delight at meeting a "security guard" from Hammerjack's. "You mean you're a bouncer?" the judge asks. "One of those people who beat people up? You're the first one I've seen in twelve years." Remarkable. History is being made all over the place.

Let the record show that after eighty-eight years, the city is closing the old Southern. And may the record further show that, at 7:39 this morning, the last police shift assembled for the last roll call. Monday, the city dedicates the new Southern District at 10 Cherry Hill Road. The characters will stay the same. Sure, one of the city's most knowledgeable prosecutors, will be in the new place but without his stool. "We're getting tables and chairs," he says. Ira Fine and Tom Klenk, the public defenders, will be there. So will the court clerks, John Neudling and Cynthia Hill. District Commander Joseph Cooke and Captain Howard Parrott get new offices. The officers get new locker rooms. The crooks get new cells. But how are we going to get by without the dreadful ambience of the old Southern?

What human history played out in that theater. The Southern had the aura of hoosegow. It could have been the set for "Barney Miller." In fact, the director of "Tin Men" recently shot a scene there, with Richard Dreyfus swearing out a warrant for Danny DeVito. Sure, it was dreary and ground-down and noisy. Sure, the third floor was condemned four years ago. It was hard to heat. Space was tight. You could hear a toilet flush when the courtroom door swung open. The public defenders didn't even have their own phones.

But history permeates these walls. In 1933, the cops cleared thirty-one drunks off the street in front of a South Baltimore saloon; they spent the night in the lockup singing, "Hail, Hail, The Gang's All Here." This was the home of Turnkey Jack Thornton, who tried to save a vagabond chicken named Biddy in the station house. Poor Thornton. He offered Biddy for adoption, then, when no offers were immediately forthcoming, he had it butchered for a meal for a needy family. Same day a chicken farmer stepped forward to offer Biddy a home. Too late for Biddy. One day a man rowed a barge across the harbor. He had his dog with him. Rowing a barge across the harbor was an infraction of some city park rule. In court, the man was asked why he did this. "I was giving my dog a ride, Your Honor."

Years ago, on my first visit ever to Southern District Court, testimony was heard about a strapping young lad who put his fist through a plate-glass window on Light Street. The judge squinted, looked at the lad, and said, "What're you? Mental?" This is where Judge Carl W. Bacharach imposed a fifty dollar fine on a man who kissed a Southern District sergeant on the lips on a dare. This is where Judge Robert J. Gerstung settled a neighborhood dispute by telling the provocateur: "Never spit in a crocodile's eye until you cross the river." This was the home of the late Froggy Floyd, leader of the gallery gawkers. Froggy used to sit in the courtroom and tap his cane, chortle, and wink when he thought a defendant was telling lies. And some judges might have shot Froggy a glance in tight calls. My favorite scene: The victim is a fat guy in a tank top; the defendant is a tattooed lady. The charge is assault. The fat guy announces he is dropping the charge. He and the tattooed lady embrace. Then they kiss. In unison, five cops on the side of the courtroom go "Awwwwwwww" at the rebirth of romance.

Yesterday, there was more of this. Moments of melancholy, moments of humor, moments of sadness. The Hour of Truce came -- as it always comes -- early in the day as domestic disputes were settled and men and women dropped charges against each other. A woman came forward to speak for her son in a sad little moment that brought silence to the room. The boy had been charged with harassing an elderly couple and breaking a court order that he stay away from them. "He's a good boy," the mother said. "He helps me support a family. He's my son and I love him." The boy got eighteen months.

A young man named Kearns was charged with disorderly conduct. He had been involved in a fight with a guy named Tony. He claimed Tony had been drunk. He said he had witnesses to prove this. But he hadn't brought them to court with him. "What did you *think* was going to happen here today?" asked Judge Welsh.

"Most likely pay a fine," Kearns said.

"Well, most likely you *will*," said Welsh. Fine was a hundred twenty dollars.

A couple of guys with shaggy hair decided not to testify against a man who had chased them down a sidewalk near The Tumble Inn. This fellow had a knife. A very *large* knife. It was displayed in the courtroom and, when Welsh saw it, he said, "Good God Almighty! That looks like Crocodile Dundee's knife."

But soon the day was gone. The sun was setting on the Southern for the last time. In the afternoon, the last case was heard at the old court on Ostend Street. Let the record show that it involved a violation of the Plumbing Code. The defendant was charged with doing something all Baltimoreans have done at some time in their lives: the practice of plumbing without a license. The defendant had messed up a job and cost his employer six hundred twenty dollars. Restitution was ordered. Then the judge went home and they closed the old courtroom doors. The old Southern went dark.

October 17, 1986

ALL DOLLED UP

She was, of course, being called upon to help the state send Robert Lee Myers to the gas chamber and so, to this end, Tina Marco dressed to kill. Madame Marco wore a black knit suit of light wool with delicate white braids at the cuffs, collar, and hem. She wore a lovely pleated peach blouse and black boots with spike heels. And she was adorned, testimony disclosed, with $8,700 worth of gold, diamonds, and sapphires -- all gifts from the man she was now fingering for murder.

The courtroom lighting was exquisite, almost theatrical yesterday. Two ceiling lamps were trained directly on Tina's handsomely trimmed auburn hair. The jewelry glittered. The round earrings danced. Had she slung a fox boa over the witness stand or filed her nails, Madame Marco could not have played the part of the conniving dame more convincingly. She pouted, giggled, batted her eyelashes, dropped her head, raised her head, pursed her lips, looked severe, adjusted her skirt, crossed her legs, clasped her hands. She spoke in an earthy candlelight voice, the kind of voice heard across a thousand nights in smoky bars.

All was proffered, of course, in an effort to convict Robert Lee Myers of murder and to save her own soft white skin. But Tina didn't look at Myers, the once successful Carroll County businessman who allegedly plotted the contract murder of his second wife, Mary Ruth, with the passionate and pathetic hopes of an eternity with Tina. Not once did she glance at the formerly chunky man who now looks like a withered Rod McKuen in a frumpy checked jacket and wrinkled chinos.

No, Tina only looked when the prosecutor, Thomas Hickman, asked the question all prosecutors love to ask their star witnesses just before concluding direct examination: "Do you see the man you have been referring to in this room today?"

Then there was the kind of breathless drama the spectators in Judge Luke Burns' snug courtroom have known only from afternoons with "One Life To Live" and "All My Children." Tina washed her moment under the lights in soap.

She pulled her plump, pouty face up and raised her right hand and brushed it toward Robert Lee Myers. "The blond-haired gentleman," she said, and then Tina sighed heavily and deeply and painfully. Oh, the pain. To sit there and point the finger at the man who had bought her furs and diamonds, and her son a dirt bike. Here was Tina, direct from drama class, sighing deeply again and pressing her left hand around her forehead. The gold wristwatch, estimated to be worth-$3,200, twinkled beneath the ceiling lamps.

"Do you still love Robert Lee Myers?" Hickman asked.

Another long, breathless pause. "I'm not sure," she sighed, and the gold earrings danced as she shook her head and pressed it against her hand. Tina Marco has large eyes that appear to have seen everything and to be bored by most of it. At times, her meticulously shaped brows whip up high. Her nose turns up a little. Her chin is a nub at the bottom of a round wide face that, by candlelight, might be considered not bad looking. There is not a single hard angle on her body. And she is the most gossiped about woman in Carroll County -- the dame who allegedly introduced Robert Lee Myers to a former supermarket mop-jockey named Daniel Chadderton, the convicted killer of Mary Ruth Myers.

There were times yesterday when mild disdain crept into Tina's smoky voice, like when she denied ever being a go-go dancer. Or when she described the large house in Silver Run where Mary Ruth and Robert Lee Myers once lived -- the house that Tina commandeered the day Mary Ruth was buried. Oh, Mary Ruth hadn't done much with the house, Tina said. The walls were bare, the furniture would never make *House Beautiful*, the china was sort of cheap, and Mary Ruth "had a lot of costume jewelry." Mary Ruth didn't have much in the way of clothes, either, Tina said. So she "bagged them" and gave some to friends, some to a mission.

Madame Marco often displayed an appreciation for the finer things in life. She testified to having had a sitting room in the Myers house converted into a large walk-in cedar closet. She kept her furs, jewelry, and Robert Myers' gun collection locked in the closet. And there were times, Tina said, when she'd go into this spacious closet and "sit at my desk and look out." Here is a woman whose idea of getting away from it all was sitting in a closet full of furs, guns, and diamonds.

Yesterday, she wore two rings -- one valued at $1,175, the other at $4,325. At the request of defense attorney Anton Keating, she held them up for the jury to see, and she did not seem embarrassed by the display. The jewels had come from Robert Lee Myers. "It was a monthly thing," Tina Marco said, "almost a weekly thing."

"You're very fond of jewelry," Keating said.

"Most women are," Tina replied.

October 14, 1982

NO DEMONSTRATIONS FOR DAVID GORDON

Black leaders rallied fifty people to remember the civil rights movement and denounce the federal indictments of Clarence and Michael Mitchell, indictments they likened to lynchings. Then the National Association for the Advancement of Colored People rallied another fifty people at the courthouse in Ellicott City to denounce the child abuse conviction of a black day care center operator. Yesterday, in Room 406 of the Mitchell Courthouse, David Gordon enjoyed no such support. He never has.

The doors to the old courtroom opened at 11:15 a.m. and Gordon walked in, manacles around his sneakers. If you were not shocked at the age of this convicted killer -- he is seventeen

-- you might have been shocked at his appearance. For he looked about thirteen. He was light-skinned, baby-faced, tall, and skinny, another manchild headed for jail.

This case slips right out of the cracks in the foundation of this city. It represents the "rot beneath the glitter." But did it provoke a rally or candlelight vigil on the courthouse steps? Were black leaders holding David Gordon up as evidence of the rot? Were they decrying his wasted life? Did they vow to break the cycle that produces violent young men in their city?

There is no past glory to recall in this story. It goes back to a Sunday evening in April a year ago. In the open-air stairwell of a Reservoir Hill apartment house, a man named Benny Sidney started to eat from a cold can of chicken noodle soup. Sidney was sixty years old, poor, and homeless. He had $4.47 in his pocket when he was shot. The bullet severed his aorta. It is believed that Sidney bled to death. Money was taken off the body. There was no public anger over the death of Benny Sidney. The city did not skip a beat when his head hit the concrete of the stairwell. There was no stop-the-killing rally following his death. No one decried the waste. No one denounced a damn thing when Benny Sidney died.

Detectives John Tewey and Errol Etting worked the case. In June, police arrested David Gordon. Gordon stood trial. A resident of the apartments said he heard the gunshot and saw Gordon scamper away from the stairwell. Two other witnesses testified that Gordon told them he had shot the old man. A jury convicted Gordon.

Yesterday, he came before Judge Thomas Ward for sentencing. His mother and grandmother sat in the front row of the gallery. Gordon wore a navy blue sweat shirt, crackling new blue jeans and sneakers. Five years down the road and Gordon's soft face could be a magazine model's.

The prosecutor, Jack Lesser, was first to speak. Once again, he told Ward, we have here a young man who, "like so many young men in this city, come into the possession of a handgun." The result was the death of Benny Sidney. The presentence report said Gordon had struggled to the ninth grade, had experimented with cocaine, had committed a theft and robbery as a juvenile, had been suspended twice from school, and had shown no remorse for the killing of Benny Sidney. Lesser asked for a life sentence.

When David Gordon stood to speak, the tips of his long, skinny fingers brushed the top of the trial table. "Guilty . . . of a crime I . . . did not commit" were the only words that could be heard in the rear of the courtroom. Suddenly, Gordon stopped. He dropped his head. His mother hunched up and cried. Gordon sat and pressed his left hand against his temple. Someone handed him a tissue.

Now there was a long, dismal pause. You could hear David Gordon whimper, hear his mother whimper. No one looked at David Gordon. And there was silence for two of the most disturbing minutes ever spent in a courtroom.

"Your Honor," he said, "I am my mother's only child like . . . like . . . Your Honor, please . . . don't give me that sentence." And there was more silence. "I can't . . . say no more," Gordon said weakly. "I can't say no more."

The judge ordered a recess. "David," Gordon's mother whispered, "pull yourself together." By the time the hearing resumed, his mother was no longer in the room and there was still no sign of the NAACP.

The judge told Gordon to stand. "This is the first time I have ever seen you show any remorse," Ward said, then sentenced Gordon to prison for "the rest of your natural life." A guard put handcuffs around Gordon's narrow wrists. The tissue paper was still packed tightly in Gordon's left hand. It was now noon, and as he was being led through the dim fourth-floor hallway of the Mitchell Courthouse, David Gordon dropped the tissue with his tears on the floor.

April 17, 1987

IN WHICH A COMMA COUNTS

UPPER MARLBORO, MD. -- His face is ugly and menacing. The eyebrows rise high on his forehead and he flashes a glare that is not pleasant to see. On the wide, pale face of William Joseph Parker there is hardly ever a casual glance, only a chilling stare.

But no matter how evil this man looks, no matter how much the prosecutors in Prince George's County want him to breathe cyanide, Joe Parker will not die.

Instead, for the rest of his life Joe Parker's name will be followed by commas. He will be called William Joseph Parker (comma) convicted rapist-murderer of an Annapolis girl who saved her pennies to buy a bike. William Joseph Parker (comma) the rapist-murderer who lived. A comma, or the lack thereof, may have saved his life.

Parker raped and murdered thirteen-year old Elizabeth Archard last summer. The jury said Parker committed rape in the second degree, which is critically different from rape in the first degree when a man faces the gas chamber. These words, taken from the capital punishment law, state circumstances under which a judge can send a man to death row: "The defendant committed the murder while committing or attempting to commit robbery, arson, or rape or sexual offense in the first degree." Notice the lack of comma after the word "rape." Under basic grammatical rules, the phrase "in the first degree" would modify the words "rape" and "sexual offense." Parker, of course, had been convicted of rape in the second-degree.

That is how Judge Howard Chasanow called it yesterday before he decided to send Parker to prison for life instead of a gas chamber for death. His ruling sounded like a high school grammar lesson because the judge had not only studied the death law but had examined English texts for rules on the use of the comma. The judge, a short, studious man of forty-two, also took a long lunch hour -- he had corned beef from Jack's of Baltimore -- to agonize over the toughest decision of his life. This was in the early afternoon, after Parker's lawyer, a blustery and long-winded man named Fred Bennett, spent three hours pleading dramatically for what might have been called mercy had it not already been predicted that Parker probably would never get death.

Joe Parker's sentencing was filled with technical jabs from Bennett as he shadow-boxed with a law that proved, in the end, to be only a paper threat. Yet, the lawyer took the death penalty on head first. He wanted his arguments in the record. He brought Parker to the stand. Parker said he was sorry.

When Parker said this, a stern-looking man in a brown three-piece summer suit took notes. The man sat strong and straight in the gallery, at the end of a bench filled with children. The man's reading glasses hung from a cord about his neck. He had a square face and a thick handlebar moustache that made him look, as he scribbled notes, like a foreign correspondent for a British newspaper. Yet this man was far from a mere reporter. He was the stepfather of Joe Parker's victim. He was Phillip Doubleday Hale, an Annapolis lawyer who, with his wife, Barbara, had somehow managed to keep his family in order through several, emotionally-treacherous months.

Fred Bennett, the defense lawyer, asked Parker how he felt. "Sorry," Parker said, and across the room Phillip Hale scribbled "sorry" on his legal pad.

Then Parker said, "Upset." Phillip Hale wrote "upset." When Parker said, "Nervous," Phillip Hale wrote "nervous." And then Joe Parker put his head down, his hard, chiseled face silhouetted in the dull morning sun from a window covered with venetian blinds. His hands shook. The prosecutor asked Parker when he started to feel sorry for the Archard family.

Then came a long, long pause. Parker said, "I can't answer that." And across the room, on Phillip Hale's notebook, there were no more words to write. No words. Not even a comma.

May 16, 1979

MR. LEVITT IN HANDCUFFS AT LAST

Here on Calvert Street yesterday, in an old courthouse with dim corridors and dingy floors, Jeffrey Levitt found himself immersed in a daytime drama familiar to habitues of the criminal justice system. He was treated like just one of the boys. Even Charles "Buck" Dranbauer, the deputy sheriff who earned himself a footnote in the history of the Maryland savings and loan scandal as the man who handcuffed Jeffrey Levitt, did not accord his prisoner any major privilege. "The only thing different," Dranbauer said, "was that he rode down instead of walking down." Dranbauer was speaking of the method deputies used to escort Levitt from a fourth floor courtroom to a first-floor lockup. Instead of taking the steps, they used a freight elevator. Dranbauer held Levitt by the arm the whole way. He then took him behind a door covered with wire mesh.

Dranbauer has been a uniformed deputy for six years. For the last eighteen months, he has been assigned to a fourth-floor courtroom wherein he is often called upon to handcuff prisoners. Yesterday, in Room 400, Dranbauer stood by patiently as Jeffrey Levitt and his attorneys took care of some business with a judge. Levitt, of course, was scheduled to start an eighteen-month sentence for contempt. But, as he also faces criminal charges of theft of other people's money from Old Court Savings & Loan, there were legal matters requiring attention.

Before Levitt arrived in Room 400, there was the usual groan of activity as another day dawned in Circuit Court. A haggard public defender called out names of young men in varying degrees of legal difficulty: "Alvin Hill, Andrew Johnson, Gregory Jameson. . . . Anyone whose name I didn't call, who thinks they're represented by the public defender, please step up."

Levitt is not eligible for representation by the public defender. So yesterday, he was accompanied by paid counsel:

Paul Mark Sandler and from Washington, the very able William Hundley.

"Is this your first appearance in Maryland?" Judge Edward Angeletti asked Hundley.

"My first appearance in state court," Hundley said, calling to mind his days as defender of W. Dale Hess in the Mandel case in the old federal courthouse across the street. Hundley's client list includes former Anne Arundel County Executive Joe Alton, former West Virginia Governor Arch Moore, and from Watergate days, former Attorney General John Mitchell. Here is further proof that Jeffrey Levitt knows the best things money can buy.

Levitt put his hands in the pockets of brown corduroy pants. He wore an aquamarine cotton pullover. On his feet were leather moccasins. He looked like a man ready for a round of drinks at the Irish Pub. There was a slightly nervous jig in his left leg. Dranbauer, the deputy sheriff, toyed with handcuffs about ten feet away.

At 9:45 a.m. the judge said, "Mr. Levitt, you are now in custody." Dranbauer stepped forward with the handcuffs. Levitt did not expect this. He backed off. Angeletti said, "You have to follow the sheriff's instructions." And then a crank and click could be heard. As Deputy Dranbauer escorted him from the room, Jeffrey Levitt, cold handcuffs on his wrists, found himself up close and personal with the criminal justice system. Soon he found himself in a room with a man charged with a handgun violation. He was fingerprinted. Deputies looked through a large green trash bag in which Levitt carried personal belongings.

Now Jeffrey Levitt, certified criminal, was being treated like one. If anyone suspected Levitt would escape all allegations of wrongdoing with a mere wrist slap, they should have been in the dim corridor of the old courthouse when at 10:40 a.m. he emerged from the lockup with twelve deputies around him. This horde of men moved swiftly down the courthouse corridor to the Lexington Street door, and Jeffrey Levitt, stuck in the middle, looked swamped, lost, trapped, and confused. You wondered if he ever believed this day would come. Men who vacation in Boca Raton do not expect the world to slip away like this.

"Bye-bye, Jeff," someone said as the entourage reached Lexington Street. At the curb was a white van with a gold star on the door. Deputies put Levitt in the back seat. The door slid shut. Levitt sat alone, surrounded by windows with wire mesh, as photographers crammed in close to capture the moment. As he sat there, waiting for the van to take him to jail, Jeffrey Levitt looked out into the cold street as if in search of a friendly face. A deputy stuffed the green trash bag in the front seat. The van drove away. Back upstairs, Deputy Dranbauer started escorting another prisoner down to the first floor. The prisoner was handcuffed. He and Dranbauer took the stairs.

January 31, 1986

TELEVISED JUSTICE

In the crook of each elbow was an intravenous needle connected to clear plastic tubes that snaked into a hidden chamber. Through these tubes an unidentified executioner injected lethal doses of sodium thiopental, Pavulon, and sodium chloride after Autry declined to make a last-minute statement and Warden Jack Pursley ordered: "Let us begin." It was 12:25 a.m.
    -- from reporter John Henry's account of the March 14 execution of convicted killer James David Autry.

Autry wanted his execution televised, claiming that such a spectacle would enhance the purported deterrent qualities of the death penalty. Such a noble desire. And such a pathetic attempt to display a social conscience at the eleventh hour.

Texas officials, on the other hand, leave me less impressed. They turned down Autry's request. Brave enough they are to kill the killer, but not to do it in public. The death penalty is a seamy secret business, and better that the warden's friends not see him at work.

At 12:28 a.m. he began breathing heavily and his chest heaved as his wind came in audible gasps. . . . Autry twisted his mouth into a tight-lipped grimace, but remained silent. It was 12:30 a.m. and Autry took a deep breath. . . . His eyes had grown cloudy and he was blinking every two or three seconds. He pursed his lips and strained his neck as if trying to swallow.

This idea of televised, as-it-happens, government-sanctioned Technicolor death has merits. The criminal justice system has come increasingly under the gaze of the public's critical eye. Several states already allow televised coverage of criminal proceedings. So why, one might ask, should we stop there? Wouldn't a telecast of a killer's execution be the fitting conclusion to the public's observance of trial, verdict, and sentence? Or is there something here we don't want to see?

At 12:32 a.m. Autry said, "Oh, it's hurtin'." Some witnesses understood him to say his arms were hurting. Except for his breathing, Autry lay still with his eyes closed. Suddenly, his head reared up from the gurney and his eyes opened widely as he scanned the faces [of witnesses].

With increasing frequency, states are killing their convicted killers. This is no longer front-page news. Perhaps that is why Autry sought to have his death televised. It was a scream for attention, a desperate plea to make his the most memorable of the nation's latest round of executions. Perhaps we would not have heard as much about James David Autry -- and his heinous crime -- if he hadn't added this bizarre twist to his walk down Death Row.

That a government allows the death penalty is probably reason enough to televise it. This is public business. To hide it is to question it. If states are going to be brazen in their efforts to kill convicted killers, then let them display the results of these legal labors. And if, as advocates claim, the death penalty serves truly as a deterrent, then let's beam this message into the criminal underworld.

Throughout America, people criticize the criminal justice system. Judges are too lenient, parole programs too liberal, criminals too vicious, the police too limited in their powers. The system stinks, they say. Rather than confront this morass, we seek to get even. Criminals are getting away with murder, the reasoning goes, so let's settle the score. Let's jail juveniles as if they were career criminals. Judges are too soft; let's establish mandatory sentences. It's too expensive to keep killers in jail; let's exterminate them. We are too much a society seeking revenge and simple answers, instead of justice and new ideas.

Autry rolled his head from side to side. His legs twitched and flexed beneath the leather restraints. His body convulsed briefly.

Roberta Roper, whose twenty-two-year-old daughter Stephanie was raped and murdered in Maryland, became titular head of one of the nation's most vocal citizens' anti-crime lobbies. Roberta Roper must understand hatred; if any woman can feel a lust for revenge it's the mother of a beautiful college girl who died a horrible death. But Roberta Roper opposes the death penalty. There are other solutions -- more complicated perhaps and certainly more expensive, but far more civilized. When we lower our standards to those of the criminal, a part of the foundation of this society sinks a little.

His eyes were almost closed, and at 12:36 a.m. he appeared to have stopped breathing. Standing next to Autry's head, Warden Pursley shifted his weight, and the barrel of his pistol stuck out beneath his blue suit coat. Walker County Sheriff Darrell White, who still wore his cowboy hat, leaned against the wall and yawned.

I wouldn't want to watch a man die on television; it would only affirm my belief that government-sanctioned killing is wrong. But perhaps our friends who advocate the death penalty should see it. Sadly, they have become too much like the sheriff in the cowboy hat, yawning while a pathetic man dies a horrible death.

March 19, 1984

GOOD SPORTS

Every once in a while, I go out to Memorial Stadium to see the Orioles, or I spend an afternoon at Pimlico Race Course, which is probably my favorite pastime. Back in college days, I wanted to be a sportswriter, but gave that up when I found that real life produced a much higher yield for a local news column. Still, I love sports and make my rounds to stadium press box and race track stable. There have been some great moments: Rick Dempsey's greatest day in the 1983 World Series, and the night I saw a thoroughbred mare produce a foal. There was also a bluefish blitz. It occurred on the Outer Banks of North Carolina but, believe you me, I practiced long and hard for it on the mosquito-smitten shores of Assateague.

BOBBY BAGS THE ELEPHANT

Bobby -- may I call him that? -- Shriver showing up yesterday as one of the four new owners of the Baltimore Orioles is a wonderful thing, for it shows how, given a second chance in life, a guy can overcome a bad start and make out. I say congratulations. And I am sure that, if we could reassemble the gallery of mugs who filled Southeastern District Court on October 6, 1983, they would give Robert Sargent Shriver 3rd a standing ovation. Never has one of their own gone so far.

I must be careful not to give the impression that Bobby himself was a Southeastern regular or that even the violation that brought him to court was of a serious nature. It wasn't. It was a misdemeanor. Bobby was charged with scalping tickets to an Oriole-White Sox playoff game.

When he came to court, his attire betrayed him as a mere visitor. A Southeastern regular (male) wears a lot of corduroy and denim, a wallet chain, and a tattoo while a Southeastern regular (female) wears halter tops and stretch polyester pants, a bare midriff, and a tattoo. Usually the ones who wear suits are lawyers; seldom are they defendants. With his pin-striped Brooks Brothers suit (or was it Britches of Georgetown?) and club tie, Bobby stood out like the America's Cup yacht at a Middle River marina.

Another distinguishing characteristic was the presence of private counsel. Bobby brought his own attorney, a very bright and congenial fellow named James Kramon. That he could afford his own counsel made the allegation against Bobby, a child of privilege, all the more peculiar.

Young Shriver, whose celebrity parents were fast friends of the late Edward Bennett Williams, had gone outside Memorial Stadium to sell three twenty-dollar tickets for a total of eighty dollars. And guess who Bobby tried to sell these tickets to? A Baltimore police officer. (The cop was in plainclothes; at least Bobby didn't try selling the tickets to a uniform.)

How embarrassing, though. Here was the son of the Shrivers getting nabbed for trying to make a twenty dollar profit on baseball tickets. And then he had to pay a $250 fine. As I say, it was a peculiar incident but it showed Bobby's potential. Scalping, in my book, is an All-American enterprise, purely capitalistic. It figures that Bobby works in investment banking up in Manhattan now. He's what they call a venture capitalist. Venturing out to scalp playoff tickets when the Memorial Stadium parking lot was crawling with cops showed the kind of capitalistic daring a guy needs to survive in the big Manhattan money circles.

Now he is called the architect of the deal to buy the Orioles. As they say on Wall Street, Bobby bagged the elephant.

Yes, young Shriver has done quite well. Other scalpers who worked the '83 playoffs have not. One, for instance, was last seen selling luggage of genuine simulated leather out of a station wagon in a parking lot. Another was spotted last Friday playing the Double-Triple at Laurel. Bobby, meanwhile, works at James D. Wolfensohn Incorporated, an investment banking firm in New York. I telephoned him there yesterday afternoon. Secretary put me right through.

"You must be a very happy man today," I started the conversation. And immediately he got snippy on me. He said that he would have no comment about his becoming a part-owner of the Orioles. He said someone had already spoken to my boss at *The Baltimore Sun* about the story -- as if, by making this phone call, I was violating some pre-ordained ground rule for the reporting of the Oriole sale -- and that all questions should be directed to the Oriole front office. "This whole conversation is off the record," he said. "I don't even want it said that he said, 'Hi,' and hung up. Understand?"

It was a very strange exchange. And a short one. Such a shame. I didn't even get a chance to tell Bobby how, as owner of one-eighths share in two Orioles season tickets, I wanted to take him out for a couple of beers and give him -- just one thirty-four-year-old to another -- my personal ideas on improving the ballclub.

Worst of all, I didn't get a chance to say what all us mugs

who witnessed his hour of darkness in the Southeastern back in '83 wanted to say: Bobby, we're proud of you. You got yourself out of a jam and went on to great things. You bagged the elephant. Now, if you want to boost the price of Oriole tickets, you don't have to scalp them in the parking lot. You can just announce a price increase. And it'll all be legal.

You done good, kid.

December 7, 1988

RICK DEMPSEY'S GREATEST DAY

PHILADELPHIA, PA. -- On the greatest day of his career, Rick Dempsey posed for a snapshot with a fan in the lobby of the Hotel Hershey, tossed a warm-up ball to a kid behind the dugout, hit a homerun that just barely escaped the Atari screen at Veterans Stadium, posed for a picture with Edward Bennett Williams, spoke to the President of the United States, held his little boy, Christian, in his arms, and said, "Let's go find Mom."

The Baltimore Orioles are the reigning lions of baseball and Rick Dempsey is the cat's meow. Write the headline, Mike. Make it read: Town Enjoying Baseball Bender, Favorite Son Makes Good. The cabbie on Thirty-third Street said McGregor pitched a swell game and Murray showed his stuff in the final round. But Dempsey. Dempsey's the Most Valuable Player of the series and ain't it great, don't that beat all? It couldn't a'happened to a nicer guy.

Yeah, Dempsey. The lunch-bucket hero. The guy that comes to play. The guy with the big ears and the sparkling eyes and the heart of a clubfighter. A dirt-faced catcher who risks life and limb for foul balls. He could hit .240 the rest of his life and Baltimore would still accord him the stature of favorite son. And Dempsey plays hard because he has to, because nothing comes easy. And maybe that's the connection. Maybe that's why fans of the Orioles love to watch him earn his pay. Most of us -- teamsters, teachers, and Tupperware salesmen -- have to bust butt to make it through a day. So we appreciate Dempsey's struggle. Couldn't a'happened to a nicer guy.

Dempsey's the generator of America's best baseball team, the heart and soul and guts of it. When it's time to go to the mattress, I'll take Dempsey in my corner. There he is, firing bullets to second when the enemy tries to steal a base, holding his ground when the enemy runs for home, scrapping in the dust, and pounding his mitt with the anxious joy of a Little Leaguer on a summertime high.

It was sixty-two degrees at Veterans Stadium, that canyonesque morgue of the 1983 Philadelphia Phillies, when the sunlight disappeared in late afternoon shadows. Dempsey, bare-armed like a longshoreman, came to the plate in the third inning and cut a pit by scraping his right shoe, *el toro* style, in the batter's box.

It was exactly 5:36 p.m. and Dempsey swung at a rookie's pitch and the ball sailed out to left field. There was nothing certain about it; it was not one of those kiss-it-goodbye jobs. But the ball landed at the juncture of the bright green left field wall and the black drapery behind it. The ball bounced above the yellow line.

Beautiful!

Dempsey trotted the bases. Favorite Son Makes Good. And then there were high-fives and then Dempsey was back in the dugout, catching his breath, sniffling a little, the cap flipped around backwards, and the chest protector flopping over his shoulders again. Up in the press box, he had a consensus. Rick Dempsey, who batted .231 in the regular season, would be MVP of the 1983 World Series, elevated to the highest ground of his career.

He hit a double and scored in the fifth inning too. But, like all the other Orioles who starred on this day, his achievements were met with near silence. There were Oriole-lovers in Veterans Stadium, but they were certainly outnumbered by mourning Phillies fans, some of whom looked for exit ramps as early as the fourth inning.

McGregor pitched magic and Murray hit homeruns, but all you could hear were the engines of the Goodyear blimp up in the three-quarter moon sky.

Then in the ninth inning, with two outs, Dempsey squatted for the last time behind home plate and shifted his body to give McGregor an inside target for Garry Maddox, the final Philadelphian. Maddox swung and the ball went out on a line to Cal Ripken Jr. and the Orioles were champions again.

Now Dempsey, coming out of an exultant bear hug at the pitcher's mound, was back in the Orioles clubhouse, on a platform for the network cameras, Reggie Jackson's hand on his shoulder, Edward Bennett Williams at his right, Bowie Kuhn beyond, and beyond that the shimmering trophy of the world champions. Cameras flashed. Dempsey's hair was matted and curly. He was still wearing shinguards when someone handed him the phone with Ronald Reagan on the other end.

"You tell the Russians we're having a good time over here playing baseball," Dempsey said, and you could use that on Dempsey's MVP trophy: Tell 'em I had a good time playing baseball. And if the Russians want to go at it, just tell me the time and the alley.

Dempsey had a towel around his neck and a bottle of Great Western in his hand now, and he was buried in reporters and TV crews, getting more attention than he ever got in his life.

"Where's your locker?" someone asked.

"Down the end on the left. I'll be there in about an hour."

Dennis Martinez was spraying champagne. Al Bumbry hung his arms over the iron bar in his dressing cage and swigged the bubbly. John Lowenstein stuck a bottle in his pants. Martinez soaked Sammy Stewart while Stewart was giving a TV interview. Ray Miller hugged Mike Flanagan and Tippy Martinez, fatherly hugs. The press had Dempsey cornered again, hung up in his locker. Great bunch of guys, he said of his teammates, classy guys, guys who go out and win ball games. "I never had a day like this before in the major leagues." He was saying all the old and perfect things that happy baseball players say so well.

His kids were with him now -- John, twelve, and Christian, five. It was a very decent little instant, the kids at his side for the greatest moment in Rick Dempsey's career. He broke from the press and went with the kids to an outer hallway to see his wife, Joani. "Let's go find Mom."

Then back in Baltimore, after the bus ride, Dempsey was wanted on stage again. It was late and the night glowed around Memorial Stadium -- TV flood lights and the police helicopter in the sky, a giant pool of Orioles fans, waves of banners and pennants, flowing from Gate E-3 out to Thirty-third Street and beyond.

The players and coaches emerged from the belly of the stadium and a tremendous roar came up out of the throat of the city. All this time, they had cheered Ed-Dee, Ed-Dee, Ed-Dee. But now there was a new two-syllable aria: Demp-See, Demp-See, Demp-See.

He came out in a long-sleeved shirt with the collar wide open and held up his hands and the roar grew louder. Dempsey spoke into a microphone and it was impossible to hear what he said but it didn't matter. The crowd on the platform moved and squeezed Dempsey tight. Still he managed to raise his arms and form an O . . . then an R . . . and an I . . . and an O . . . and an L . . . and an E . . . and an S. He was a cheerleader again, down to the end, down to the last happy shout of the greatest day of his life.

October 17, 1983

THE LAST KISS

Hey, Bartender. Gimme a beer, and make it a Boh. Put a fat head on it, too. I don't care. And while you're at it, get my buddy here a shot of Calvert. Burn his belly, bartender. He needs it. Tonight, we're sad so we're gonna drown. A beautiful summer love just ended with a jab to the jaw and one last kiss.

But let me tell ya, it wasn't always like this. Last Friday, things were looking up. We were down at the Waterfront Hotel in Fells Point with Gene-The-Vote-Toter, Brooks-The-Lawyer, Bald-Bill-The-Tugboat-Magician, and Sandy-The-Surgeon-From-Shock-Trauma. They just fixed the place up; years ago, they rented rooms by the hour. Last Friday, the TV was on and you wouldn't believe it. People yelled and screamed and there was this imitation Wild Bill who stood up and spelled O-R-I-O-L-E-S in body language. We beat the Pirates. Then Saturday, we're all sitting around Nick's Place getting depressed when what happens? The Orioles come back with six runs and win another cardiac case. It went like that all summer, bartender. A long, corny and passionate summer with rainy weekends and a lot of romance.

Hey, how's about another belt for me and my buddy here.

All summer long, we were out there in the stadium and we were in love. There were McBride and Phyllis; The Italian and Frenchy; Cookie and Cat Lady; Fat Vincent and Sir Butch of Arbutus; Gabby from the Essex Elks; Smokey and Weasel; Turkey-Breath and Fred; some guys from the Greenmount Pleasure Club; Royal Rangers TCL -- Baltimore Forest No. 45; Perry House; and Optimists International. Mike, Steve, Rick, Jackie, and Sandra. Up in Section 34 you could see Wild Bill's orange beer-belly. And so what if he always led a cheer while the stadium stereo was on? We were loud anyway.

I tell ya, bartender, there was nothing like it. There's never been anything like it, though I know you go back a long way. But didn't this latest fling beat all?

Get me another brew, chief, and see about my buddy here.

This season . . . she was great. She beat the Colts' sudden death game in '58, and she beat '66 and '70 when we won the Series. She made you feel like a champ, made you swig many fat beers, made you say you're proud to come from Baltimore. We don't need champagne either. So what if we blew the World Series? Last night, Baltimore was in the big leagues.

Know what I mean, barkeep? Give us another round.

You shoulda been there. There were all these limousines outside the stadium; the fast money had come to town. We had an Eisenhower throw out the first ball. Even Jimmy Carter showed up, which I wish he hadn't done. He didn't come all year and then he shows up for the most important game, and look what happens? The guy's a disaster.

Anyway, the fans stayed strong throughout the last date, though they knew they were courting a heartbreak. And that guy from Washington, the new owner, saw these two teams from two union towns -- two beer-guzzling, bowling league towns -- battle it out til the last kiss. Dauer hit a home run in the third and you shoulda heard the place. It looked like we were gonna get back together and beat the Pirates. But then, at ten o'clock, Stargell sent the killer out to right field.

And you could feel the summer go out of us. We were on the road to Mudville, 53,000-plus lovebirds on the final leg of a great summer fling. We tried to patch things up. We got the bases loaded in the bottom on the eighth. The love was still there, but things just didn't work out. So the loud speaker played an Elvis song and we made one last embrace. Then we kissed and said good-by.

That's all, bartender. I've had enough. A guy's gotta pick himself up and get on with the world. Besides, you always have next summer. And you can always chase a summer love again.

October 18, 1979

BALLS

About twenty people, including a young priest from St. Leo's, stepped out of the black cold last night to say a few prayers for a little man known to his family as Theodore and to the rest of the world as Balls. The people came to the Della Noce & Sons Funeral Home, 322 South High Street, shortly after seven o'clock, hung up their heavy coats, knelt by the open casket, and made signs of the cross. It was a short, soft gathering, with the brothers of Theodore Peter Maggio Jr. passing around memories like so many wallet-size photographs.

Theodore Maggio, who was sixty-five, died of an apparent heart attack last Friday morning in his bed in his house in the 1000 block of East Baltimore Street. His house was more than his sanctuary and his room; it was his treasure trove, his headquarters. Balls Maggio, a man of moderate fame in this town, was what newspaper people and regular people call "a character." He won this description largely because he lived the life he obviously adored and didn't really care what the wincing masses thought. And it was fun to watch him. He found a lot of happiness roaming the back streets and cracked alleys, scouting the leftover merchandise of a throw-away urban society. And if he didn't have to shave every day, that was good too.

Ask just about anyone from around the harbor on East Baltimore Street or Fells Point about the little man on the bike, and they'll say, "Oh yeah, Balls. Mr. Balls." His most famous activity was what gave Theodore Maggio his nickname. More than one kid from Little Italy or thereabouts can recall seeing Balls Maggio, in his old clothes and heavy shoes, fishing for balls out of the Jones Falls. Since childhood, the river was his happy hunting ground. Balls would stand on a concrete wall, perhaps in back of the pumping station over by President Street, and scout floating balls that had plopped into a storm drain up river.

Over the years, he became a marksman. He had the eye of a hawk. He would stand on the concrete wall, or on a bridge, and drop a long, light string into the murky water. At the end of the string was a coiled wire, usually made from an old coat hanger. Balls would drop the prop ahead of the ball, gently pull on the string and scoop his prize. Just like that. He was very good at it. His coiled device -- the construction of which I was once allowed to witness -- could handle a ball of any size, from a basketball to those tiny red balls kids use with jacks. There was no ball too big or too small for Balls Maggio. Throughout his career, Balls captured thousands of balls -- five thousand, his brothers say -- and he'd trade them to kids for soda bottles. Then he'd trade the soda bottles for cash; a friend who ran a lunchroom used to swing the deals.

I remember visiting the House of Balls one day about a year and a half ago. It's in a block of East Baltimore Street where only strong-hearted, mugging veterans like Balls Maggio would hold court. "He never moved. He loved the city," said his brother Frank. "He was happy there." The first floor was an amazing cavern of throw-away baubles. Balls had dozens of cardboard boxes and milk crates and bushel baskets, and each one would be filled with balls. Tennis balls. Lacrosse balls. Baseballs. Footballs. Big kiddie balls with stars. Pinkies.

I opened up an old cabinet. In the cabinet were a couple of shoe boxes, and in the shoe boxes were dozens of little red balls. I never saw so many balls in my life. This was the Maggio Museum, his life's work. He had a lot of plastic jugs, onion bags, potato sacks, old clothes, scrap metal, a lot of cans, lamps, and cigar boxes full of pens and pencils. He collected scrap lumber for an iron stove. He kept just one light bulb burning on the first floor, and he would point to this as evidence of his keen ability to make do on very little.

Balls Maggio boasted that he could live a happy life without much money. Money just caused a lot of problems anyway, he said. His advice to a young man was abstinence -- from drinking, smoking, women, dancing, gambling, bowling (because the balls didn't float), and one other thing that I forget. Balls pedaled his big bicycle like an Italian racer on a ten-speed. He had tremendous leg muscles. He could be seen early in the morning on the side streets, from Canton to Fells Point and Market Place, and he could be seen chasing the dusk back to his house. The bike had a big, warped basket up front, and on a good day it would be full of balls or other notions. There were days, he said, when twenty balls an hour from the Jones Falls was nothing. He was a proud man with vibrant eyes, completely free in his own corner of the universe.

He's survived by eight brothers and sisters. They were talking about him last night at Della Noce's. The young priest, Father Charles Marrone, noted that the memories had made Balls Maggio, a man he'd never met, very real. And if anyone ever doubts, there are a few thousand balls in a house on East

Baltimore Street that will attest to the full life of a happy little man.

January 11, 1982

FOUL BALL

Cal Ripken Jr.'s classic opening day duel with Roger Clemens of the Red Sox -- the outcome of which was most satisfying to the home team -- was a lesson in patience and foul balls. Ripken is one of those highly disciplined batters who, blessed with keen eyes and killer swing, are patient enough to foul off evil-looking pitches until they see the one that smiles. Last Monday afternoon, Ripken hit several fouls off Clemens before ending the confrontation decisively with a three-run homer to left. Thursday night, when he faced his former teammate Mike Boddicker, Ripken again was a nuisance, carefully guarding the plate, swatting away fouls as if they were gnats.

Suddenly, however, one of these foul balls made a high arch toward the stands down the third base line, about where I was sitting. It was certain, from the instant Ripken made contact, that the ball was headed our way. And so, with the ball reaching its apex, everything seemed to freeze, and ten different thoughts tumbled into my head: There's going to be a scene, grown men are going to drop their beers to reach for the ball, women and children are going to be crushed, beer-bloated thugs are going to grope and claw through the throng, there will be a fight, someone is going to bang his knees against the back of a seat, fingers will be broken, nice trousers will be torn ... and everyone else is going to be watching. What if the ball comes to me? Do I try to catch it? What if I drop it? What if it lands on my head? Maybe I should just get out of the way.

By now, of course, the ball was making its descent. I could sense people jostling for position. This ball was about to become a souvenir, and everyone wants a souvenir, especially off the bat of a star whose name might one day grace the Hall of Fame. Nothing new there.

Twenty-nine years ago, I attended my first major league game in Fenway Park, Boston. The Red Sox were playing the Yankees and, though the Sox were terrible, the Yankees were sensational, and the place was packed to see Whitey Ford pitch against Ted Williams. I went with my father and his loud Kiwanis buddies. We sat up in the stands behind the first baseline, and Williams, the most talented and crafty hitter of his time, fouled several our way, all well out of reach. But one of them finally came toward us and, for a moment that has remained a fresco in the back of my mind all these years, it looked like my father had a shot at it. A foul ball off the bat of Ted Williams! My father was sitting at the end of a row, twelve feet above a concrete ramp. The ball looped into the ramp, bounced thirty feet high. Good old dad stuck out his short, hairy, muscle-bound left arm. And missed the ball by two feet.

Now, twenty-nine years later in Baltimore, I had to make up for the loss. Ripken's ball was coming down fast. Nearly everyone was on their feet. Arms stretched skyward. Is this any way for grown men to behave?

Eleven years ago, before the birth of Orioles Magic, this would not have been such a big deal. Before Baltimore became a baseball town, the seats around mine were often empty. If a foul ball bounced in there, an ambitious runt sitting two sections away could scamper and get himself a souvenir easily. Now, however, there is greater competition for a foul ball at Memorial Stadium, thus increasing the ball's value.

But it's not just for the sake of a souvenir that grown men risk their lives for fouls. It's because a big league baseball gives them a connection to those young men on the field. And those young men are living a life that was a dream for the rest of us. Hold and rub the ball that Boddicker pitched, that Ripken hit -- it represents what it represented that long-ago night when Joe Rodricks reached for the ball that Ford pitched, that Williams hit: the longing of men to be part of a glorious moment, to be the hero and not just the observer, and to live free of everything except a game and to have the game be baseball, and to have it be a complete and total joy.

The feel of a major league baseball will do that to you. Its stitching and texture remind you of the days, however fleeting, when you thought you had a chance for baseball, when you went to bed to dream of it, when you slept with a ball in your hand.

Ripken's ball bounced off a hand and over heads and landed under the seat behind mine. I reached and snatched it up. It wasn't the prettiest snare of a major league foul, but the ball was mine. It took twenty-nine years, and a lot of patience, for it to get here. I wasn't about to let go of it. That night, I fell asleep with it in my hand.

April 10, 1989

THE LEGEND AS LEGACY

Some day in the next century, when Baltimoreans yet unborn ask their elders about the decision to build a new baseball stadium at Camden Yards, the name Edward Bennett Williams will spring from lips. Should children of the future wonder why Baltimore, at great expense, decided to abandon its fine old stadium at 900 East Thirty-third Street, those who live to tell the story will explain about the formidable Mr. Williams and, in so doing, underwrite his immortality. For that, of course, was part of the deal.

The new stadium probably will not bear his name (though it would not shock anyone to find such a stipulation in the fine print). But the new stadium will certainly bear the Williams legend, if not the Williams shadow. It will go down -- or up, as it were -- as the Stadium EBW built. Or deigned. Or decreed. Or demanded.

Of course, his representatives will claim that Williams never demanded a new stadium as a condition for keeping the Orioles in Baltimore. (And, of course, Richard Nixon never demanded a pardon from Gerald Ford before resigning as President.) But Williams refused to sign a long-term lease at Memorial Stadium. For years, Baltimoreans analyzed his every public utterance in search of secret agenda. He didn't like the drive to Memorial Stadium. He didn't like the "egress," and we all scurried to look the word up. His chums from Washington, who'd never been north of Harborplace, thought the trek to Thirty-third Street a miserable excursion through hot traffic. Watch, we all worried, the O's will soon be playing pepper in RFK. And George Will will be the batboy.

But all that was just part of the ingenious lawyer's game, and he played it out even after the state agreed to build a new stadium. When the fifteen-year lease was finally announced by William Donald Schaefer on May second, the cheers in Memorial Stadium were laced with sighs of relief. The game was over.

It is impossible to say whether Baltimore would have been forced to play that game had someone less driven than Williams purchased the team in 1979. But when one examines the man's long, lush life, one sees a series of contests. "Contest living," a Jesuit idea spurned by Trappist monks, is how the old Holy Cross grad put it. In courtrooms or board rooms, perhaps even in living rooms, Williams loved The Contest. Here was a man who probably considered Monopoly a war game. So when he came here in 1979, most Baltimoreans, especially those who were going to have to deal with Williams directly, were intimidated. No local individual, or consortium for that matter, managed to raise the pocket money needed to buy the team from Jerold Hoffberger. And suddenly this Limousine Legend owned the Orioles, and the Baltimore political and business establishment, a decidedly unsophisticated bunch, hadn't seen anyone as brilliant as him. They probably never will.

The same with the rest of us. Like it or not, with his cosmopolitan designs for the Orioles, Williams did a lot to bring Baltimore into the modern baseball century. It might have happened anyway, but 1979 was the year the Orioles became the Team that Ate Baltimore. The incoming owner, a Certified Celebrity, added to the drama.

It has been said that Williams was disruptive to the steady, smart operation of the Baltimore Orioles. He "intervened" where the previous owner presumably hadn't. But, of course, if the Orioles were today contending for the division, instead of being Les Miserables of the American League, Williams would be considered a giant of sports. That's baseball. That's the game.

Throughout his life, the obituary writers make clear, Williams knew what he wanted, fought hard for it, and usually got it. Toward the end, he probably wanted immortality, as the rest of us do, and he probably wanted it in a big way. That might have been why he played out the game on the new stadium for so long.

August 15, 1988

BUSH HOG BUILDS CHARACTER

Even with the kielbasa in his hand, Bush Hog James is my friend. A big brother really. And never mind that his brotherly love is sometimes cruel and unusual. Never mind that he grosses me out. I am a better person for knowing Bush Hog James. He has helped make me the person I am today. He wants me to be a man of strong character. So he always treats me to character-building experiences. Consider our recent fishing trip on the Chesapeake Bay. Bush Hog loves to fish. He believes that fishing -- especially when the chance of catching fish is remote -- builds character. So he always invites me. The other day we went after bluefish. "You gotta pay your dues," Bush Hog said, "if you wanna catch the blues."

We left Chesapeake Beach at seven a.m. aboard the Miss Shady Oak, with Captain Junior Tayloe at the helm. The conditions were atrocious: steady wind out of the southeast, slate-gray sky, clouds spitting rain, water rough and rocky. And I mean rock 'n' roll city. Once it gets into your stomach, the queasiness never leaves. It may just play along like a mild rhythm-and-blues tune. It may explode into full-fledged acid rock. Either way, there's no getting rid of it. The boat rocks. Your stomach rolls.

It was under these conditions that Bush Hog James, who has a stomach made of Samsonite, decided to do some character-building. At eight a.m. he opened an ice chest, extracted a twelve-ounce can of Wiedemann Light, popped it open, and chugged. Bush Hog stood, legs firm as pilings, on the deck of the Miss Shady Oak, one hand on his hip, the other wrapped around the Wiedemann -- the macho mariner in morning. The bay rocked. The warm-up band started playing in my stomach.

"Ahhhrrr, me bucko," Bush Hog said. "It don't get much better than this." We trolled for bluefish, caught a big one in the first hour, then settled in for a long dry spell. It was a lousy day and the fish didn't feel like feeding. But Bush Hog did.

At nine a.m. he opened the ice chest again. "Let's see what we have here," he said, reaching for another character-building tool. This time it was a jar of little red sausages embalmed in vinegar. "They're made from beef lips," Bush Hog added. He unscrewed the lid. I could hear the second warm-up band kick in. James Brown was now singing in my stomach. Bush Hog stuck one of the sausages in his mouth and let it dangle there like a rancid, red stogie. "Have one," he said. The bay swelled up. Rock 'n' roll was here to stay.

"Get that away from me," I said. "I don't wanna even look at it."

"What's a'matter?" Bush Hog asked with a cheshire grin.

"Don't ya like beef lips?" The boat plowed through the rough water. Up and down, the engines going rugga-chugga-chugga, my stomach keeping pace. Up and down, up and down. "Time for Tostitos and salsa," Bush Hog said. He dipped corn chips in red Mexican sauce -- which he declared "a little too mild" -- and washed it down with another Wiedemann. It was ten a.m.

The rest of us tried to concentrate on fishing. But there was no ignoring the rock concerts cranking up in our stomachs. I had Bruce Springsteen with me now, singing his new song "Trapped," which is exactly how I felt. "You look a little green around the gills," Bush Hog observed. And he seemed more pleased than sympathetic. "Time for pickles," he declared. He unscrewed a jar of cold kosher dills, squishy green belly bombs. He gave one to Captain Tayloe, then sucked on one himself. "Wonnerful," Bush Hog said.

We caught three more fish. The bay kept rocking. Suddenly I was experiencing abdominal Woodstock. After Springsteen came Iron Maiden and Twisted Sister. After the pickles came the kielbasa, "the piece de resistance." The kielbasa was smoked, orange-pink, long, and nasty. Bush Hog stood on the deck -- up and down, up and down -- cut off a hunk of kielbasa and pushed it into his mouth. "Delicious," he declared.

For the last hour of the fishing trip I was lethargic. I didn't look at Bush Hog. I couldn't face him any more. We returned to the dock. The concert in my stomach ended. And I was a better person. Yes, indeed, I owe a lot to Bush Hog James. He has made me what I am today. "You look a little pale," a guy said at dockside. "You have no color." How wrong he was. You don't judge a man by the color of his skin, but by the content of his character. On that day, I was full of character. Managed to keep it all down, too.

May 29, 1985

MORE TO FISHIN' THAN CATCHIN'

AVON, N.C. -- Eight Aprils ago, a Carolina good ole boy looked at me and my vacationing fishing buddies, one of whom was wearing cutoffs and wingtips at the time, and said, "Y'all gotta pay your dues if you wanna catch the blues."

That good ole boy, a hard-bitten Cape Hatteras Fisherman, was speaking of bluefish. He felt that a tourist from the north can't simply walk down to the beach in street shoes, throw a line in the water, and expect those big bad blues to give themselves up. You've got to visit the Outer Banks often, do some hard time on the beach. So all these years, we've been making a trip here, paying annual dues, hoping to hook the blues. We never had much luck and consoled ourselves in the philosophy of my fishing chum, Bush Hog James, who, on our first surf-fishing trip, cast a line unto the water, sat down, popped a Pabst, and declared, "Fishin' ain't catchin."

Anyone who's tried to catch a fish from a beach knows that there's a whole lot more to fishin' than just catchin'. But last week, I finally found out what the local good ole boys were paying their dues for. More than that, I had one of those "life experiences" that inflate the soul. As a matter of fact, there was a day -- a "moment" really -- when I felt like the first person to wake up in a world that seemed to have been created the night before. It was an experience of damn-near-biblical proportions. Know what I mean, Vern?

It was six a.m. The seabirds were calling. I grabbed my fishing rods and walked across the high dunes. Straight ahead was the big morning sun, rising like a kite and leaving a rippling tail of orange on the ocean horizon. The breeze was from the east and gentle. Gulls and pelicans circled in the air about thirty yards off the beach. A pretty picture; looked like the good Lord had just been there and gone.

Above the crashing surf, five bluefish -- not one, I swear, under ten pounds -- were flopping in the wet sand. I stopped about twenty yards from the water and at my feet was the treasure the hungry blues had been after when they beached themselves -- hundreds of Atlantic herring, flickering like silver and turquoise jewelry in the sand. They had been chased into the surf, then up the beach. Just moments before I awoke, all of this had happened -- a violent and natural ritual as old as the Earth: Big fish gobble little fish, and life goes on.

Feeling some pity for the overzealous bluefish, I intruded into this episode by grabbing two of them by the tails. They were still very much alive and as I read somewhere that bluefish can see as clearly out of water as in it, I assumed they were as aghast at the sight of this large, goofy human as I was at their gaping, snapping, barbed-wire mouths. I hurled the first two back into the surf and watched them both swish-tail off toward the sun. I did the same for the remaining three. The little herring jittered at my feet and as the surf crashed up on the beach, some of them managed to squirm back into the tide, resuming their unhappy stature as prey to bluefish.

I had walked into what sporting guys call a bluefish blitz. One of the good ole boys here calls the blue "a saltwater piranha." They are big, strong, maniacal fish. Along the beach, I found the ravaged carcasses of half-eaten herring.

The day before, half-eaten sea trout had been discovered in the sand, a sure sign of blitzing blues. A blitz occurs when the blues chase small fish toward the surf, where they become traumatized by crashing waves and easy prey for the razor teeth. If you happen to have a fishing pole with a line and a hook, there's a pretty good chance a blitzing blue will eat it. So there I was, throwing a shiny Hopkins lure into the water, hooking a blue on almost every cast. One of them actually snapped a large baited hook in half. Three of them busted my lines. I was at least ten minutes beaching each of them. I beached twelve before I stopped counting. I kept five for the freezer and returned the rest, including a very fat cow that appeared to be loaded with eggs.

By then, the good ole boys had arrived to fish. One of them stopped by and said he had been watching cable TV the night before, and there had been a program about the sick, polluted waters of America. It was one of those documentaries that leave you depressed about the state of the earth. But shortly after that, some dolphins swam by. And dozens of birds lunched on the dead herring in the sand. I walked off the beach with five suppers of bluefish. The sun was high and golden, which about describes the state of my soul at the time.

April 6, 1988

NATIVE FLESH AND BLOOD

A gangling grandson of the late great Native Dancer was born under a frosty moon at Sagamore Farm Monday night, and barely a hungry railbird noticed. The bay colt with two white socks and a spot of cream between the eyes pushed his way out of an eleven-year-old mare named Star Strewn at nine p.m. Foal boss Leroy "Skeeter" Figgins, his uncle Raymond, farm manager Harold Ferguson, and a nameless feline connoisseur of barn mice attended the ceremony.

The colt's mother is among the last crop of children by Native Dancer, the Vanderbilt stallion who won twenty-one of twenty-two races in the early 1950's (his only loss was the Kentucky Derby) and cast about his family jewels at Sagamore until he died in 1967. Monday night's birth was far from an historic event; Native Dancer's flesh and blood have been making the big leagues for years.

Horseplayers follow the big leagues, but they seldom pay much attention to the farm system. They detect the coming of spring by a brief look at the color scheme of whatever clubhouse they happen to visit. They know the red-and-white of Bowie ends where the yellow-and-black of Pimlico begins, somewhere around the first of April.

But spring already has begun up in the valley. Skeeter Figgins and his wife Jean are tending the mares. The other day, Skeeter made a slip of his tackroom tongue. During a discussion of birth rites, he looked over another crop of motherhood and recalled the time his wife "was in foal. . . .

Do you believe I said that?" he asks. "She was in foal. . . . I mean my wife was gonna have a baby. It was in February and about three o'clock in the morning, you know, she said it was time to go. We were getting ready when the night man called me down at the foaling barn.

"He says, 'Skeeter, you better come down here. I think Star [Star Strewn] is ready to foal.' So I went down and stayed through the foal. I took my wife to the hospital about seven o'clock. She was as unpredictable as these mares. The baby didn't come till the next day."

Down past the graveyard where Native Dancer and some of his illustrious relatives are buried is the foaling barn. In one of the 20 x 20 stalls, with her belly nearly rubbing hay, is Star Strewn. She was one of twins by Native Dancer and Staretta, a top race mare. She has the Dancer gray but she's a little smaller than most thoroughbred mares. Still, for seven straight years she's been a resident of the Sagamore maternity ward. And she's been placed in that position by some high class gentlemen -- Damascus, What A Pleasure, and Le Fabuleux, the latter being "a wild Frenchman," according to Skeeter Figgins.

This year, Star Strewn was in foal to Iron Ruler, a stud she met during a brief vacation in Florida last winter. Monday night, both her 1978 boyfriend and her owner -- A. G. Vanderbilt is currently sailing under a sultry moon in the South Pacific -- were nowhere to be found. But around eight p.m. steam started coming off Star Strewn's neck and Skeeter Figgins said, "Think we're gonna have a foal tonight."

While Skeeter wrapped Star Strewn's tail with a bandage, another mare named Sugar Dot offered a groan from across the hall. Skeeter flicked on the stall light. "What're you doing, ma?. . . . Good Lord, looks like we're gonna have two."

While Sugar Dot let her foal loose, Star Strewn strutted about her stall, gave out a dull moan, dropped to the hay, and started night labor. Skeeter took hold of the foal's tender hooves and pulled. A pair of wet, black legs slipped out. Then the long black snout, covered in a filmy sack. Star Strewn rested her head in the hay, taking deep, almost unnatural breaths.

"Come on, Star," said Skeeter. More heaving, moaning, more breathing, pushing, more driving. Then, like black paste out of a tube, the rest of the foal appeared. Skeeter's big hands gave a final tug and the newest grandchild of Native Dancer was in the hay, extending his legs like a seventy-five-pound spider, fighting for all four. An hour later, he wobbled on his feet, and the moon somehow seemed warmer.

February 14, 1979

THE NEIGHBORHOOD

It's a cliche but, as cliches carry much truth, Baltimore really is -- still manages to be - a city of neighborhoods. It doesn't take long to learn where the lines are drawn, to appreciate what makes each neighborhood distinct from the next. I find the most telling stories about old Baltimore and the emerging Baltimore right where everyone says they are -- in the neighborhoods. So I get out of the city room, park my car on some side street, and walk and talk. The neighborhoods are where people grow up and marry and die. It's where they wait for something better or enjoy the simple, intimate lives they've made for themselves. It's where they lean out over the window boxes and see life, as it happens.

THE RIPE STUFF

I go to Mugavero's lunchroom for the phone booth. It's a wooden phone booth. A phone booth out of a George Raft movie. You can shut the door, sit down, and talk. Or you can shut the door, sit down, and hide. I like the phone booth in Mugs' place. It suits me. So the other day, a beautiful day, I go to Mugs' to use the phone booth. The door to the lunchroom is open to Fawn Street, which I take as a sign of spring. Two guys are playing pinball in the back. Mugs is behind the counter, as usual. He's wearing an apron, as usual. He's wearing his handsome, friendly smile -- as usual. And he's got something in his mouth.

"How ya doin'?" he asks.

"I'm OK, Mugs."

"What'll it be?"

"Can you make me a sandwich?"

"Anything, boss, anything. I just ate a tomata. One of the best tomatas I ever ate."

"It's not from Chile, is it?"

"From Mexico. I just had to eat one. Look." Mugs holds out his hand. In the palm sits a plump, bright red tomato. It has been many months since such an exquisite tomato was seen in Baltimore. I take this as a sign of spring. Mugs raves about this tomato. And he does this with full mouth.

"Mmmm," Mugs says, "mmmm, mmmm, mmmm, that's good. You gotta taste it. What kind of sandwich you want, babe?"

"How about salami and provolone?"

"You got it, babe."

"Can you make it to go?"

"Go? Ah, come on. Siediti," Mugs says, and several times he repeats this word -- which is pronounced "si-ed-atee" and means "Sit down, slow down, you shouldn't eat and run at the same time."

Mugs is adamant about this. "Siediti," he says. "Siediti, siediti. I'll fix y'a beautiful sandwich with one of these tomatas. You gotta taste it. Mmmm, are they good." Mugs smears olive oil across a hard roll. He slices the salami and cheese at the slicer behind the counter. He slices one of those Mexican tomatoes. He makes a gorgeous sandwich. Just then, a guy named Joe comes in.

"What'll it be?" asks Mugs. I love the language of the lunchroom. I love to hear a guy in an apron behind a counter ask, "What'll it be?"

"Gimme a hot dog and a coffee," says Joe, who takes a seat at the stool one stool removed from mine.

"Hey, Mugs," I say, "this sandwich is delicious. What kind of olive oil you use?"

"What? You want my recipe? Hey!" Mugs yells to the two guys playing pinball, "he wants my recipes!" Just then, a woman named Maria comes in. Mugs sees her right away and remembers a phone call.

"Maria! Maria! Maria!" sings the middle-aged hunk behind the counter.

"Hey, Mugs," says Maria, "is my hot dog ready?"

"Comin' right up, Maria. I had to eat a tomata."

Maria apparently phoned ahead for her hot dog. She works at a big wholesaler in Little Italy, a couple of blocks away. "I can't eat Italian food all the time," she says. "I eat pasta every night. I like to have something different for lunch. Hey, Mugs, is my hot dog ready? You haven't even cooked it, have you?"

"I had these tomatas, Maria," says Mugs, with the innocence of an altar boy. "They looked so good, I just had to eat one. I hope we get 'em like this all summer. . . . How's that sandwich, babe?"

"Good," I say with full mouth.

"Come on, Mugs!" urges Maria.

"The hot dog's gotta cook, babe."

"What kind of hot dogs you use?" I ask.

"You want all my recipes, don't ya?" says Mugs. "Hey, that tomata good or what?"

"Where'd you get that tomato?" I ask.

"My cousin brought 'em in," says Mugs. "Chalky they call him. He's a produce man. From Caroline Street."

"Come on, Mugs!" says Maria. She's getting increasingly impatient. She'd phoned in her order before noon. Her hot dog should have been ready when she arrived. All Mugs can do is talk about tomatoes.

"What time did the tomatoes get here?" I ask.

"Which one?" says Mugs.

"The one in my sandwich."

"Noon," he says. And that explains everything, doesn't it? Mugs gave himself a moment for a tomato on a beautiful day when he should have been putting the hot dog in the kettle for Maria. He lost his head. I take this as a sign of spring.

March 17, 1989

INVENTIVE LOOK AT FUTURE PAST

I walk through the Great Caputo's joint on South Broadway -- well, really, I tiptoe and slither through the joint because of all the clutter -- and I am struck by two things: the fierce march of twentieth century technology and the historic right of men to invent whatever the hell comes into their heads. Cigarette lighters shaped like the torsos and heads of women? Cigarette lighters with names? Flashing Flora? Glowing

Gertie? Why not? It's a free country, and here in the Great Caputo's secondhand store, this purgatory for bric-a-brac, it is the inventive mind that looms awesome. In fact, it haunts the place. It haunts the earth.

Imagine the road to South Broadway. Imagine the man who sat in a workshop some years ago and actually designed cigarette lighters shaped like women. Glowing Gertie! What an idea! The idea probably crashed through the man's brain one Tuesday morning and stunned him. So he donned tie and fedora, packed his invention in a suitcase, and presented it to cigarette lighter executives. And they loved it! The lighters went out into commerce, then into American homes. Now they reside at the Great Caputo's, on sale as "collectibles."

There are many such items in this cluttered shop on Broadway. Some are junk. Most are so unusual you must marvel at the anonymous minds that invented them. The radios, for example. From the back to the front, the store is a scattered and sloppy museum of the instruments of mass communication. On the floor I find two black boxes with leather handles and latches. They look like old doctor's bags. I open them. They turn out to be early portable radios that can either be plugged into a socket or operated on batteries. The dials indicate setting by time of day: Set it here for morning listening, here for afternoon, here for evening, and here for the weather. The antenna stays hidden until you extend it. The Great Caputo thinks these radios go back to the 1930s. As he says this, I imagine some RCA technician in lab coat rushing down a hallway exclaiming his happiness with these radios, his claim to immortality.

The RCA techs were probably just as pleased with the duck radio, a truly amazing piece that makes you appreciate the wonder of a man with an idea. Some inventive mind decided to take a cheap print of winged ducks rising from a pond and make it "practical." He built a radio behind it. The on/off switch and the tuning dial appear in the lower right-hand corner of the print. The whole thing is framed and suitable for hanging. At the time it first appeared in stores, the duck radio was undoubtedly considered a thing of great beauty and ingenuity. Today, it would be considered junk, but I remain in awe of the mind that developed it. Someone actually looked at a picture of ducks and thought to attach a radio. Amazing.

The horse clock conjures the same feelings. It is a framed corral of horse heads circling the hands of an electric clock. You marvel at the kind of mind that united horse heads with clocks. Who knows? At one time, such a product might have been all the rage. Today it would probably be considered tacky. *But just try to find one in Hunt Valley!*

I was stunned by another assemblage of moving parts at the front of the store. Back when small television sets were new to the world, some mastermind at General Electric decided to test the outer boundaries of technical imagination. He brought together a nine-inch TV, an alarm clock, and an AM radio, all in one box the size of an overnight bag. Marvelous. The fellow who formulated this design probably received a Christmas bonus.

Where do we find such men? Where did the captains of consumer sales find the 1930's wunderkind who invented what the Great Caputo calls "a very rare ship's clock." Actually, it is not a clock from a ship. It is a chrome-colored, cast-metal sculpture of lighthouse and Cape Cod home. An electric clock sits in the roof of the house. The light tower glows. So does the house. In fact, when the bulb inside the house gets warm enough, you start to see little sailboats. They move on a cylindrical slice of plastic, 'round and 'round they go. Ahoy! It is an amusing piece that when considered long enough, draws up a happy appreciation for the man who labored over its extraordinary design. I do not know the chap's name or his whereabouts today. But his lighthouse still glows, his clock still tells time, his boats still sail -- all because one day long ago, he executed his right to invent whatever the hell came into his head. It's a great country.

December 2, 1987

O YE GREAT URBAN HOMESTEADER

He is, from his Sherwin-Williams cap down to his steel-shanked boots, the most obnoxious, know-it-all urban homesteader in the joint. In fact, he's the only urban homesteader in the joint. He stands more than six feet tall, with plaster dust clinging to his moustache, his right hand in dirty pants, his left holding a Heineken, and his belly stuffed into a corduroy jacket. A leather sheath hangs on his hip.

It has been a rough Saturday for the urban homesteader, and now this macho man of the new Baltimore, this slayer of termites and rotten floor, joists wants to talk. He wants to talk about exposing brick because the Great Urban Homesteader has seen the enemy and it is paneling. Indeed, he is a sought-after cocktail party speaker these renaissance days. So the folks gather about him just as the radical chic once cuddled up to the Black Panthers and other urban pioneers. They want to hear what it is like to be a trail blazer out there, in the new Baltimore. After all, he has survived the great wilderness of Otterbein, Barre Circle, and yes, even Federal Hill. His accomplishments in the real property world of the new Baltimore make the Louisiana Purchase look like a 7-Eleven stick-up. He has been beyond and back. So please speak to us now, Mr. Gentrification.

"You have to be careful when you're exposing," he says.

The ladies in the room coo.

"You can chisel too deep and gouge the brick. Oh God, have I chiseled too deep in my day. . . . You can knock out too much mortar and then you'll have to repair the joints and you won't be able to match the color so you'll have to re-mortar all the joints."

The men in the room harumph with jealousy. They feel like sissies. They know that, no matter how they try, they will never be able to expose as much brick as the Great Urban Homesteader.

"Sometimes," says the Great Urban Homesteader, "you find that the bricks in the wall are two or three different colors, so you'll have to paint the whole wall. . . . Then there's the horsehair plaster." He shakes his head and adds, "Boy, oh boy, could I tell tales about horsehair plaster."

One of the women rushes up with raw broccoli and yogurt dip. She knows the Great Urban Homesteader needs sustenance.

A man in the room raises his hand. "Sir," the man says. "Speak to us now of walls."

The Great Urban Homesteader gulps his broccoli, washing it down with another Heineken. He assumes the posture of a prophet looking over the router bit section at Hardware Fair. "Taking out interior walls can open up the appearance of your house. But then you can take out too much and the whole thing might collapse. See, you have to know -- as I do -- the difference between a bearing wall and a non-bearing wall. Take the time I took out our curved wall, for instance."

He chuckles with a side glance at his wife.

"I don't mind admitting I left one beam standing. Then I find out that it's a bearing wall and that one four-by-four is holding up the whole house. . . . Well, I had to laminate three two-by-twelves together, cut into the brick, and put them crosswise to support the second floor. This is, of course, after I jacked up the whole house, leveled it, and dropped an eight-by-eight in the basement to support everything."

He pauses, swigs from his Heineken, surveying through the green glass the looks of envy in his audience. "Too bad we had to cover up the hand-hewn joists. But in life we must all make trade-offs."

A woman in the room lurches from beneath a hanging spider plant. "Sir," she says. "Speak to us now of cement."

The Great Urban Homesteader grins. Cement is his specialty. Cement is his raison d'etre. Even Mayor Schaefer has marveled at his ability to mix. "I've always said that mixing cement is like making a good pie crust -- when you think you've got enough water it's probably too much."

Giggles. The women in the room scribble notes. The men scowl. There is talk about publishing the sayings of the Great Urban Homesteader in *Baltimore Magazine.*

But now it is time for him to return to the wilderness -- hammer, Heineken, and crowbar in hand -- to destroy more Formstone and paneling, to slay more termites, and above all, raise the price of housing in the new Baltimore. He knows that somewhere there is brick yet to be exposed. A pioneer's work is never done.

April 17, 1980

THE GOOD DOCTOR

The good man, though he may die before his time, will always find rest. A long life is not what really makes life worth living, nor the number of years the true measure of a good life. . . . This person has sought to please God, and so God has loved him.

-- The Book of Wisdom

The bright light of a winter morning bounced off Harford Road, streamed through the glass doors of Saint Dominic's Church, and cast a pale wash on the wall above the sanctuary. There, the shadows of men and women moved separately, then blended together. They transformed a small usher at the front door into a giant silhouette. One by one, new shadows appeared on the wall. A woman with a cane walked through the doorway, and her shadow blessed itself with holy water. Then the woman moved out of the angle of light and up the aisle of the church. "Some man, some man," she said as she genuflected, shook her head, slid into a pew, and sobbed. "Some man. Where'm I gonna get another doctor like that? He made me walk and talk."

Slowly, the church filled with people -- the friends, family, and patients of Dr. Sebastian Russo of Hamilton. Women and girls in wool coats and knit hats. Men and boys in raincoats and ski jackets. Then the ushers, looking professionally somber, closed the doors in the front of the church. The light from the street vanished and so did the shadows. And now the shadows were all people, about seven hundred.

The women in Sebastian Russo's family were small and dark, with shiny black hair and eyes swollen crazy with tears. They hugged each other as the procession moved down the endless aisle. The congregation sobbed and coughed and twisted handkerchiefs. Father Michael Roach, a large priest who resembles Pavarotti, met the casket of Sebastian Russo at the middle of the church. The priest's vestment, satin-white with black trim, sparkled under the lights in the church.

"He was living in the midst of the world and so God took him away unto himself. And he has been taken away so evil may not warp his understanding, nor treachery ever seduce his soul. . . . His soul was pleasing to God, so God took him from the wickedness around him."

Seldom in the annals of the city have we seen such a generous man who was caught in the cross-fire of insanity. Hundreds paid deep respects this week to Sebastian Russo. He was, they say, a great doctor whose tirelessness was outdistanced only by his humanity. You could call him at any time, they say. He visited the old and the sick. He would treat anyone, Father Roach said, even a "thuggy creature from the street." It didn't matter. If you couldn't pay, Sebastian Russo let it slide. He studied his patients and avoided prescribing pills as a quick solution to their problems. He never operated in the world of modern medicine, with its computerized billing and weekend answering service.

He was -- they say over and over -- a very good, very decent, very serene man. But this good and very decent, serene man was murdered by a handgun in an instance of terror on a Friday night in Hamilton. There was shock, and then the people Sebastian Russo treated for so long held a vigil with candles. Yesterday, when those people filled Saint Dominic's Church with sobs and tears, a strong spirit of community emerged from the mourning. Hundreds of people with different lives, different problems, and different frustrations could look around and share a solitude. They had all come to the church for the same reason and they were united in ninety minutes of prayer. Their shadows blended together on the sanctuary wall.

"Sebastian Russo made believing in a loving God a good bit easier," Father Roach said. "He was not a pious man, not a churchy type. How he cared for his patients was a reflection of God's love. . . . Falling asleep amidst pain and confusion, he awakened in the loving arms of our Savior."

Then the doors opened and once again the morning light from Harford Road poured into the church. As the people turned to leave, the light made their faces white and soft. A March breeze chilled Harford Road, where the pallbearers put Sebastian Russo's coffin in a hearse. Dozens of cars followed the hearse to Moreland Memorial Park, which was wide and bright on the winter day. Men and women, at least a hundred fifty, parked their cars and walked across a lawn to the mausoleum. There was little standing room in the building, so people crowded into doorways and tried to listen to Father Roach's final words.

The wind turned the collars of coats, and people shivered. The women in Sebastian Russo's family continued to cry and speak in Italian whispers. When the service ended, each person walked by the coffin and touched it. Father Roach held his prayer book against his chest and stared at the coffin a very long time. "Hopefully, he will have inspired someone to be the kind of doctor he was," Father Roach said. "But it will be a long time before Hamilton has another like him."

The people turned from the mausoleum and walked away, spreading evenly across the grass. The morning light was rising now and, as the people went off in different directions, there were long shadows on the ground.

March 4, 1981

PIGTOWN WILL SHINE TONIGHT

So it's a rainy, wind-swept, smoke-stink, traffic-jam day in Pigtown. There's a big fire on West Pratt Street, playing havoc with the masses and sending mud-brown smoke into the mouse-gray sky. It's a lousy day. Which is a fine reason to stop by the 1019 Pleasure Club. So let's go. We can dry off, have a drink, shoot some pool, shoot some bull, and maybe listen to the latest pronouncements of the Mayor of Cleveland Street. There's the mayor now, Bobby Kloch. Cloak is how he pronounces it.

"It's Kloch!" says his press secretary, George Gerver, making it sound like Clutch.

Clutch or Cloak, Bobby is the mayor of Cleveland Street. When he ran for office back in 1963, his campaign slogan was: "Remember Your Coat and Vote For Kloch." He was running for state central committee. But that's nothing. His true calling is chief executive of Cleveland Street, which is where Bobby Kloch comes from. He's a back-street politician. He knows everybody. He does things for people. Right now, he's entertaining three friends in the 1019 Pleasure Club, which is on James Street. The mayor is sitting at a table playing solitaire while three guys watch. You never have to do much to entertain your pals in Pigtown.

"They help me," the mayor says. "This here is Mr. Bell; you know, like ring the bell. This here is George Gerver. And this gentleman here is Mr. Lashley, Eddie."

They are all dues-paying members of the 1019 Pleasure Club. It's a big airy rowhouse converted into a clubhouse. There's a bar and a jukebox and a pool table and a lot of folding chairs. "Whiskey and pickles and anything you want," says the Mayor. They have parties here. Each member pays twenty-four dollars a year. The bar works on the honor system. The club was formed in 1939 at a bar at 1019 West Cross Street.

"Louie Roe's Bar," says the Mayor. "Roe like shad roe."

"Not *Louie!*" says Gerver, the press secretary.

"Oh. Floyd," says the Mayor. "Floyd Roe."

"Not *Floyd* Roe! *Roy* Roe!"

"I got a tooth out in front," the Mayor explains. "I can't pronounce right."

The founding fathers of the club were Archie Miller, Charlie Durham, and Harry Riesset.

"They're all dead," says the Mayor.

"No! No! *They're not all dead!*" says Gerver. "Jeesh!"

Without Gerver, we'd never get this right. For the record: Mr. Durham and Mr. Riesett are still active members of 1019. The Mayor of Cleveland Street, who is approaching sixty-nine, usually gets all this straight. He knows everybody. In fact, he knows a lot of historical facts about people and Pigtown. For instance, the Mayor says Jimmy O'Neil was the man who wrote the Pigtown theme song:

Pigtown will shine tonight
Pigtown will shine
Pigtown will shine tonight
All up and down the line
Pigtown will shine
With a bar of soap and a Turkish towel
Pigtown will shine.

O'Neil had the voice of an angel. All the nuns at St. Jerome's School used to make him sing, "I'm Looking Over A Four-Leaf Clover."

Now the Mayor of Cleveland Street recalls another famous Pigtown character, fella by the name of Pineapple Murphy. "They used to call him Hepner's Mule, too, 'cause Pineapple used to pull an ice wagon for a man named Hepner." Legend has it that Pineapple Murphy once cleaned fish in a tub with soap and a scrub board. "Then he hung them out to dry," the Mayor says.

These older guys, who now pass the day sitting around the 1019 Pleasure Club, used to walk out to Gwynns Falls Park for a swim. "There was a man there with a brush. He made you scrub your feet before going in the pool," the Mayor says. They also swam in the duck pond in Carroll Park. They had a buddy named Buzz Pettit who could swim under water -- but not on top. Swear to God. The kids used to drink from the horse trough at Cross Street and Washington Boulevard too. "There was a trough in front of Number 10 Firehouse," says the Mayor.

Don't forget Ba-Ba Benson from Scott Street. He was the custodian at 1019 for years. "He's dead now but I still see him from time to time," says the Mayor. "He breezes through here. Never says hi. Just slams the door. And I'm always telling him: 'Hey Ba-Ba, don't slam that door.'"

Pigtown is most famous for the pigs that used to hustle down Ostend Street on their way to the slaughterhouse. "If the pigs got tired they'd give 'em a ride in the truck," the mayor says. "I used to follow the pigs to school. They had cattle too. They brought them through here and one time they got loose and busted up all the people's steps."

Bobby Kloch, Mayor of Cleveland Street, comes to the 1019 Pleasure Club every afternoon. But he starts each day with a cup of coffee at Pete's Confectionery. "Except Wednesday and Sunday," he says.

And why not Wednesday and Sunday?

"They're closed."

The Mayor goes to the store and sits around. His friend George Stoffel sits around there too. "Don't ever say Hungry Jack Pancakes or Jell-O to George," the mayor says.

What?

"Don't ever say Hungry Jacks or Jell-O."

Why?

"He gets mad."

Why?

"George never eats the stuff himself. If you say it to him, he gets mad. Pete makes Hungry Jacks and asks George if he wants some and George gets mad. He's like that. He doesn't like Hungry Jacks, Jell-O, or the people who eat 'em."

Rain or shine, the Mayor of Cleveland Street knows his public.

November 11, 1983

THE KOREAN DOWN THE STREET

It is a splendid day on a quiet street in East Baltimore and the sun is shining into rowhouse windows filled with ceramic birds. There's a child in a black-and-yellow checkered hat, twenty dollars in her hand, out for bread and soda. Another one, with a dollar, has been dispatched for two loaves of white bread. They go to the corner grocery store and when they push the door and fresh air comes in with them, you are reminded what a beautiful day it is here in the Promised Land.

At this moment, I am standing at the counter of the grocery store, fresh bananas from Colombia at my fingertips, talking to the store's owner. He is sitting behind the cash register, smoking a cigarette. His wife is assisting the children with bread and soda.

"Korea?" I ask.

"Yes," he says. "Nineteen seventy-four . . . February tenth." He came here with his wife and three children. He didn't speak English. Today, he speaks fine English with an accent and tells a proud story.

When he was first in America, he kept three jobs. He repaired refrigerators for a department store for $4.13 an hour. He washed dishes in a hotel restaurant. He worked as a painter's helper. He saved his money "penny by penny." He bought a new car, a station wagon, in 1976. A couple years later, he and his wife became citizens of the United States of America. He opened a grocery store in Pigtown in 1982. He stayed there three years, until the lease was up. He moved to this new corner location in East Baltimore last fall. He put his name on the store, over the front door. He sells groceries and candy and cigarettes. He seems very content in this little world. His children are now in college. He still has the '76 station wagon.

I have come here on this day because of curiosity about a sign down the street. At the next corner, there is a competing grocery store, a larger one, a brighter one, an older one. There is a sign in the front window. It stands out like a flag. "We're Still Americans," it says. "We Speak English."

Is there some animosity here, between the two corner grocery stores, on this marvelous day in East Baltimore? Is something more than allegiance to native country being declared here? And does the Korean-born gentleman, eight years a citizen of America, feel even mildly insulted by this sign, or is that a thought occurring only to me, who passes through this neighborhood just now and then?

"I don't care," the man from Korea says. "I don't care. What am I going to do? Start something? No, I don't care. Why should I?" And there is a laugh and a sigh and a shrug. "You hear me," he says. "I speak English."

At the competing store, I ask about the sign. The proprietor, a friendly and witty middle-aged man with a pencil behind his right ear, says he has been on this corner thirty-two years, and he says this with the same proud tone I heard in the voice of his competitor up the block. "That's right," he says, "thirty-two years, raised four kids . . . and I've watched the neighborhood change." He says he survived the flood that hit his street when the storm drains overflowed. He's done many things for the neighborhood -- bought Girl Scout cookies from local children, got involved in a crime-watch program. He stayed right here all these years. Country life was not for him.

"You got to put up with crickets," he says. "And it's dark. You can't find your way home at night, can't put the key in the door. Here, we got police helicopters lighting up the streets. We got police dogs to show you the way home."

But what about the sign? The neighborhood has changed, he says. Some "hillbilly" moved in down the street. Had a barbecue on the roof. Cooked hot dogs and grits. Almost cooked the whole house. Fire Department came.

And the sign? That was the idea of a guy named "Willie the Whale." Willie, I am told, walked into this store one day, hugged the proprietor, and said, "You're the only American left around here." So Willie got the sign made. And it's in the front window. Been there a few months now. No complaints until this columnist showed up with all the questions.

"I went along with it," the proprietor says. "I love the Koreans. Christ, they're hard-working people and all. I love them guys. I'm just letting people know we're still American." But so is the Korean-born gentleman down the street.

Before I leave, I ask the proprietor of the store with the sign where his father was from.

"Highlandtown," he says.

"I mean, where was he born?"

"Munich, Germany."

March 19, 1986

KINDNESS STILL A FEAST OF LIFE

The name is Anne and she lives alone on South Mount Street, and there are days when Anne sees things from her window that make her wonder about the American character, things that leave her bewildered about human nature. She left Lithuania during the war and went to Germany. After the war, she came to the United States. She's been in southwest Baltimore ever since. She's sixty-five now and loves America as much as anyone, but there are days when she wonders sadly about its people and how they treat each other.

For one thing, she never expected to see much cruelty in America. Not, at least, like the cruelty she saw about three weeks ago, just a few yards from her house. A woman had been left on Lombard Street, apparently because she and her children and grandchildren had been evicted from a nearby house. As the story goes, the woman's family packed their belongings into a small trailer and left, and the woman stayed behind.

No one that I talked to knows exactly why. No one in the neighborhood knows all the details. From the outside, it appeared to be an act of cruelty. But it might also have been the result of family disaster, a bitter epilogue to a tale of bad relations. The reasons almost don't matter. The woman, said to be in her fifties, was on the street. Some say she stayed there, with her belongings, for three days.

Anne watched this from her window, and the more she watched the more her view of the world grew dim. In the old country, people didn't treat each other like this. Especially family. Maybe, in all her years in the great country, Anne came to expect a minimum standard of decency from Americans. But most human nature -- both the good and the bad of it -- has nothing to do with nationality. You can't lay borders around goodness and badness, can't chart the human heart.

So just as it might not have been surprising to see a woman left to the street, it was not surprising to see people come out of their houses to try and help her. Three workers from a nearby shelter talked to the woman and brought her food. A young man named Tom, Anne's next-door neighbor, tried to see what he could do. But the woman was, at times, belligerent and profane, even hostile. She didn't want any help. She kept saying that someone would come for her. She said she was waiting. While she waited, Anne brought her breakfast. Of all the people who approached her that last week of July, Anne seemed to be the one the woman came to trust a little. Someone finally called the local social services office, and by July 26, the woman was off the street. The people who witnessed this sad sidewalk drama do not know what became of the woman but they seem certain she finally received some help. It was a pathetic little episode.

July 26 also happened to be an important day in Anne's life. It was the feast day of St. Anne, which meant, by Old World custom, that July 26 was Anne's "name day." Instead of celebrating birthdays, many Europeans celebrate the feast days of the saints whose names they bear. In America, this is not the custom. So Anne had long since given up on the idea of anyone beyond kin remembering her saint's day. And in her broken English, she told Tom, the young man from next door, that greeting card companies rarely made cards to honor the feast days of saints. So she wasn't expecting any.

The day passed quietly, and Anne didn't seem much in the mood for celebrating. The sidewalk theater left her pretty sour about things. She had never seen anyone evicted from a home in the old country, and never expected to see it in America. On that day, Anne could have been excused for being full of gloom. Later that afternoon, there was a knock on the door. It was Tom, the young man from next door. Anne thought he had come to get ice, as he does regularly. But just as she started to tell him she was out of the stuff, Tom swung his arms around and presented Anne with a big piece of apple pie, freshly baked by his wife Joline. Then he gave her a homemade card in honor of the seven-centuries-old feast of St. Anne. The card thanked Anne for being a terrific neighbor -- and for always being generous with the ice.

Suddenly the day, the world, the country, the neighborhood, and the people in it didn't seem so gloomy to old Anne of Mount Street. People had brought her down, people had raised her up again. The day was saved. Ah, it was a grand moment for the old woman. "No matter how hard I try," says Anne's daughter, "I will never understand people. And here are two examples from everyday life that make people even more of an enigma than they already are."

August 13, 1984

WHITE MARBLE STEPS

The aluminum storm door was smeared with black fingerprint dust and now, the day after Antoinette Zavadil's long and decent life ended in a sad and brutal death, a cop with a moustache stood in the doorway, the door braced open and rain washing streaks of the black dust onto the white marble steps. White marble steps line both sides of North Streeper, which is a narrow street a block north of East Monument. Antoinette Zavadil had lived here since 1940, and there was a time when she and the other women of the street bent their knees and scrubbed their white marble steps. There is probably no greater symbol of the perseverance of old Baltimore than the women on their knees scrubbing -- and no greater symbol of its infirmity than the cop in the open doorway.

"The old folks have their habits," said Officer John Lorme, standing in the drizzle and blocking the entrance to Antoinette Zavadil's living room. "You try to tell them they have to change their ways -- 'You can't walk home alone through that alley any more' -- but they can't change. For years they've been doing things a certain way, and they can't break their habits." And they stay in their neighborhoods long after all their friends have moved out or died, after their kids have grown up and gone, after they've been warned about dangers. Some are stuck. Some are defiant. Some stay because the neighborhood is their home -- old, tough, and familiar.

Antoinette Zavadil was eighty-six. She lived alone at 709

North Streeper. Her husband died years ago. Her daughter moved to Florida. She kept her house clean and neat. She walked to the store, to the bank, to the coin laundry, to church. Everyone in the 700 block knew her. Everyone liked her. Wednesday evening she was found on the living room floor of her rowhouse. She had been stabbed to death. The police think someone followed her into the house in the afternoon. The keys were still in the door. Mrs. Zavadil was still dressed in her rose-colored coat.

Now it was raining again on Streeper Street and people poked their faces out of windows and doors. Maurice Carroll, who moved two doors from Mrs. Zavadil about six years ago, pointed across the street. "You know what makes me feel so bad?" he said. "Look over there, see the door to 704? She was standing over there talking to her friend. She was standing right there and she asked me how my baby, Sherrah, was. 'How's that child?' she asked me. And I was telling her that Sherrah had just got an award from her school for being the outstanding student. She loved the children on this street.

"She was standing there with her cart. She looked like she had just come from the Laundromat. And in the other hand she had her check. You know, it was first of the month, and she had her check in a brown envelope. And I said she shouldn't be having that check in her hand, the way things are out here. 'What are you doing, standing out there with your check in your hand?' I said. 'Why're you standing there like that? Go inside with that check. You don't know who's watching you.'"

The neighborhood has changed in recent years. Elderly white people and younger black people with children live on this block. "Miss Teenie -- that's what we called her -- she didn't care anything about race," Carroll said. "She did everything she could for everybody. Gave my kids cookies on the holidays, like Valentine's Day, Christmas."

"Miss Teenie treated my kids like they were her own," said Wycal Carter, a truck driver who moved next to Mrs. Zavadil ten years ago. "She'd been like family. Any holiday that came by, she had something for my kids. From Day One when we moved here, she'd been like that. . . . She had a lady friend, a lady who used to live here, who came by to check on her. She didn't go out at night at all, except maybe a little in the summer."

Carter works for a moving company. He's been thinking about moving his family out of here. "Last few years it started to change," he said. "More people hanging out, more drugs, more noise. My wife and I been talking about moving out, finding another place. Last night we talked about it again. We never had anything like this before."

Across the street, Elaine Dolch, seventy-one, sat in her doorway at 704 and watched the police hovering about Mrs. Zavadil's house. She and Mrs. Zavadil were old friends. "My son was ten months old when we moved here," Mrs. Dolch said. "That was forty-eight years ago. He lives in Dundalk. He came by to see me this morning, he was so worried. . . . Ten years ago he told me, 'Get the hell away from there.'. . ." And she waved her hand as if to say the debate about moving was finished years and years ago, before it ever started really. "It was always a nice neighborhood," she said. "We scrubbed the pavement, scrubbed the steps, the white marble. Oh, yes, a very nice neighborhood. Very clean."

"But you've thought about moving?"

"Oh, yes," Mrs. Dolch said. "Oh, yes. But Miss Zavadil -- Abigail some called her -- she begged me not to go. 'Please don't leave me,' she used to say. But there aren't many left from the old neighborhood. They either moved or died or went in the nursing home. . . . Margaret, across the street, she moved. They tried to break into her house, she turned white, and her son took her out to Rosedale. . . . Mildred, they had mice in the house; they moved out. I got mice now, too. You know, you're on Social Security, you don't have money to make repairs."

"And a new place costs money," said Ellen Dernetz, who has lived on Streeper Street for thirty-one years and who now stood in Mrs. Dolch's doorway, raindrops on her eyeglasses. "One place was four hundred fifty dollars a month, with a five hundred dollar deposit. That's $950. Where you gonna get $950 at?" So they don't move. They stay. And the neighborhood changes. The police come around looking for drug dealers. The sun goes down and the older folks lock their doors.

"We go shopping just a few blocks from here," Mrs. Dernetz said. "Miss Zavadil just went to the bank, Golden Prague, at McElderry and Curley, to get a money order."

"They said it was a hundred sixty dollars," Mrs. Dolch said.

"She needed it for something for the house," added Mrs. Dernetz. "She just had had her hair fixed, too. . . ."

"Oh, yes," said Mrs. Dolch. "Just had a perm. . . . She was a wonderful woman. Oh, God. They were wonderful people. And she had one daughter, a sweet girl, looked just like her. Her husband drove a truck for a milk company. He died, oh, that's been many years ago, quite a few years ago."

A little girl came in from the rain. "My granddaughter, Heather," Mrs. Dolch said. "She's seven. She just had her First Holy Communion at St. Elizabeth's. She just gave a picture from her First Communion to Miss Zavadil. They said she had the picture in her coat, that rose-colored coat, when they found her." Across the street, Antoinette Zavadil's daughter, just in from Florida, walked up the white marble steps, smeared with the dust and the rain, and into the house with the cop in the doorway.

May 6, 1988

THE CLOCK STOPPED

When they rolled over at the sensation of morning and looked up from their beds, the children saw pink. If they slept in the rear room of the house at the end of the block, they saw yellow. These were the colors someone once decided to paint the walls. It was years ago, long before the people left their neighborhood at the scare of a new highway and the demolition of their homes, when things were safe and it made sense to redecorate the bedrooms.

Today in Sharp-Leadenhall, there's no time capsule to say who did the paint jobs or built the houses in the first place. No clock says exactly how much life elapsed here before the people vanished. There's no trace of the children who slept in the beds that now lie in the trash. No record of their fights or triumphs or holidays, or their growing up and heading off to Southern High. There's no history of the old folks who made soup in the kitchens that were once each of them unique but that now share the same pile of dust. The houses are very fragile, very old. "A hundred and fifty easy," says Dick Ayres, the man in charge of bringing the final ruin to the last eight rowhouses in Sharp-Leadenhall.

You can come down to South Baltimore, past the Inner Harbor, to the west of Federal Hill, south of the homes being renovated by the young couples at the end of Lee Street, and watch Dick Ayres remove an entire block from city history. It's all in the bricks. The pile grows with every heave of a backloader as it tugs a chain strapped through a window. One thrust, and a bit of long-ago falls. There are strips of gray wood, rusty pipes, and the smell of dust, the same musty aroma you get from an old box once it's taken from a desolate corner of an attic and reopened.

Sharp-Leadenhall used to be full of people. Two centuries ago, it was one of the first black communities in the city, a segregated bedroom community for the servants of wealthy uptown whites. In 1960, there were five thousand people here; today most are gone. They left under the threat of a new highway. Time passed and brilliant engineers decided to change the route of the highway, but not until after the landlords had sold out and the people disappeared. It was a chapter in what Dick Ayres calls "the rape of the city."

He's a big man, a round man. They call him Ducky. When his men work on a job, he plants his trailer nearby and holds court with his two lhasa apsos at his feet. One he calls Ming; the other -- the midget -- he calls Poco. "I'm a gypsy in the city," he says. Ducky Ayres has been in the business thirty-four years, the last five on contract from the city. He's renovated old homes and torn them down. He handled the "Solar House" that Jimmy Carter visited during his trip here last August.

In his work, Ducky Ayres sees great irony. But he doesn't speak with anger; he sits back and points. "They built the Beltway so people could bypass the city," he says, reaching down to Ming. "They built the tunnel so people could go under it. They built malls so the merchants could leave, too. It was a rape of the city and now they're trying to bring it back to life." James Rouse, the famous developer, comes up during this conversation. He was among the great suburban mall-makers. But now he's returned, heralded as a hero come to save the city with Harborplace.

Ducky, who stayed in the city all along, says, "We've gone back to where the whole thing started. It started at the harbor and everything developed around it. The history repeats itself. We have to tear down the old to make way for the second cycle." Ducky Ayres and his men will build six new rowhouses where the eight are falling. There will be, then, a lapse in time until their work ends in June, new families move in, and the clock starts again.

September 28, 1979

SOCIAL STUDIES

The early 1980s will be remembered on the streets of Baltimore for three things: cheese lines, the election of another millionaire to the White House, and the deinstitutionalization of mental patients into society. It all seemed to hit at once. The vagrant population soared. The unemployment lines grew. Ronald Reagan came up with a simple-minded game plan: cut social spending, give tax relief to the rich, sit back, and hope the crumbs fall off the table. Meanwhile, the middle-class found itself threatened again by recession. The unemployment lines looked as if they would wind right through their middle-class living rooms. Eventually, the economy recovered, but at a terrible human price -- especially in poor urban centers like Baltimore. By the time Reagan was re-elected in 1984, the misery of his first term was almost completely forgotten, except in the sad underworld of the city.

MR. PRESIDENT, GET A JOB

Ronald Reagan hasn't looked for a job in decades, so no wonder he can't understand why people complain about being out of work when the Sunday classifieds scream for help. "How do we explain that in the Sunday [New York] *Times* there were 45 1/2 pages of help-wanted ads and in the Washington *Post* Sunday there were 33 1/2 pages of help-wanted ads and these were jobs calling for people of every range that you could make?" the new President asked. "How does a person in any of these skills justify calling themselves unemployed when there's a fellow spending money and saying, 'I've got a job. Come fill my job'?"

Amazing things happen when President Reagan decides to read something besides the Sunday comics. He comes up with a startling revelation: The classifieds are full, but people are still unemployed, and what does it mean? The answer is simple if you follow the simple and time-worn reasoning of economists who agree with Reagan: The government pays people for not working, so why should they bother.

If you dig a little deeper, you might find a deeper and just as time-worn answer: Most of the ads listed in the Sunday classifieds are aimed at people already working and looking for a step up. Very few offer employment to people at the bottom of the ladder -- those with no marketable skills, little education or experience, who are too old or too young, teenagers leaving high school with no plans (or money) for college, housewives looking for badly-needed extra income. In three sections of yesterday's Sunday *Sun*, I counted 1,972 job opportunities. Of those, 418 did not require experience.

Most of the ads were for people who have college degrees and experience in fields like computer programming, electronics, dentistry, mechanics, nursing, engineering, or management. Of the 418 non-experienced job opportunities, many required a high school diploma while others required that the applicant type or relocate or travel or have no children. The jobs included baby sitter, barmaid, cab driver, car washer, chimney sweep, and "Girl Friday." One asked for participants in an aspirin study. Another needed someone to sell adult books. One job, for a groundskeeper at Hunt Valley, required two years experience.

No doubt, even some non-skilled jobs will go begging. The American society has more than enough freeloaders to go around. And those are the people, along with welfare cheats, who President Reagan points to when he beefs about the economic state of America. But what American wants to concede that a large portion of the country's work force is not willing to work, that we are a nation of lazy goofs and good-for-nothings? Most of us feel lucky, even proud, to say we have a job. As Walter Heller stated in a news dispatch last week, "Thank heavens that being unemployed and on the dole still carries a lot of social disapproval."

If there are so many jobs around, as Reagan suggests from his quick-read of the Sunday papers, then why did twenty-six thousand people show up last fall for seventy-two entry-level jobs at the new Social Security complex? And why, just this month, did five thousand residents of Toldeo, Ohio, line up in the cold for ninety jobs at a Johnson Controls battery plant? Most Americans still want to work, and finding a job isn't easy.

Martha Thomason called here two weeks ago, just as new statistics showed 156,806 Marylanders were unemployed in January, the highest number in state history. Martha Thomason is an extreme case: a fifty-five-year-old widow who supports her thirteen-year-old granddaughter and ninety-one-year-old father. "But I honestly want to work," she said. "I have to."

She worked for Exxon's accounting division in Towson until it relocated to Houston. She took a job with Durrett-Sheppard Steel for a year, but was terminated one Friday night "because of economic reasons." She found a temporary inventory job with Diamond Shamrock Corporation, but the woman she had replaced came back to work. She spotted a newspaper ad for an entry-level job at a Baltimore bank, but learned she was unqualified because "I couldn't type thirty-five words a minute." She tried to get another job with the bank, the salary for which was $137 a week. She tried to get a job with the city, but was told she had to be a city resident.

She applied for a job as an inventory clerk with a computer rental firm, but was told she was too old. She went to Pantry Pride. "They told me I was qualified, but I didn't get the job." She went to Blue Cross and applied for a job as an accounting clerk. She applied for a job in Timonium and the man who received her application asked: "Are you going to retire soon?" She went to the Baltimore office of Senator Paul Sarbanes to complain that she was a victim of age discrimination. A member of Sarbanes' staff said nothing could be done and suggested she go to the state Office of Aging. "I'm getting old," Martha Thomason said. "So I went there and filled out an application but they told me there were no jobs."

Just for kicks, Ronald Reagan ought to step out of the presidency for a day and do what Martha Thomason does -- look for a job through the help-wanted section. I wish him luck. In yesterday's Sunday *Sun*, there were no openings for politicians and only one for actors. It said, "ACTORS. Out of work? Need a job? Make an appt. Call 265-6460. Ask for Bill Johnson."

March 23, 1981

STATE OF THE UNION

On State of the Union Day, the path to cheese turned to mud. Sticky, cold mud. They were handing out cheese at the Victory Villa Community Center in Middle River, and feet were treading relentlessly on the path to the door. Just before noon, some workmen came out and placed two large pieces of one-inch plywood on the ground by the steps, and as soon as they did this, twenty feet shuffled from the mud to the wood. "That's better," a woman said. "Much better. Thank you."

Actually, the path had been whipped into mud from the waiting. The first seekers of cheese arrived at the door about seven-thirty a.m. Three hours went by before big yellow county trucks unloaded the brown boxes. And it was at least eleven before they actually gave away the cheese.

Everybody waited. Hundreds of people. Young women holding children. Old women holding purses. Old men. Young men. The line went from the door of the delivery room, down four steps, across a wet lawn, then down a driveway, and onto a sidewalk around the community center.

The intersection of Compass Road and Martin Boulevard was jammed with cars the way streets around high schools are jammed on Homecoming Day. And the wind was picking up, and the sky was dingy gray.

Allan Walls, in a big blue snorkel coat, came down the steps with two long boxes, each containing a five-pound block of All-American cheese. He had two one-pound bricks of butter, and he was fidgeting to get a better hold of it all. "I figure I paid for it with my taxes while I was working, so why not?" said Walls, who is thirty-six years old and the father of three children. He put the blocks of cheese in the pockets of the big coat. "It's a little degrading, I guess. I worked all my adult life and now it's the pits, standing in line for a couple of pounds of cheese."

In 1980, which was the last time Walls worked a full year, he went into a voting booth, flicked a switch, and ordered up Ronald Reagan. "I've always been a little conservative and I thought Ronald Reagan was going to turn the country around," he said. "His main thrust was to cut government spending. And that's all the Democrats seemed to be doing -- spend, spend, spend. He seemed like he was going to get the thing back together. You can't blame all the problems on him, but he hasn't done very much, has he? He doesn't seem to have much sympathy for the working man."

Allan Walls got the cheese because, aside from mowing lawns in summer and shovelling driveways in winter, he hasn't worked a serious job since September, 1981. He had fourteen good years installing drive shafts at General Motors when the layoff notice came. And those were fourteen pretty good years for Walls and his family. "I had a rowhouse in Dundalk all paid for. I made about twenty-three, twenty-four thousand dollars a year. I was proud of the fact my wife could stay home and take care of the kids while I went to work." Walls had two cars, both Chevies. He had little trouble getting credit, too. In those days, you told a credit manager you worked at General Motors and you just about walked away with money in your pocket.

In 1979, Walls moved out of Dundalk. He bought a house with three bedrooms and a two-car garage in a new development near Perry Hall. In today's market, the houses there sell for seventy to a hundred thousand dollars. His neighbors have mostly white-collar jobs. "This is the first time I've ever been out of work, and I think I can hold on. But I'm getting worried. It doesn't seem like anything's coming our way."

Walls figures he has three more weeks of unemployment benefits. His wife keeps a part-time job in a department store, so they're still making mortgage payments. "I haven't filed for food stamps yet. Others need it more. And I guess that's where my pride gets in the way. I heard the interview is pretty degrading. You've got to tell them everything, tell them every penny you have."

In the meantime, Walls, who has a degree in business administration, keeps looking for work. "I've got all the places written down somewhere. Mostly places like insurance companies and banking. But most places don't even take applications. You send in resumes, and most of the time you don't even hear back from them. . . . I get tired of sitting around. A lot of times it seems like I've got nothing to look forward to."

Given a chance to make a State of the Union address, what would Allan Walls, with the blocks of cheese, have told the nation last night? "I'd tell the President and the Congress to stop fighting each other and get the country back together. Stop worrying about aircraft carriers and get some job training programs. I'm all for defense, but you get to the point where it's just throwing money down a hole. And the MX, that's money that'll be buried in the ground.

"It's going to take a cooperative effort with government, industry, and labor. And it's got to be different than before. No leaf - raking jobs; they don't amount to much. I think the government should give a job credit to industry, where a business gets credit for hiring someone who's out of work and training him. . . . I don't know. Maybe I'm lucky. I still got my health and my family's in good health. But I'm not better off than I was two years ago. Remember that? That's what Reagan used to ask us. Are we better off?"

January 26, 1983

THE STORY OF FRANK

The face came out of the whiskers and the lips quivered. He was Frank -- Frank of the street, address unknown -- and he tried to explain how his first life ended and his second life began. "You know," he said, "I can't look people in the face no more." His Fagin nose had been beaten by the weather, his clothes were ragged and infested with insects. "I don't know what it is. A year ago, I wasn't like this. I had a job, worked for Social Security out there in Woodlawn. I was special police." A long stringy beard was in knots, thick and permanent.

"Don't know. One morning I woke up and I was like this. I had a car and a steady job, and then I didn't have them no more." He rested a bottle of Sprite and a cigarette on his knee. "Just gave up I guess." He said these things on a Sunday in September, from a bench in Marketplace. Last week, Francis Michling, address unknown, came in off the street to die. His friends called him Midge and he would have been sixty in March. He was a gentle person, a religious man, a part-time loner who fell out of contact with his family. He grew up in Overlea. His sister lives in Florida now, and there is a niece in Baltimore. Michling was a veteran of the Army, World War II. He worked in Woodlawn as an officer in the Federal Protective Service. He directed traffic. Each day, he left his rented room on Pelham Avenue and drove to work with his friend Milton Ross. On Sundays, he went to church.

"He never drank a drop, long's I knew him," says Bill Kroeger, another federal policeman. "He was neat and clean and always on time. I'd say, 'Let's go out and get drunk,' and he'd refuse. He was a very religious Catholic and I think he said he used to be an altar boy."

There was never a wife, only lady friends. And one special one, in New Jersey. A year ago September, Frank borrowed some change for a phone call. "He came back and said she'd married someone else," Milton Ross recalls. "He took it very hard. For three or four years he traveled up to New Jersey to see her. And then that happened. He went into a daze."

Federal policemen carry guns, and they have to pass a shooting test each year. Last year, Frank couldn't shoot straight, and it was late summer when Bill Kroeger drove him to Bladensburg so Frank could turn in his uniform. Something happened; something snapped inside Frank Michling. He told Kroeger he could not even handle a desk job. "We tried to help him," Kroeger says. "But it was sickness, nerves, I guess. We tried to get him to see a doctor, but he refused. After a while, he didn't come to work any more and he lost his job."

Here, as Frank Michling's first life ends and the second one begins, the facts become fuzzy. There is no record of the last year, except the one that comes from friends. They know he left his car and all other possessions at the house on Pelham Avenue. Milton Ross saw Frank several months ago.

"On Belair Road," he says. "He was walking around. He talked to me and started to cry; then he walked away. He said he didn't want his friends to know what he turned out to be. That was the last I saw him."

Bill Kroeger hadn't been in touch with Frank for many months, so he started a search. He found Frank a week ago Tuesday, on Lombard Street. "I recognized his nose," says Kroeger. "That was all. I said, 'Do you know me?' He started to choke up. I cried when I seen a man like that: it took the wind out of my sails. He said, 'Oh Kroeger, where you been? Can you take me home?'"

People who look like Frank aren't allowed in restaurants, so he asked his old friend Kroeger to take some money, go to a carry-out, and buy some food. "I got him a big Coke, a cup of vegetable soup, and a big piece of pie," Kroeger says. "Then that night I brought him some nice sweet rolls, and he was crying. I think he slept in a doorway." With the telephone, Kroeger's mother and Milton Ross tried to get Frank some help, get him off the street. Wednesday, Kroeger looked for his old friend again, but Frank was gone.

Thursday, Frank was found on South Street, in front of a building, a big building. The sort of building that looks as though it could step on small men like Frank Michling. But, there are nice people who work there, like Jim Ryan, Lou Moseley, and Dianne White, employees of the Social Security Administration. Jim, Lou, and Dianne found Frank Michling sitting against a wall, shaking. Someone called an ambulance. "He kept saying, 'I'm scared. I'm scared,'" Jim Ryan recalls. "I helped persuade him to go to the hospital. Lou went with him." Mercy Hospital took Frank. They shaved him and they bathed him and they burned his filthy clothes. But he was very sick and they couldn't bathe or burn the pneumonia.

His personal effects consisted of a wallet with three dollar bills, another three dollars in change, a watch with a broken wristband, cigarettes, a family photo, his federal employee card, Blue Cross and Social Security cards, car keys that hadn't been used in a year, a little address book with an out-of-date telephone number for his sister, a miraculous medal, prayer cards, and his eyeglasses. A Mercy social worker located Frank Michling's niece. She had not seen her uncle for several years. And last week she was sad about having lost touch with a man who once cared for her and her brother very much, a man who took them on trips when they were kids. Now she would take him on one last trip and wonder why Frank Michling had to live and die twice.

November 9, 1979

DOLLARS AND CENTS

The first time she went through the check-out line, the woman in the sleeveless cotton dress stepped beyond her limits by eight dollars and change. She was in the Giant at Yorktowne Plaza, Cockeysville, and on this day she was down to her last twenty dollars in United States food stamps. Even with a fat handful of coupons -- and the store's standing offer to double their worth -- the woman in the sleeveless cotton dress had come up eight dollars short. Eight dollars and change.

She was anxious because there were other shoppers in line. The other shoppers had been thumbing through magazines, but now they had stopped and closed the magazines and they were all looking. Rather than negotiate with the cashier, rather than stand there and sort out necessary items from the unnecessary and the marginally necessary, the woman in the sleeveless cotton dress pulled her shopping cart out of line and went back into the aisles. The cashier voided the sale.

The woman was somewhere in her forties, lean and well groomed. The white cotton dress, with its green and orange print, could have passed for a house coat. She had placed three brown paper bags in her shopping cart. Each bag was about half full and each bag had been assigned a different priority. The first bag contained food items. The second carried toiletries. The third held a few household items.

The woman had twenty dollars worth of food stamps and a handful of coupons clipped from newspapers. So if she had to leave some items behind -- if the double-value coupons couldn't carry her much beyond the twenty dollars in food stamps -- at least there would be an order to the madness. First bag, second bag, third. . . . In the aisles, the woman parted with some items. Then she returned to the same check-out counter and the same patient cashier.

This time, the cashier agreed to give the woman a running tally. "I'll subtotal as I go along, okay?" she said. The woman nodded. And the process began, and people who usually read magazines in the check-out line were watching again. There were two women and a man. The first bag contained mostly packaged food items such as cake mixes and cereals. There was a bottle of corn syrup. There was a small waxpaper bag with doughnuts. The woman in the sleeveless cotton dress kept her eyes down on the check-out counter, her back to the other shoppers.

Soon the cashier announced the score on the first half-bag of groceries: seven dollars and change.

Now the woman in the sleeveless cotton dress emptied the contents of the second bag onto the check-out counter: bath soap and deodorant, tooth paste and shampoo. Some of the items were the type you buy only when there is a coupon to match, which is about the main reason for the existence of coupons. The other people in line watched as each item went into the hands of the cashier and across the computerized scanner. The woman in the sleeveless cotton dress kept her eyes between the groceries and the cash register. She did not look at the other people in line. The tally after the second bag meant the process could continue. The woman was still safe, a feeling common to shoppers who have limits, who play guessing games as they fill carts with groceries. One of the great embarrassments of the recession is standing in a supermarket check-out line and finding yourself surrounded by eyes, short of money, and long on detergent. This time, though, the woman in the sleeveless cotton dress had been more precise in her calculations. Each step of the way, the cashier gave her double credit for a coupon. And each step of the way, the woman asked for the running score. If she was still safe, she selected an item and slid it toward the cashier.

"Okay, add these," she said. Together, the coupons were a dollar and twenty cents. This meant the woman's absolute spending limit, including tax, was $21.20 -- that is, twenty dollars in food stamps, with a dollar twenty cent credit in coupons. The other people in line were still watching and waiting, and the woman in the sleeveless cotton dress pulled her last food stamps from a book. The cashier rang up the final total. The woman was still safe.

But there was one more item and the woman in the sleeveless cotton dress wanted it. Memory fails at this juncture. It may have been a bar of soap. Whatever, it meant only another fifty-six cents. "I'll pay for this separately," she said.

The cashier nodded. There was another pause as the woman rummaged through her purse. She took out a checkbook and a courtesy card. She wrote a check for two dollars and fifty-six cents. The cashier handed her two dollars, which went into an empty wallet. The woman in the sleeveless cotton dress pushed the shopping cart out of the store. Then the cashier looked up at the next customer, a young woman who had been reading a magazine, and apologized for the delay.

July 26, 1982

OUR DAILY BREAD

"I lost my hat in the library," the man said. "I was there yesterday, sitting a while, and I think I left it there. A stocking hat. It was a nice hat." But a lousy day for losing it. And that's because the day the man was talking about was Monday and Monday came to Baltimore with a lot of rain, heavy and ferocious rain. It was not a day to be on the streets. So the man went to the library on Cathedral Street and sat a while, waiting for the hour when the missions open. "I went in a bookstore, too," he said. "Maybe I left the hat there. I went back to check and no one had returned it yet. I'm gonna keep checking."

A hat is not something an acquaintance of the street wants to be without as winter approaches. Someone told the man he could buy a new one. "Not 'til my check comes first of the month," he said. The man had a plump paper bag under his left arm. He pointed to it. "I was out in the rain all day with one of these. It gets wet and falls apart, you know." He was a fairly young man, with a fatigued and whiskered face, and he had just finished lunch at Our Daily Bread, the place on West Franklin Street with the long line. People come in off the streets to eat there. Every day they start lining up about ten-thirty. The volunteers serve hot meals between eleven a.m. and one p.m.

This has been going on for a few years now, and the lines haven't been getting any smaller. There's a phone booth down the street from the place and that's how they measure the hardness of the day -- by the amount of time the line stays solid to the phone booth. Yesterday, some ninety minutes after the door opened, the line still backed up to the phone booth.

The lines always grow toward the end of a month. But in November, right from the beginning, Our Daily Bread was serving four hundred meals a day, which is a lot more than usual. Yesterday, they served 475 meals. The food came from about sixty casseroles that had been prepared by people from St. Thomas More in Hamilton. There were noodles and beef, noodles and chicken, noodles with vegetables, cheese, and Spam. The meals were served on plastic plates with canned Bartlett pears, a piece of cake, a cup of tea, all the bread a man or woman or child could eat.

When the door opened, two tidy old women clutching bags and newspapers came in. They ate slowly, with a smile, always polite, always saying please and thank you. "Darlin', could I have a plastic bag please?" one of them asked. She wanted to take her cake with her and eat it later. There was an old man with a psychology textbook under his arm, pressed against his wool coat. He wore baggy blue chinos and shoes without laces. There was a man with rimless glasses and a round red face, then a man with buck teeth and a watchcap atop his head, then a man with eyeglasses held together by paper clips. The paper clips had been twisted into a wire and pulled around the man's ears. They all ate in silence.

Some of the guests asked for more bread. On this day, there was a variety of bread -- white H&S, pumpernickel, hot dog rolls, or large round dinner rolls. There seemed to be a preference for white bread. An old man sat at a table near the front of the dining room and handed his meal ticket to a volunteer. When the plate of food went on the table before him, he bowed his head, closed his eyes, and moved his lips -- a moment of grace. Another old man sat on a bench, taking a little rest before lunch. "I'm doing better now that I'm sittin'," he said. "This leg . . ." He raised his right leg and pointed to the ankle. "This leg gives me fits. I got medication for it. It swells up when I'm on it all day." Yet another old man said he was going to "the Western Union park" to sleep after lunch.

There were young men in there, too -- one with a crazy yellow beard, one with a Murphy-for-Mayor cap, another with a hitchhiker's placard. He said he had to eat in a hurry because he had to be in Philadelphia by three o'clock. There were young women -- one with a puffy face and pitch-black hair, another with knee-high laced boots, another with two kids who patiently waited for a table so she could eat with her children.

Kids come to Our Daily Bread. Some walk in. Some are carried in. Yesterday one child came in a stroller, which was as sad a sight as there could be on the American continent. He couldn't have been a year old. His mother, a young Oriental woman, pushed the stroller. She had an older woman, most likely her mother, with her. They sat at the same table and ate the casserole and pears. The young woman put the child in her lap and fed it from a fork until a volunteer brought a spoon. A baby and strollers do not belong in these places. No one does. But they come all the time now, which is another way to measure the hardness of the day.

Around a quarter to one, a large man demanded a new cup of tea because he was certain someone had stuck a finger in the one he had been given. A minor argument ensued, then was quickly quelled. He was the only complainer among a group of people who have plenty to complain about but don't. "Thank you" and "Could I have some bread?" is about all they say.

November 30, 1983

A WISH FOR CHARLIE

Walking away from the graveyard, and knowing that mere men cannot turn back clocks and change what was, I held the quiet wish that Charlie Turner's life could have been different. It should have been lived some other way. It should not have been spent behind the cinder block walls of a home for the mentally retarded. That was the frustrating thing about meeting Charlie so late in his life. He was seventy-nine when I first shook his hand in a private room at Rosewood Center. That was 1983. By then, the damage had been done. All the dramatic reforms that took place in mental health in the 1960s and 1970s could not correct a dramatic truth: Charlie Turner was doomed to institutional life when he was nineteen.

In 1924, his stepmother brought him to Rosewood when the place was called the Asylum and Training School for the Feeble-Minded. In those dark days of treatment for the mentally handicapped, many children ended up at the asylum for a variety of reasons. Some were not mentally retarded at all; they were simply unwanted or too expensive for their parents to keep. Charlie was not profoundly retarded, just a little slow. He spoke with slightly slurred speech and he walked with a limp. His parents either did not know what to do with him or did not want to be bothered.

And, over the years, the institution misdiagnosed him.

"I've got more sense than a lot of people," Charlie said. "I couldn't read nor write nor keep up with the class. I was way behind the other children." His parents took Charlie out of school after the fifth grade. He was seventeen at the time. Two years later, he was in the asylum. He did not see much of his stepmother -- or any relatives -- after that. Charlie lived in a place called Stump Cottage and worked as hard -- if not harder -- than he had as a teenager in East Baltimore, where he sold produce from a horse-drawn wagon.

"All the big boys who could work lived in Stump Cottage in those days," Charlie said. "They were roughnecks. They worked, those Stump boys. If you couldn't keep up, you had to get out.

They didn't take no foolishness. They drove us to the barn where you got your work detail. They had some boys for the farm and some lawn boys. I worked on the farm from seven-thirty in the morning 'til six at night every day but Sunday. I carried plants out to the fields for planting. We'd bring in hay, bring in vegetables from the fields." He drove a team of horses to a depot in Owings Mills to pick up coal for the asylum and training school. "I never got paid. No one did," Charlie said. "They never paid the patients in them days."

That was because institutional peonage was accepted practice. It was not until 1978 that legal reforms brought Rosewood patients a wage for their work. By then, Charlie had lost both his legs as a result of circulatory problems and infection. His legs had been smashed when Charlie was struck by two cars on Reisterstown Road in 1945. Charlie stayed at Rosewood -- he had no relatives to care for him -- and worked in a laundry room. He bought himself a radio and some sweets. But what made him most happy was buying small gifts for Suzie. She lived in Charlie's building at Rosewood. She was far younger and far more handicapped than Charlie, and I think he considered himself her granddaddy. He really loved her. Suzie was in a chair at the gravesite yesterday in Oak Lawn Cemetery. Charlie died last Friday of cancer.

About a dozen men and women who were his friends and advocates at Rosewood attended the burial. So did Stan Herr, a law professor whose students won a $16,500 settlement (about a dollar a day) from the state for Charlie's long labors at Rosewood. "You waited for us a long time," Herr's "Tribute To A Tolerant Man" began. "Waited for us to discover your abundant potential. Waited for us to discover your tortured rights. . . . Gentle good man, you knew we would do better one day." And it was a beautiful tribute for the old man. But still there was that damnable regret. Charlie's life should have been different. He should have been out in the free air, working hard, living an ordinary life. But mere men cannot turn back clocks and change what was.

So at least Charlie Turner could smile. And he made others smile. At least, in a long life behind the cinder block walls, he enjoyed the gentleness of strangers. At least he finally got out of Rosewood.

October 21, 1987

COUPLE DOLLARS, OLD FRIEND

His hand, puffy and the color of oysters, was as cold as the steel fire escape he'd slept on the night before. He felt cold, he looked cold, he even smelled cold. He smelled of brisk air, the strong fragrance of the street.

"Breaking your heart, ain't I?" Now the grin -- that childish, lip-silly, jack-o-lantern grin. He was a cartoon. He was the stumblebum from central casting with one line in the script: "Gotta a nickel for an old altar boy, Fadda?" He was a bag of whiskers and wool. He was standing there, in the lobby of the newspaper building, a ghost come back to haunt.

"I look like hell, don't I?" The gray hair was matted now. The middle-aged face had been burned orange by winter wind. His tongue kept smacking his lips through the grin. And he breathed heavily, sucking hard through the nostrils, puckering and twisting his mouth. He spoke again.

"How's that wife a'yours?" Now the laugh, that husky cigarette laugh. But there was nothing funny, old friend, don't you see? Nothing funny at all. You look terrible. You've blown it again. You've died a little again. You went back to the gutter, didn't you?

"That wife, what's her name? Oh hell, I forget. Does she still have that streak of gray in her hair? What's her name? What is that lady's name?"

He plopped down in a big comfortable chair in the lobby, a lump in a wool topcoat. He put his fingers to his face. People were starting to stare. He rubbed his face with his hands, trying to wipe away the fatigue. There was a long embarrassing pause. What can you say? We were at the bottom of the roller coaster again. The roller coaster had taken this man down into the gutter, down into the very rancid bottom of the city. He was a drunk. He panhandled wine money. He slept in vacant buildings. He slept on the streets. He slept in alleys where rats picked at him.

But that was years ago, wasn't it? That was the past, old man. One day, you latched on to the roller coaster when it was headed up. You had people pushing you and pulling you. You stopped drinking. You turned to God, and there was a young priest who gave you faith and instilled a spirit for change. Pretty soon you had a job. And then a car. And then a suit. And the people at the church -- the ones who worked with you and believed in you -- gave a big party to celebrate. There were front-page articles about you in two Baltimore daily newspapers. There were before and after photographs. One showed the blue suit, the cool smile, and the clean, proud look of a man on the rise. The other picture showed the old man of the streets, the ragged troll of the gutter. It was a great day. The story had a happy ending. People were inspired. People believed.

People took a liking to you. A lot of people went the distance for you. They gave you clothes and furniture and rides to job interviews. They kept you working. You took a janitor's job. You moved when the job moved. You went away for a while, but you kept in touch with the people who were there when you rose from the ashes in Baltimore. Then you came back to town and, when there was no job, you slipped a little. But you resisted the booze. You stayed strong. And people were there to help you again. They gave you a little money for food. They put a job-wanted ad in the paper for you. One of them, Vince Bagli, found a job for you. You swept and washed floors on the night shift. But that was months ago, wasn't it?

You vanished again, didn't you? And some of us were busy and barely noticed. And maybe some of us didn't want to know what became of you. Maybe we didn't want to be disappointed. We had invested in you and wanted results. There were emotional strings attached to all of our efforts.

Now the old man reached over across the chair in the lobby. His left hand was very cold.

"Gimme a couple dollars. . . ." Don't ask, old man, please don't ask. Not now, not this time.

And it was a cruel thing to say, but it seemed the only thing to say. There was too much disappointment right now. If the dollars would buy food or a night's lodging, then maybe. But not now, not with this smell of doom in the air. Maybe some other day. You're a better person than this. Maybe we can start again . . . some other day.

He got up from the chair and pulled a watchcap over his head. And still he grinned. And still he gave a husky laugh. *"You tell that wife a'yours I said hello. . . . And God bless ya."*

January 27, 1984

THEY TRIED TO SAVE MARGARET

It was fifteen minutes after seven, and Evan Selsky had just stepped from the cold into the lobby of Mercy Hospital when a voice on a loudspeaker cracked the quiet of Thursday morning.

"Code 99, emergency room!"

Selsky, twenty-eight years old and a third-year resident, knew what that meant: adult in cardiac arrest. He ran to the emergency room. So did Selsky's "code team." The voice chased them there: *"Code 99!"*

In the emergency room, a doctor slipped a plastic tube down the throat of a woman on a table. The woman had collapsed on Charles Street. She'd been brought in by ambulance. "It's Margaret," Selsky said to himself.

Margaret Meinl, fifty-nine years old. She was a woman of the street and had every symptom of the homeless lifestyle: aged beyond her years, dirty and matted hair, abrasions all over her body, trench feet, a bad hip, and the fresh, cold aroma of a cruel night. "I touched her skin," Selsky said, "and it was just like touching ice." Selsky knew Margaret because, just three days earlier, he'd treated her in the same emergency room for a urinary tract infection. Margaret had spent the night in the hospital, eaten a breakfast of scrambled eggs, received some clean clothes, and left.

Now she was back, and she wasn't breathing. A monitor showed her heart rhythm: the dangerous, jagged waves of "ventricular fibrillation." Her heart twitched wildly. The code team surrounded Margaret at the table. Dr. Margaret Keeler was there. So were the interns working under Selsky, and the emergency room nurses. They took turns thumping Margaret's chest. They hooked her up with a respirator. They gave her electric shock. They gave her a dose of drugs. Still the heart fibrillated. In another minute, Selsky heard Margaret's body temperature: seventy-three degrees.

Selsky was astounded. In his three years at Mercy, he'd seen several cases of hypothermia -- most afflicting street people like Margaret -- but never one with such a low body temperature. The reading had come from deep within Margaret's body. It meant Selsky would have to warm Margaret from the inside. It's called "core warming." Core warming would be extra difficult with Margaret. She'd been exposed to hundreds of nights of cold over the years. She was an alcoholic. She was a weak and sick woman to begin with, and the terrible cold in her body now was trying to kill her.

Ten years ago, Margaret lived in the Armistead Hotel. She'd been among the many turned out when the old hotel was torn down. Then she'd lived in the Edison Hotel and gotten her disability checks cashed at Pines Pharmacy on The Block. Both places are gone now. In recent years, Margaret stayed at the

Congress Hotel. Or, she went to Charles Street, near Read or Madison, and sat on a bench with her stainless steel walker in front of her. Sometimes, she visited My Sister's Place, a day shelter on Mulberry Street. Of all the people who'd known her -- Page Stack, a social worker at Mercy Hospital, Sister Patricia McLaughlin, director of My Sister's Place -- none can really say much about Margaret's life. She'd been in psychiatric clinics and sometimes in jail, but Margaret revealed little else about herself. She had no family, though a social worker thinks Margaret had a son who died long ago.

At times, she was well-spoken and sounded like an educated woman. Other times, smelling of alcohol, she was incoherent, unpredictable, unable to make a sound judgment for her own well-being. Most of the time, she was on the street, panhandling for change or cigarettes. She slept on benches in Mount Vernon. She stood in doorways for hours. Having become known for strange and angry behavior, there were few -- if any -- shelters available to her.

Now, in the emergency room, Margaret was dying, and Evan Selsky and the nurses were trying to save her. Selsky knew an emergency room rule: "You're not dead until you're *warm* and dead." He was dealing with two demons: severe hypothermia and the cardiac arrest it brought on. He had, of course, lost patients to cardiac arrest before. But Selsky would not assume Margaret was a lost cause until he had at least tried to raise her body temperature. He had to see if that could make any difference. Nurses warmed intravenous fluid in a microwave oven, a blood warmer, and a dialysis warmer. Selsky turned up the temperature of air flowing into Margaret's lungs. He ran a tube into her stomach and filled it with a warm saline solution.

Then a city paramedic brought "The Thumper" into the emergency room. "The Thumper" is an automatic chest compressor powered by air pressure. The code team lifted Margaret and slid her under it, and, with a loud and sustained *click-click, click-click,* the machine started thumping against Margaret's chest. This relieved the code team from its exhausting resuscitation efforts. Later, the Mercy nurses moved Margaret to the coronary care unit.

Some of the women who knew Margaret arrived at the hospital. Margaret may not have had a family, but she had friends. Some were from My Sister's Place, where Margaret had often gone for relief from the cold and where she'd met Regina Morano. It was Morano who wrote this poem about Margaret.

*Old woman, come sit down
and tell me
where you have been walking...*

*Tell me there was a home you lost
with carpeting and a big warm bed
a pot of soup on the stove
teacups rimmed in gold
a radio on the table
some books on the shelves
and neighbors
who came for coffee in the morning...*

*Tell me
that you remember something
before threadbare clothes
translucent skin
swollen ankle
these bruises on your face
a drink of gin in a paper cup
your body soaked in urine
your eyes flinching at nothing...*

*Tell me
there is a place
you can run to
where memory never sleeps
where your breath and words and
stories live
where you live.*

By noon, Margaret's body temperature had climbed only a couple of degrees. Selsky asked another doctor, Steve Zemmel, to run a catheter into the thin peritoneal cavity around Margaret's abdomen. It was a risky thing to do with "The Thumper" still putting -- *click-click, click-click* -- pressure on

Margaret's chest. But Selsky thought he'd already tried everything else. When the plastic catheter was in place, warm water filled the cavity. Margaret's body temperature started to rise. But in the early afternoon, the jagged line on the heart monitor went flat. And it stayed that way. Selsky tried drugs again. He stopped "The Thumper" and tried electric shock again.

It was close to five o'clock and the city was going dark when Selsky and the nurses stopped trying to save Margaret. They'd tried for ten hours. They'd given her more human attention than she'd had in years, and they'd given the most to the least. They'd raised her body temperature to eighty-eight degrees. Margaret Meinl died, but she died fifteen degrees warmer than the streets had left her.

February 16, 1987

THE VICAR DIED WITH AIDS

He had several months to put his affairs in order, to say farewell to friends, and to arrange his own funeral. Ricardo Palomares, young vicar of the Chapel of the Holy Evangelists, knew back in late winter he was going to die. In April, he selected the man to deliver the homily at his funeral. He picked the Reverend Canon Edwin G. Bennett, canon administrator of the Episcopal Diocese of Maryland. Everyone calls him Ted.

Bennett, a middle-aged man with a gift for distilling the many words of the Gospel into beautiful human thoughts, had preached at the ordination of Palomares just two years ago. The ordination was held in the Episcopal Cathedral of the Incarnation at Charles and University. Yesterday, they held Palomares' funeral there, and it was an exquisite tribute to a man's life and the power of love.

By eleven a.m. the aroma of incense was in the air, the cathedral was filled with people, and a procession of eighty-two clergy, including Bishop A. Theodore Eastman, moved melodically with music up the main aisle. There was a sixteenth-century kyrie, then a reading from Isaiah, a psalm, a reading from the first lesson of Paul to the Corinthians, a hallelujah. The Gospel was according to John. There was a lovely Spanish song "Gracias a la Vida" during communion. All of this had been selected by Palomares.

He had come here from Cuba in 1961. For several years he had been a teacher. Five years ago, he entered the seminary. He was ordained a deacon in June, 1984, a priest the following December. He had been vicar at an old church with a small parish in Canton. He also served La Mission Episcopal Hispana on Broadway. He had been a busy man and, judging from the size of the congregation at his funeral, had touched many lives in his short time as a priest. He was forty-four when he died.

Phil Quarrier, a communicant of the Chapel of the Holy Evangelists, carried a candle for Palomares in the procession yesterday. He said the small parish had benefited from Palomares' drive and spirit. "At first we thought he was sent over here to give the place a nice death. But he really turned the place around. We're an old neighborhood congregation, and people really liked him. A lot of older people came back just for him. He was still active in the Spanish services til, I guess, July. August was his vacation month. In September he did a service or two." But by then Palomares was terribly sick. He died from complications associated with acquired immune deficiency syndrome. Phil Quarrier said the nature of Palomares' illness became known to his close friends in the parish, then to everyone. No one turned away because of it. "We're a fellowship of Christians," Quarrier said.

Now Ted Bennett went to the pulpit to deliver the homily he'd been thinking about for seven months, but wrote only this week. He knew what was on so many minds, why so many had come to this funeral though they had already said their farewells to Ricardo Palomares. "Perhaps we weep," he said, "because of Ricardo's death from this dread plague afflicting so many in our world. We prayed for his healing but Ricardo died, and yet I say to you, 'Did not God answer our prayer?' Where is the disease? Where is the pain? Where is the brokenness? Where is the disfigurement? All are gone from Ricardo now.

"I say to you God has healed Ricardo and never again will he be threatened by virus, by illness, or by anything. . . . Ricardo lives in joy and peace. We gather here as a church to make absolutely clear the truth of God by which we live and that truth is the gospel we proclaim, enshrined in the promise we heard -- the love and care of God for all his people, no matter who, no matter what."

Later, Bennett reached out still further. "I know many in this cathedral have long felt alienated from the church -- the preachings of many, who I believe misunderstand the Gospel, have made you feel unwelcome, unwanted, and unloved. But the gospel message seems to me unequivocal: 'God so loved the world that he gave his own son. All who believe in him shall not perish but have everlasting life.' No one is excluded from the love of God and if the church is faithful none is excluded from the care of the church.

"I know that many in this cathedral live in fear of the plague that afflicted Ricardo, the fear of getting sick, the fear of being rejected because of your sickness, the fear of being alone when you most need the love of friends. But let this service this morning be witness to the fact you need not be afraid -- we have heard the Gospel message -- and as you are not excluded from the love of God, so you are not excluded from the love of those who love and serve the Lord.

"For we know that every human being, no matter how you live or what your pain, is someone God thought worth the death of his son. . . . And more than this -- more than being loved by God, more than being cared for by his church -- the promise of eternal life is yours. . . . We celebrate not only Ricardo's life today but yours and mine as well."

And you left the cathedral at peace, grateful for Ted Bennett, who wrote this message . . . grateful for Ricardo Palomares, whose life provided it.

November 19, 1986

EVERY CREATURE BORN

The young man's blue suit clung to him like old pajamas and when he stood before the judge in Southeastern District Court, his long arms fell out of the sleeves of the suit and the big knuckles of his hands dangled down by his knees. A shock of dirty blond hair looked as if it hadn't felt the caress of a comb in a week of jail. The young man's face was pink, centered with a large nose. His mouth formed a weak smile. He shifted his weight from one foot to the other, flexed his knees, and tapped the sides of his thighs with his fists. He did not say a word.

The public defender said the young man was a busboy in an East Baltimore restaurant. He said the young man had an IQ of seventy-eight and that a report from Crownsville State Hospital had described him as "borderline retarded." Putting the young man in jail wouldn't do any good, the public defender said. The young man, head bowed, said nothing and kept flexing his knees and tapping his thighs.

A police officer said the young man had been discovered, one busy Baltimore day, in the middle of Eastern Avenue, waving a stick at cars. For this, he was brought to the lockup, and now the court. The judge shook his head. The prosecutor said nothing. The tapping of the hands, the shifting feet, the flexing knees, the bowed head -- all of that spoke deep, dark paragraphs. For there are times like these, in the district courts of Maryland, the chapels of community justice, when the state of man seems especially dreary, when there is little to say, nothing to scorn, but much for a human to feel.

Somewhere in the humanities section of the Enoch Pratt Free Library is a book with the translated words of Bertold Brecht: *"But sirs, I beg, do not give way to indignation/ Each creature needs the help of all creation."* I have heard this translated another way: *"You, I beg, hold back your scorn/ For man needs help from every creature born."*

Those words belong on plaques in courtrooms and living rooms. The world is never black and white; it is full of gray ness. Who knows the minutes and seconds that make a life and establish its color and character? Who knows the road which our brothers and sisters have traveled? Who knows what makes them do what they do? Who really understands why a young man waves a stick at cars?

Humanity carries the responsibility of holding back scorn. Human justice demands that judgments be leavened with fairness. And in our lives, there must always be tears, for tears are the Wonder-Grow of humanity. Of course, seeing the world black and white is easier. Feeling another man's pain is difficult, often dreary. Indignation is always at our fingertips. Understanding lies deep in the soul.

There are troubled lives all around us. Look into the sad, hard eyes of the tall young man in Southeastern District Court and you see the signature of a troubled life. The rest of us have obligations to understand the road to such pain, to remember it after we walk it ourselves, to recognize it in the future, and if possible, lessen a brother's pain.

No crusades are required for this. Just open minds and hearts. When a young woman left her two children in the city courthouse, it was perfectly natural to allow scorn to command our feelings. Emotions are powerful forces. But so are thoughts, so is thinking. And thinking leads to better understanding of the troubled life, and better understanding leads to greater justice for all of us.

Understand the quiet suffering of a neighbor -- the tragedy of a woman abandoning children -- and you understand yourself better. You become better equipped to handle the trouble that comes, inevitably, into your own life. You won't surrender to indignation. You won't live in the tower of intolerance. You will come closer to the center of understanding. *"You, I beg, hold back your scorn/ For man needs help from every creature born."*

July 26, 1985

AT HOME

I was never much for writing in the first-person (he said, with a sentence beginning with the first person). I had a couple of rules: don't write more than a couple of columns a year about yourself, and don't write columns about writing.

I've never broken the latter, but violated the former more often than I wish to remember. What follows is evidence of those misdeeds. Here are a few tales from the personal file, the life and times of my alter-ego Joey Amalfitano, and some comments on domestic issues, my own in particular.

SWEPT AWAY

To tell the truth, I thought the last door-to-door vacuum cleaner salesman disappeared back when "I Love Lucy" went off the air. I thought they were all dead and that only their fossils remained deep within the frozen tundra of that nostalgic America of Edsels, hula hoops, whiffle sticks, and nickel Cokes. But hold on, America! Who's that coming up my driveway on a bright and balmy Sunday afternoon? Who's that stepping out of a pickup truck? Who's that skinny fellow in the shirt and slacks and a baseball cap that says, "I'm So Excited About Electrolux"?

It's none other than a door-to-door vacuum cleaner salesman, a living and breathing American anachronism, with his goods in the back of his truck and a business card in his hand and an opening line that goes something like: "I don't want to come any closer because of the dog. I got nipped by one a couple of weeks ago." His name is Tom Strycharz and, believe it or not, he's been knocking on doors to sell vacuum cleaners (upright and tank-style) for sixteen years. Made a living at it, too. Sold a vacuum cleaner and rug shampooer to Johnny Unitas. If he makes two more sales this month, Tom says, that'll make fifty and qualify him for a nice bonus. So, no matter what happens here and now, Tom isn't going to bed unless he makes two more sales.

The vacuum cleaner salesman could not have picked a more opportune time to visit my house. The place was a mess and I'd spent most of the day cleaning it. My vacuum cleaner was not, of course, the brand Tom was trying to sell, a fact that put a gleam in his eyes. "Would you get mad," he asked, "if I brought in our rug shampooer and demonstrated?"

"Okay," I said, "but if you think you're going to sell us a vacuum cleaner, forget it." The braided rug in the kitchen needed a good shampooing, so why not? This rug was particularly filthy so before Tom attacked it with the shampooer, I volunteered to go over it with my vacuum cleaner. Which I did. And then Tom got quiet, scratched his beard and said,

"Would you get mad if I brought in our vacuum cleaner and went over that rug a little?" Why not?

He brought the gray upright model into the kitchen. Before starting the engine, he placed a small piece of white cloth over the bag hole. This way, I guess, he'd be able to show whatever dirt my vacuum cleaner might have missed.

Well, I don't know quite how to describe the dirt that showed up on that little white cloth after about thirty seconds of vacuuming. Let's just say you could grow carrots in it. And there was an assortment of dog hair, cat hair, watermelon seed, and the remains of someone who must have died while I was away one weekend several years ago. Three demonstrations later, three more clumps of dirty dirt on little white pieces of cloth, and Tom was drawing closer to a sale. You could smell it.

I couldn't believe this was happening. Of all the experiences my old man warned me to expect in life, he never once mentioned the door-to-door vacuum cleaner salesman. That's probably because the vacuum cleaner salesman of my father's day didn't work Sundays. And, as I said, I thought all the door-to-door hucksters were extinct, pioneers who had wandered into the last golden sunset of the American Dream after the company closed out the line or laid off all the salesmen and opened a store in a shopping mall. Who knew that men still made a living selling vacuum cleaners door to door?

Tom pulled out order forms from the previous day to show that he had made six sales, to show that I was not alone. Some people had purchased both the vacuum cleaner and the rug shampooer. Tom said he sold five hundred machines last year and was aiming for six hundred this year. I found this startling. He went upstairs, vacuumed, and shampooed another rug. "We are having," I said, "a truly American experience."

Suddenly, we were talking price. Then we were talking about installment payments. At some point, it became obvious that, yes, I was indeed about to buy a vacuum cleaner from a man who, thirty minutes earlier, had been a stranger in my driveway with barking dogs at his feet. Now, he was telling me how to order bags for the upright model. And now I was writing a check.

And now Tom was packing up the shampooer (which I did NOT buy) and driving the truck into the sunset, another success on that long lonesome highway to the Electrolux Hall of Fame. Beautiful. The American Dream lives on. And folks, it was great to be a part of it. Even if it cost me three hundred bucks.

September 4, 1985

GREENHOUSE AFFECT

Now the story can be told. Now is the time to come out of the greenhouse and tell how I went from riches to ragweed, how my victory garden went down to defeat. I'm feeling better and I think I can talk now. Talking, my analyst says, is good therapy. So lend me an ear. I just need someone to talk to. This is how it started.

The day in February was white and bright. I climbed atop the skeleton of a greenhouse with a fresh roll of plastic and worked for hours like the emperor's tailor, stretching and binding a new set of transparent clothes for the old, abandoned arboretum. Once complete, the greenhouse became an instant sauna. The thermal energy was there. Plants for my vegetable garden would soon sprout. Slowly and painstakingly, your hero prepared a batch of rich, black potting soil and filled three large trays with the stuff.

Next I removed seeds from their small packets. Early Girl tomatoes. California Wonder green peppers. And, of course, eggplants -- an old Italian favorite. With the simple tool of index-finger-against-thumb, I dropped two seeds in each of the little seedling pots in the trays, covered them with a fine layer of soil, and set them out. With much glee, your hero set off at a trot for the nearest bar to celebrate the upcoming birth of his victory garden.

Time went by. Good sun broke the blustery days of February. One by one, the seedlings sprouted. When the temperatures in early March dipped frightfully low, your hero pulled all his seedling trays indoors. I nurtured the plants, gave them a lot of love, bedchecked them each morning and night, and became a Norm Lewis Weather Expert in the process.

All this time, your hero bragged to the world, boring one and all with stories about his chlorophyll kids. I told my friends Bush Hog and Captain Ozone that the plants were doing fine, just fine, and that I would probably be able to provide them with a dozen or so each in the spring. "Don't buy any tomato plants," I told Ozone. "The way my greenhouse is going, we'll be in tomato city by April." April came and the plants were four to five inches high, a splendid, luscious green. The sun pulled them skyward.

On May sixth your hero plopped his best tomato plants in the garden. Then I took a dozen other plants to a friend's house, leaving them on the front doorstep. Next day, the friend called. "Hey," he said, "what was that you left on my front steps?"

"What?"

"Those plants. What are they?"

Full of pride, your hero said, "You've got your basic tomato plants, Early Girls, of course. And pepper plants, California Wonders, of course. And, of course, eggplants."

"What is this? A joke?"

"What do you mean?"

"I hate to tell you this," said the friend. "But unless I'm terribly mistaken, or unless someone came by and stole the tomato plants while I was gone, you just gave me three dozen weeds. Ya'turkey."

The smelling salts worked fine. Your hero was on his feet in no time. I scoffed at this assertion I'd just spent three months growing two hundred weeds. "Don't you know a tomato plant when you see one?" I asked my friend.

I ran home, fetched a sample from the greenhouse, and took it to an expert. The expert said: "That's a weed!"

Another expert said: "Yup, that's a weed all right."

Yet another expert said: "That's your basic weed."

And a fourth expert said: "Maybe you can smoke it."

I was crushed. For three months, the greenhouse had been stocked with two hundred healthy, vibrant, very very green, chlorophyll-producing ... weeds! And they each had their own little pot. And they were weeds! Someone said I had used bad soil. They were weeds! Someone said the air in the greenhouse may have been contaminated. . . . They were weeds! Weeds! All weeds! Within a day word was out that your hero had pulled one of the biggest boners in botanical history. Weeds! But time heals all.

Last week, I bought some tomato plants, and now I know what they look like. I've handled the embarrassment pretty well though Bush Hog now calls me "Luther Burbank Jr." and the guys in the office sing "I Beg Your Pardon, I Never Promised You A Tomato Garden." But I can take it. Weeds! They were all weeds! Weeds! As for the plants that I planted thinking they were plants only to be told they were weeds, weeds, they're slowly roasting to death in the greenhouse.

Weeds! Weeds! They were all weeds! You hear me? They were all weeds . . . don't touch me . . . they were all weeds . . . stay back, back! . . . weeds, fat mama, weeds . . . weeds . . . no, no, not tomatoes, not peppers, not even eggplants . . . just %&'$#&*%*&##*!!!!!**&&## wwwwwwww-wwweeeeeeeeeeddddddddddssssssssssssss.

May 23, 1980

PIT BULLS THEY'RE NOT

I stayed home to see what my dogs do all day. I have been curious about this for years. Most weekday mornings, I say bye-bye to them on the front porch and they sit there looking terribly sad to see me go. I come home at night and they are still on the porch, terribly happy to see me again. But I think it's all a big show. I think my dogs are really very bad dogs. So I want to know what they do all day.

If your dogs are loose all day, and no one is there to watch them, do they behave themselves or do they dress in leather and join a gang of outlaw canines, chasing postal carriers, terrorizing children, trashing trash cans, and committing other acts of evil? Are my dogs just pit bulls with glad-ta-see-ya wags? So I stayed home to see what my dogs do all day.

They are both mutts. One is named Molly. She is small, chubby, and black. She barks at anything that moves, including clouds and wounded moths. She begs a lot. Sit down with a gin and tonic and Molly wants a sip. The other dog is Rose. She is large, long-haired, and black. Ellen Hawks, the pet columnist of *The Evening Sun*, saved her from the city streets eight years ago. She -- Rose, not Ellen -- was found on a rainy, freezing day on Calvert Street, a thick rope around her neck. Ellen talked me into taking her. So I brought Rose out to the house and gave her space. She does not bark as much as Molly does, but she yawns an awful lot. Molly and Rose hang out together -- at least when I'm around. They stay on the porch and wag their tails. Such nice dogs. But they are *too* nice, and I fear they are only nice when I'm around because, after all, mine is the hand that feeds them Jerky Treats.

So I stayed home to see what evil my dogs do all day. I parked my car in a neighbor's driveway and slipped back into the house without my dogs seeing me. They did not see me because they were napping. This is what my dogs do almost all day. A home security system they are not -- unless, of course, you consider Molly's barking at wounded moths a helpful early warning system. The napping went from midmorning to well past noon. The mailman's arrival did not disturb them. My presence inside the house did not stir them. Molly slept on the porch, her pork-barrel belly spreading like a hairy blob over the concrete. Rose napped under a forsythia bush.

Shortly after one p.m. a golden retriever named Sammy showed up. This dog traveled from a distant neighbor's home to get here. Rose came out from the forsythia bush and sniffed Sammy. Sammy sniffed back. Molly rose from her nap and yawned. Sammy let loose on my azalea bush. Rose wagged her tail. Sammy and Rose jogged off together. Molly went back to sleep.

And so, I thought, it's Rose that goes marauding through the neighborhood with this wise guy Sammy. I followed them. They went out to the road. Sammy let loose on a telephone pole. Rose wagged her tail. They sniffed at a privet hedge. They sniffed a neighbor's lawn. Then they went under a maple tree and took a nap. Rose, I discovered, sleeps around.

Back on the porch, Molly had sat up. She was staring at something. I spotted a young rabbit at the edge of tall grass about twenty yards from the porch. This is the thing at which Molly was staring. Ordinarily a dog -- especially a semi-hound like Molly -- would run after a rabbit. But she did not do this. She just sat on her ample rear end and stared at the rabbit. Poor Molly. She must have learned through trial that she cannot catch rabbits; she doesn't even chase them anymore. She is too heavy. Plus, her legs are only about five inches long, so it takes her the better part of an hour to cover twenty yards. Poor Molly. She probably wanted to tear that rabbit apart but knew she had no chance of catching it. She just stared.

An hour later Rose returned. The rabbit hopped within ten yards of her. Rose paid no attention. She went under the forsythia bush and took another nap. By now Molly was spreading the pork-barrel belly on the porch again and napping again.

About three p.m. some kids walked by the house. Molly got up from her nap, sat on her wide rear end, and barked. Then she plopped down for another nap. Molly did not move more than a foot or two the whole day. Rose stayed under the forsythia bush. I had stayed home to see what my dogs do all day. They don't do much. In fact, they are basically dead. What a life.

September 2, 1987

GARLIC EARNS BOUQUETS

Anthony Mangino, ninety-nine when the Lord finally called him home, was an honorable man from the old country who wore suits with big shoulders and wide lapels and flowery neckties, held a cigar between his fingers, and wore a necklace of garlic. Relatives and friends remembered him for his smile, his rascality, his generosity, and his aroma. A quick sniff told you when Anthony was visiting for the weekend.

He wore the garlic because he had arthritis. He cleaned two dozen cloves and strung them on a string. He wore the garlic necklace and ate garlic every day. I believe he slept with the garlic. His wife slept in another room. After six months, the garlic necklace came off and Anthony announced to everyone that the arthritis was gone from his body forever. This, of course, guaranteed that the remedy Anthony brought from the old country -- an herbal heirloom, really -- would remain in the family for at least another generation. Now his descendants, of which I am one, believe in garlic. Cook with garlic. Eat garlic. Do almost everything but play poker with garlic.

And this very week, there is further evidence that Great-Uncle Anthony was no disciple of quackery. Researchers at a small, private cancer treatment clinic in Panama City, Florida, report that garlic boosts the body's immune system to fight cancer and infection. Once again, Lovers of the Stinking Rose and other garlic-breaths have reason to feel good about their past dietary habits. And they can relish the good news, however preliminary it may be, that something they love to eat is actually good for them, too. Can chocolate addicts make such a boast?

The researchers say garlic stimulates the cells that attack other tumor cells and virus-infected cells. They gave doses of garlic to volunteers. Three of the volunteers ate the equivalent of two raw bulbs of garlic daily for three weeks. Three took the equivalent dose in capsule form. Another three abstained. Testing blood samples, the researchers found that natural killer cells from the raw garlic eaters killed 139 percent more tumor cells in culture than those from non-garlic eaters. Immune cells from the volunteers who took garlic capsules killed 155 percent more tumor cells than the same cells taken from the non-garlic group. How do you like dem bulbs?

Lovers of the Stinking Rose should never get too clinical about their passion for garlic; that takes some of the romance out of it. But since so many things we eat -- including chicken, if you watched "60 Minutes" last Sunday -- turn out to be such disappointments once they're analyzed, the good news about garlic must be savored. When you think that something that produces such a wonderful flavor can also be good for the little soldier cells of your body -- that's reason enough to throw a party with a garlic buffet. You think back over a life of eating and you recall doughnuts and potato chips and french fries and bacon grease, and you fear for your future, not to mention your arteries. But now, Lovers of the Stinking Rose can figure that every piece of junk food they ever ate might have been offset by a clove of garlic. That's how you spell relief, friends.

I grew up with garlic. My mother, the former Rose Popolo, put it in everything except brownies and Jell-O. For a treat, she scrambled eggs with chopped garlic. Her mother-in-law, the late Justina Gomes Rodriques, never started a soup without garlic. She boiled garlic in water and drank it down. She was not very approachable, but she lived to be ninety-six.

Just last week, I was in the kitchen of the Trattoria Petrucci restaurant in Little Italy watching the chef, Nilo Negapatan, experiment with a new fish chowder. He started off by firing up a quarter-inch of olive oil in the bottom of a copper kettle. And what was the first thing Nilo threw into the sizzling oil? Two fat handfuls of fresh garlic, and Nilo has big hands. The aroma created by garlic sizzling in olive oil is absolutely intoxicating. I wish more women would wear this fragrance. It is far more appealing than the Eau de Phew! you smell in crowded elevators.

There is much folklore associated with garlic. It has been said to heal scorpion bites and kill mosquitoes. Siberian citizens used it for money. Eleanor Roosevelt supposedly ate chocolate-covered garlic to keep her memory lively. It has been used since ancient times to prevent and treat diseases. Now, the scientists of the twentieth century have caught on and, on behalf of Lovers of the Stinking Rose everywhere, I welcome them to the club. The more this nation stinks of garlic, the healthier it will be.

April 1, 1987

JOEY -- BORN AGAIN

The oil slick on his chin indicated that, after a year of promise, Joey Amalfitano's diet was finished. You don't have to be Mike Hammer to know that a wet, greasy chin with a quarter-inch sliver of noodle stuck to it is proof of linguini intake. The grand jury could indict on such evidence.

I caught Joey red-handed. Or white-handed, as it were, since he had obviously decided on white clam sauce. Either way, the diet was over. "No speeches," Joey said. He was sitting in a restaurant in Little Italy, where you can gain five pounds simply by yawning. "No speeches. I don't wanna hear no speeches." Amalfitano, napkin in the collar of his shirt, twirled slippery white noodles on his fork. "You can sit s'long's you don't give no speeches."

But Joseph, you were doing so well.

"Don't start," he said. "I get enougha' that over the racquet club. It's another world over there. Those people are obsessed. Every time you pick up a fork, they stare at ya. They give speeches about eatin' too much. I been hearin' that for a year."

In fact, Joey was part of the chorus. He started out fat, noticed that he was a cheeseball in a world of celery stalks, saw America going skinny, and felt left behind. In fact, he was mostly behind. When he walked, he felt like a walrus wearing an inner tube. Then, someone gave him a copy of the Scarsdale Diet. He tried it, and it worked.

Joseph Amalfitano, who hadn't weighed a hundred eighty pounds since he was ten, found himself trim and slim and fitting into size thirty-four pants again. He went to Old Joe, the tailor on East Baltimore Street, and had him take in the waist of his pants.

He avoided visiting his mother, who is chef to the gods, for fear that he would become a Balloon Over Baltimore again. This caused some tension in the family because Joey's not eating his mother's cooking was a high insult. In fact, it broke his mother's heart. Only after being threatened by his father did Joey go home for lasagna. That was last fall, his only deviation from the diet. Next day, he went back to melba toast. Now here he was, oil slick on the chin, the cheeks swollen. Word was out that Amalfitano was eating again so, being a concerned friend, I decided to track him down. I found him sucking linguini.

What gives?

"Basically," he said, "I'm sick of grapefruit. That's the short version. You want the long version?"

Sure.

"The long version is life is too short. It's too short to argue with friends, too short to save your money where you never even spring for a trip to Wild Kingdom. It's too short to go around worrying about what you look like, as if anybody really cares. And it's way too short to miss linguini. Linguini is the greatest thing to come outta' Italy since Sophia Loren." This certainly was a different Joey.

Only two weeks ago, I'd found him tapping into a nice big fruit salad at Lexington Market. "Yeah," he said, "but did you see what those people next to me were eating? It was incredible! They were wolfin' down those fat cheese steak subs from the stand next to the Greek's over there." But Joey seemed to possess great will power. He ate only lean meat. He avoided bread and beer. He laid off sweets. He ate salad like a foraging elk. He was jubilant and cocky, felt light and slim, and he even made snobby comments about his friends who were still chubby.

"I know, I know," he said now. "I've seen the error of my ways. If people wanna be skinny and starve themselves to stay that way, fine. Bein' skinny is great if you like it. But they shouldn't foist their beliefs on other people, like they were in EST or something. . . . I went to Washington and during lunch hour, you shoulda' seen all the people joggin' down there. I said, 'Who's runnin' the guvmint? What happened to power-- lunchin'? No wonder the deficit's so big."

But Joseph, you'll be just as big if you keep eating like this.

"Save it," he said. "This weekend, for the first time in a year, I ate graham crackers with peanut butter -- melted peanut butter! -- and I washed it all down with milk. I had bacon and eggs. I had cheese ravioli. I had French bread, a burrito, and some Doritos. I had several dishes of ice cream and chocolate peanut clusters. I had a grilled cheese sandwich. I went to Jack's and had a corned beef sandwich. I went to Wendy's and ate some big beef, some serious beef! Sunday night, I watched "Alien" on TV with a giant bowl of popcorn with butter. It was beautiful. A lost weekend. I found myself."

As he ordered a cannoli, Joseph Amalfitano never looked so jubilant. "Life," he said, "is delicious. You should try some."

May 28, 1984

SCREWDRIVER WILL DO, IN A PINCH

This is how a guy had some bad luck and some good luck on Thursday and ended up holding onion bagels and dish detergent in a shopping bag on Saturday, snow whipping his face, thankful that it takes a screwdriver to start a boosted car. It was a caper, I tell ya, a story that slipped right out of the cracks in the sidewalks of the city they call Baltimore. Goes like this:

Thursday I finish work early. Three o'clock in the afternoon, I'm meeting with my friend Dave. We're drinking beverages with little bubbles and chewing the rag. Everything's cool. Meanwhile, my car is a block away, and everything is not so cool. I had parked on the metered lot across Guilford Avenue from *The Baltimore Sun* newspaper building, which is where I work when things are slow down the shipyard.

Now it's getting to be about 3:30, and I think my meter is about to expire and the meter maids around Guilford Avenue -- they're very tough -- they don't miss a thing. So I'm worried about getting another parking ticket. I'm scrounging around for change for the meter when -- what happens? -- I get a phone call that interrupts my important business meeting with Dave. The call's from Elaine from my office.

"Dan," she tells me, "I got some good news and some bad news. The bad news is your car was stolen. The good news is they got your car and arrested the guy."

I hang up. "Well," I tell Dave, "I won't have to worry about getting a parking ticket."

"Why?"

"Some runt's boosted my car." Me, I stay cool as a chilled dill pickle. I'm lucky.

The keen police work of a couple plainclothes officers out of Central District, Jim Eigner and Kerry Councill, saved me a lot of hassle. They were scouting around the Guilford Avenue parking lot -- I hear they do this so often that a punk would have to be a complete dork to try and boost a car there -- when they spotted three young men hanging out. They watched the lads for about fifteen or twenty minutes. Apparently, these youths already had popped the lock and the ignition on my car and were now waiting for the coast to clear.

Councill and Eigner watched them. One got in my car. Then another. Then the car pulled out. A third youth hopped in the back seat. Zoom! Off they went. Councill and Eigner, Police Officers of the Year in 1980, followed. They radioed for registration information. The owner was listed as a certain yours truly. The cops, knowing yours truly from his mug shot in *The Evening Sun,* determined immediately they had a stolen car on their hands. They moved in, spotted the popped ignition, and radioed for uniformed support. No high-speed chase. No gunfire. Not a trace of Miami Vice, which was nice. The car ended up on Gough Street, not far from Little Italy. Councill and Eigner took an eighteen-year-old city youth into custody. The two other runts scampered away.

Now it's around six p.m. and we're all in the garage at police headquarters. Frank Blackwell, from the city crime lab, is dusting the car for fingerprints. The youths had fled in such haste they left the tools of their trade behind. "Are those your tools?" Councill asks, and he points to a screwdriver, vise grip, and hammer on the floor of the car.

"Nah," I say. "I never carry tools in my car. I could use a vise grip, though." It turns out that this particular make of car is very popular among joyriding youths. They like the stereo system. I read where some of these delinquents even bring their own cassette tapes to play in the cars they steal. Now it's seven o'clock. We start my car with a screwdriver.

"What's the world coming to?" I ask myself, shaking my head, driving away from the police headquarters, and finding the radio turned up full blast, tuned to V-103. Jeesh! By Saturday, I'm still using a screwdriver to start my car -- just as the thieves had. It's stupid, I know. I should take care of this right away. But, hey, I'm a busy guy.

So it's Saturday morning at my house and the snow is whipping my face and I've just come back from Super Fresh. I've got groceries. I burst into my house, set two bags on the kitchen counter. I return to the car, gather up two more bags. I run back to the house. The door's locked. I reach for my keys. *The keys are inside the house. On the kitchen counter!* But I don't panic. I reach for the screwdriver in my back pocket. I break into my own house. Good thing Councill and Eigner are off duty.

November 23, 1987

MARYLAND'S BEST KEPT SECRET

I took a New York City girl out to Prettyboy Reservoir the other night for the romantic adventure of fishing for crappie. We went out across Beckleysville Road, to the old steel bridge where the people fish. After dusk, this is one of the prettiest sites in Maryland, and I report this, convinced that I'm spoiling somebody else's secret.

Men and boys, a few women and girls, stand along the bridge, and the only light comes from gas lanterns. They tie these lanterns to chains and lower them down off the bridge, to a point about one foot above the surface of the water. This, it is said, attracts bugs and small bait fish, which, in turn, attract crappie. Friday, there were enough lights out there to make the old bridge pass for a secret entrance to Manhattan.

As the New York City girl and I approached the bridge, we could see these lights, hanging still, just off the surface, making the water bright green. On the north side of the bridge, there were twelve lanterns in a row, all, except one, the same height off the water. "That one outta' line's ours," a friendly young fellow from Westminster said.

He was standing by the road leading to the bridge. His buddy was there too. They came looking for crappie. They had to stop talking every now and then to spit; and when they spit, one fellow spit to the left, the other to the right.

"What're you using?" they were asked.

"Minnows," one of them said.

"No luck yet," said the other. "Just a little perch is all."

There were about sixty people fishing off the bridge. Every once in a while a car or truck would come drumrolling over the steel grates and interrupt the soft sounds out there. Someone had a radio tuned to the Orioles-Yankees game. That far from New York City -- and twenty-six miles from the local station that sends the sound out to a bridge too far -- the radio signal weakened, so you had to concentrate to hear the score. At the time, it was 4-1 Baltimore. "I've never seen anything like this," the New York City girl said.

"Like what?"

"People out at a bridge fishing on a Friday night in the middle of nowhere."

"Well," I said. "It's nice here."

"This is definitely not New York," she said.

We stopped about ten feet from some young men who had a lantern down. My line dropped just beyond their circle of light, in a spot illuminated enough so I could see the line in the water. Along the bridge, the lines of two dozen fishermen glistened in the bright glow from the lanterns. The lines moved gently and, at times, jerked suddenly. The light from the lanterns made the fishing lines look like falling laser beams.

Out in front, fish were splashing in the black water. The sound of the baseball game faded in and out. Down to our right, along the banks of the reservoir, I heard a sort of swooshing sound in the thick grass. In a squint, you could see something dark and fat move up the bank, deeper into the overgrown grass. "There's something over there," I said, nudging my shoulders to the right.

The New York City girl took the flashlight and moved down the bridge, to where it becomes road again. She stood on her tiptoes and leaned over the concrete wall and trained the flashlight down on the steep bank. The light found the brown glob in the grass. "It's a beaver."

In the battery-powered light now we could see the big, flat wet tail and the chunky body. The New York City girl softly said, "Wow," which is something I said, only louder, the first time I saw Grand Central Terminal.

I went back to fishing. The beaver, after foraging for about fifteen minutes, started crawling back down the bank, to the water. The New York City girl whispered, "He's leaving." And with nothing more than a tender splash and a gurgle, the beaver slipped into the water and swam under the bridge, away from the light of the fishermen's lanterns.

Up along the bridge, one of the laser-beam lines jerked out of the water with a fish. And in the light, you could see a man's big hand reach out and gather it in. A fat cat prowled along the bridge looking for leftovers. The man on the radio said the Orioles were still leading. One of the fishermen pulled, hand over hand, the chain attached to his lantern. He brought the lantern onto the bridge and, in the glow, pinched some fresh bait on his hook. Convinced I wasn't using the proper lure -- crappie must have something against worms -- I reeled in and said, "Let's go."

As we drove back across the bridge, I counted thirty-one anglers, with tackle boxes and white plastic buckets, on the north side. There must have been at least this number on the south side, too. On the pine-adorned road out of the reservoir, the high beams caught a young deer, moving gracefully back into the woods. The New York City girl was amazed at this and said, "Wow" again. She liked going out to the bridge. Didn't at all mind that the Yankees lost.

June 21, 1982

HISTORY LESSONS

I do not usually stray very far from Baltimore. But in these columns I did. One of these columns was wired home from Normandy during the last day of week-long observances marking the fortieth anniversary of the D-Day invasion. That, I'll never forget, was a full week of history lessons. There have been many other times when, reaching for the coattails of a national or international story, I still find myself with a Baltimore dateline. There's a local angle on almost everything that happens on the globe -- if only because Baltimoreans have some reaction to it. Or because, as in the case of the 1983 Beirut truck-bombing of the United States Marines barracks, it comes home the hard way from a distant land.

SEARCH FOR THE PRIDE

AGUADILLA, PUERTO RICO -- On the second day of the search, the tropical waters north of here, the same waters that had growled and swallowed the Pride of Baltimore six days earlier, lay calm and blue and bright under the sun. Fourteen eyes, including mine, gazed down on the sea from a wide-body airplane a thousand feet up, looking for man, woman, wood, sail, something, anything. They found nothing.

For eight hours, seven Coast Guardsmen sat calm, quiet, and deliberate in their search, nothing desperate in their search, nothing desperate or frantic about them. They had performed this task countless times before. They sat at windows and stared into waves.

The plane was a Coast Guard C-130, a large white, hollow craft that moved slowly and evenly over 1,000 square miles of ocean. The pilot was a twenty-nine-year-old lieutenant named Steve Ruta.

The plane left here shortly after ten a.m. yesterday and flew about 350 miles north of the Coast Guard air station called Borinquen. The flight took ninety minutes and put the plane within the Bermuda Triangle.

It was one of five aircraft assigned to search an area that, given proper allowance for drift and winds, was considered the best possible place to search for Armin E. Elsaesser 3rd, captain of the Pride; Vincent Lazzaro; Barry Duckworth; and Nina Schack. All were among the missing.

If any were alive and drifting, they were probably headed this way -- to the north-northwest, toward the Florida coast. The Pride had gone down in waters -- estimated to be five thousand meters in depth -- to the southeast of this search area. Eight surviving crew members had been found Monday in that northwesterly drift.

Now time was getting short. On this day, the Coast Guard had been told to concentrate on searching for two possible survivors in particular -- one last seen in a pink shirt, the other in a yellow rain slicker. If they were alive, this would have been their seventh day in the water. "A lot of this," said Scott Schlieffer, the co-pilot, "depends on an individual's will to live."

If they were not clinging to raft or debris from the Pride, they would be very hard to spot. In fact, official calculations by the Coast Guard gave the C-130 searchers only a five percent chance of finding free-drifting humans alive in these seas. If they were in a four-man raft, the chances shoot up to seventy-five percent. Rafts are much easier for the human eye to spot.

The waters were calm. By noon, the mild wind of morning had faded. The sky was high and bright. The sea could put you to sleep.

Below the flight deck of the C-130, in a section just in front of the wings of the four-engine plane, two crewmen, Dave Brum and Bo Aplin, sat in high Star Trek captain's chairs, back-to-back, one looking into the waters east, the other west, as the plane traversed its search sector. They sat there, in headsets, leaning into windows like two workmen on lunch hour daydreaming out a high factory window at the city below.

Only they weren't daydreaming and there was no city. Below these windows was blue, and blue, and blue, an occasional whitecap, maybe an oil slick, maybe a passing powder-puff of cloud, maybe a white bird or a stretch of floating Sargasso weed. Mostly blue. Monotonous blue. Blue that filled the windows as the plane banked toward the water. Blue that, with the daydreaming eye, started to look like dark cemetery marble, blue that looked like crumpled wrapping paper, blue that began to look like night, with the whitecaps of waves twinkling like stars. "You can't look at any one spot too long," Dave Brum said. "You've got to move your eyes or you fall asleep. If you fall asleep that's when you miss a person in the water."

In the late morning, Bo Aplin thought he spotted something. The plane turned and made another pass over the area. When the plane turned and banked like that, your eyeballs seemed to be almost parallel with the surface of the sea. And all below you was that blue with the twinkling white caps. It filled the windows of the plane. The sea looked so peaceful, so innocent, from a thousand safe feet away.

The second pass showed the object of Aplin's eye was a giant Portuguese man-of-war. Later, the co-pilot, Schlieffer, thought he saw an eight-foot plank in the water. Additional passes over the area, which the crew marked by firing smoky flares, turned up nothing. There was another false alarm later in the day when the crew spotted what turned out to be a huge chunk of Styrofoam adrift in the sea.

It was around one p.m. when Schlieffer suggested contacting a Russian freighter that had passed beneath the C-130, probably on its way from Cuba. He consulted, via headset, with the pilot, Ruta. "You want me to talk to him, Steve?" the co-pilot asked.

"If you can do it in English," Ruta said.

"Soviet freighter," the co-pilot said, "this is the United States Coast Guard." He asked if they were picking him up on Channel Sixteen; a mumbled, broken English response came back.

"We are a Coast Guard rescue aircraft," Schlieffer explained. "We are conducting a search for a sunken sailing vessel. We are requesting that, as you traverse this area for the next eighty to a hundred miles, that you keep a sharp lookout for persons or debris from the sailing vessel, Pride of Baltimore."

"Just a minute's waiting, please," the voice shot back. "I talk to the captain."

In a minute, another voice was heard; it asked for further instructions. Schlieffer answered, "This is United States Coast Guard aircraft one-seven-one-four. We are conducting a search for four persons in the water or on a raft or on debris of an American sailing vessel, Pride of Baltimore, which sank in this vicinity last week. Eight persons were rescued in this vicinity yesterday. We are looking for remaining personnel. As you traverse through this area, until you pass east of sixty-seven-west or north of twenty-five-north, until you pass one of these lines, if you see anything, we'd appreciate it if you contacted us on Channel Sixteen."

"Okay," said the Soviet captain, "that I shall let you know and look sharp out and call Coast Guard on Channel Sixteen."

Now even the Soviets were helping with this search for what remained of the Pride and her crew.

"A lot of strange things have happened down here," said Brum. "Sometimes you get a call, get the coordinates, and right away, you're there, and no raft, no debris, no people, no boat. Sometimes I think there're still pirates."

The pirates are gone. The sea remains, and you could look through the window where Dave Brum sat yesterday and see nothing but the blue for fifteen miles. You couldn't see the Pride, or pieces of it. You couldn't see its remaining crew members, dead or alive. All you could see was the water -- which growled and swallowed a boat -- calm and blue and bright under the sun.

May 21, 1986

HOMETOWN BOY

WASHINGTON, D.C. -- A young man stood on the green lawn in front of the Vietnam Veterans Memorial and he carried a book as thick as the Manhattan telephone directory. He said his name was Mike Hamlett, from Pulaski, Tennessee. He said he was twenty-six years old, which means he was eleven when his father died. Eleven is about the fifth or sixth grade. Mike Hamlett's father was Sergeant First Class Byron D. Hamlett. He was in a flight crew and he was killed October 8, 1967, somewhere over the Mekong Delta.

So Mike Hamlett volunteered his time yesterday to direct people to the names on the big polished black granite wall. The names are not in alphabetical order. They are listed chronologically, from 1959 to 1975. As one man said, "They're all on the wall next to the men they died with."

So you had to give Hamlett a name and have him look it up.

When I got there, Hamlett was surrounded by men and women who were whispering names and looking over his shoulder into the book. What I did next had nothing to do with newspaper work or the assignment of the day. I wanted to see a name of a man I didn't even know. He was the man from my hometown who was killed in Vietnam. His name plays on the ears of the people in that small town every Memorial Day, every high school graduation when they announce an annual scholarship in his honor.

"Peter Moskos," I said. "M-O-S-K-O-S."

Hamlett thumbed through the book, stopped in the M's somewhere. "M-O-S-what?" he asked.

"M-O-S-K-O-S."

His right index finger slid down a page, stopped in the middle, and then Mike Hamlett said, "Here it is. Moskos, Peter. East Bridgewater, Massachusetts? . . . corporal. Marines 7 July '67. He's on 23-East, Line 29." This was code for one of the granite slabs on the eastern wing of the stark memorial. There is a little number carved into the bottom of each slab. I burrowed through the crowd of people near the memorial. They were all staring hard into the wall. There was a young man with a red sweater and blue jeans that ended at the knees; he was staring at the wall from a wheelchair.

Right near slab E-23 stood a large middle-aged man in a brown tweed jacket, black polo shirt, and brown slacks. He was a big burly guy, the construction-foreman type. He looked, at that moment, like a man who might be standing on the sidelines of a high school football game, watching his boy make tackles. But his top lip pressed hard against his bottom lip, and he looked at a name in the wall, then he turned his eyes away and pressed his lips together again. His face started to break, so he pulled out a handkerchief. He gazed around to see if anyone was looking. Then, after about five minutes of exchanging glances with the wall, he disappeared.

Now it was time to find Line 29 on E-23. From the top, I counted down, found the right line, then skipped across to the only name that was familiar, the only name that, given a chance, could reveal the power of the Vietnam Veterans Memorial. Peter Moskos. A gray name in polished black stone.

Suddenly, like a thrashing wind, the name swept me back fifteen grainy years -- to the small town in Massachusetts, to the grown-ups talking about Peter Moskos, and the priest telling altar boys to lay out funeral vestments, and me and the other altar boys in the sacristy preparing the incense, and one of the church workers flicking a switch to start the carillon as the procession came up the street, toward St. John's Church. I could see packed pews, townspeople from every stride, men in uniform, a widow, a father, a mother, younger brothers of Peter Moskos I went to school with. That was the day the Vietnam War came home to East Bridgewater. And, like a friend said over the phone last night, "That's the way all wars come home."

So there I was, with this name on a wall in Washington. I didn't even know Peter Moskos, didn't go to Vietnam, didn't lose a brother, a father, a son. But I was standing there, fighting away the embarrassment of public tears for a reason I couldn't grasp, a reason left in the small peaceful towns of big warring nations. Now the only thing to do was to move away.

A ceremony started. Teenage children of Vietnam's American dead were placing flowers at the base of the wall. A young boy from Baltimore was there. His name was Alton Gibson, and his mother, Georgia Gibson, said he was eighteen years old. Which means Alton was five when his father died. Five might be kindergarten. His father was Sergeant Alton Gibson. He died in Vietnam eighteen days into 1969. When the ceremony was finished, Alton Gibson wanted to see his father's name. So we found another young man with another big book and the young man said: "Gibson, Alton. Sergeant. He's on 34-West, Line 48."

Alton Gibson moved through a crowd of much taller people, looking through legs at the base of walls to find the right number. At slab 34, he pointed to the top and counted down forty-eight lines.

"There he is," Alton Gibson whispered. And, at that, Alton Gibson, eighteen, was looking straight into the name of Alton Gibson, who was thirty-one. Young Alton didn't cry. He didn't say anything for a very long time, which meant he was braver than me.

Because much later in the day, I was still thinking about Peter Moskos. So I called some people in East Bridgewater. When I heard their voices, the town was there again and so was the day of the funeral and so was the gray name in the Vietnam Veterans Memorial.

The memorial is an experience. It made me feel, at last, a very small, very real piece of the pain. A piece of what mothers and fathers and sisters and wives and brothers and sons and daughters must feel whenever they remember young men from the small peaceful towns of big warring nations.

November 12, 1982

HOME FROM BEIRUT

The morning had begun in fog and rain but now, as the hour of the first burial approached, the sun appeared in the autumn sky and ignited the crimson and orange in the leaves on the oak and wild cherry trees in Baltimore National Cemetery. This day of sorrow -- when the United States Marine Corps would bury two lance corporals, and two mothers would bury two sons -- had become a warm, bright day.

Twenty-four hours earlier, graves had been prepared for both Lance Corporal Jeffrey James and Lance Corporal Ulysses Parker, Baltimore boys, at the foot of a grassy knoll in a special section of the cemetery on Frederick Road. "Section O," said Maurice Page, a member of the cemetery's field crew. He stood by a truck with a canvas-covered trailer. He wore work clothes and a yellow hard hat. Page, a young, lean, friendly man, has worked at the cemetery for three years. This was the first time he performed his chores for American servicemen killed in the line of duty. It hasn't happened here since Vietnam days. Now Page pointed to Section O, where a Marine honor guard waited for the arrival of the hearse bearing the casket of Jeffrey James, twenty. "Over there," Maurice Page said. "It's like a memorial section. The flag pole's there, and there's a Medal of Honor veteran buried there. He'll be in the front row."

Maurice Page said he had a special feeling as he went about his work this week. He's dug burial places before. He's maintained the grounds around graves of veterans who died of natural causes, the wives and children of veterans and servicemen who died while on active duty. But this day he and the other members of the field crew -- Thomas Allen, Jesse Bagley, Gerald Skrine, Louis Hite, John Law Jr. -- knew that something special was about to take place. And they knew they could trace it all back to a truck-bomb in Beirut. They knew. Everyone knew. "I feel for him," Page said of Jeffrey James, whom he knew only from news accounts. "I'm sorry it had to happen. I consider what I do a service for him."

The flag at the center of Section O hung at half staff and it flapped when the breeze picked up. This is a special time of year for leaves of trees, a fragile time. So, whenever the breeze stirred, there was a rain of leaves to the ground. And the leaves already on the ground crackled as they fluttered across the road at the foot of the grassy knoll. In this special place you can find the grave of Laddie Stupka, a Navy man who won the Medal of Honor while in service to his country during World War II. The letters on his stone are etched in gold. The stone stands under a wild cherry tree, its leaves burned by the season. In this special place, where they would bury Jeffrey James and Ulysses Parker, you can find a large plaque with the words of Lincoln at Gettysburg: "We have come to dedicate a portion of that field as a final resting place for those that gave their lives that that nation might live. It is altogether fitting and proper that we should do this."

In this special place are the graves of men who performed a distinguished service: David R. Cook, corporal, 319th Artillery, Vietnam, August 8, 1950-November 7, 1969; Michael Steffe, specialist, 319th Artillery, Vietnam, November 23, 1948-November 3, 1969. There is another plaque beyond the flagpole, inscribed with the words of the commander of the Grand Army of the Republic, May 5, 1868. The words command that the nation remember its war dead each May by "decorating graves of comrades who died in defense of their country . . . and whose bodies now lie in almost every city, village and hamlet churchyard in the land."

It was just about eleven and the men from the field crew took off their hard hats and held them against their chests. They directed traffic with their free hands. Cars came up the smooth, winding road around Section O. The honor guard, led by a young Marine captain named John Bower, stood at attention. There is, of course, a precise method for the burial of an American soldier. And this day, all the parts were in place: six Marine pallbearers and a sergeant to give them orders, then a Marine firing detail for the twenty-one-gun salute. The only missing piece was the Army bugler from Fort Meade; because of a mixup, he never showed at Jeffrey James' burial. But the burial went on. Not a single politician was present.

The pallbearers faced each other by the open door of the hearse. They side-stepped toward the flag-draped coffin, then each man carefully reached under the flag. White gloves grasped the handle of Jeffrey James' coffin. On command, the pallbearers turned and carried the coffin to the grave, under a temporary tent, and placed it on the straps of the lowering device. Then the family and friends of Jeffrey James gathered close. His mother sat about four feet from her son's coffin. The minister spoke. He said Jeffrey's mother and grandparents had raised him, that he was loved, and that he loved them back. He came out of Northwestern High School and, three months later, joined the Marines. "It was something he wanted to do, that he looked forward to," the minister said. He said Jeffrey was a "jovial, warm, and friendly lad." The pallbearers lifted the flag and held it over the gray coffin, and a woman from the funeral home placed four red carnations on the lid.

Then came the rite that is by now old and familiar in America, a rite that has been around for as long as mothers and widows have sat by graves in special places. Three of the pallbearers -- Staff Sergeant Francis Daugherty, Sergeant Roy

Johnson, Corporal Anthony Cole -- folded the flag into a triangular stack. Gunnery Sergeant David Goode handed it to the young Captain Bower. Bower stepped up under the tent, bowed, and handed the folded flag to the mother of Jeffrey James, saying softly that this was a gift "from a grateful nation . . . in honor of the honest and faithful service of your son."

There were so many people, ordinary people, standing there now and staring at the coffin after the honor detail marched away. They were crying and holding each other. Women came up and touched the coffin. Men looked at the ground as they walked away. The breeze stirred and leaves fell through the warm air. When everyone had gone, the cemetery men lowered the coffin into the vault in the grave. Then they prepared for the burial of Ulysses Parker at two. An older workman, Thomas Allen, pulled iron stakes out of the ground and walked the distance of twelve burial plots to the front row grave that had been prepared for Ulysses Parker. Allen rammed the stakes into the ground. They were hammered into the ground. And then the four hollow aluminum tubes that hold up the tent were placed over the iron stakes.

"I knew him," Jesse Bagley, one of the cemetery workers, said of Ulysses Parker. "We called him Greg. We came from the same area. I lived on Etting. He's from McCulloh Street. I knew him from playing ball in the neighborhood." When it was two o'clock, Jesse Bagley removed his hard hat and held it against his chest in honor of the young man who was once a boy playing ball in a neighborhood.

Another hearse, another funeral procession, another weeping mother, another crowd of tears and somber faces, another folding of the flag. The minister said to reflect on the joys and happiness that Ulysses Parker brought his family and friends. This time, there was a bugler and when he played taps those who mourned for the young lance corporal mourned extra hard, embraced each other, and held carnations in their hands. The breeze came over the knoll again and above the tent, the leaves of a tall oak tree rustled, then sprinkled into the air one by one, then fell to the earth, onto the grass of the very special place.

November 4, 1983

REAGAN'S TRIBUTE TO THE BEIRUT DEAD

You can tell the two graves are not old graves by the absence of clover. The grass on the graves is new and thin, free of the dandelions and clover that creep over the older, surrounding burial plots. You can still see the outline of the digger's work. You can still hear whispers, too, like the whispers of mourners at a wake. A year ago, when two Baltimore families buried two sons in Section O of Baltimore National Cemetery, there was a breeze in the autumn air. And when the breeze whisked brittle oak leaves across the encircling asphalt driveway, the leaves made a hollow scraping whisper. It's a sound that will always accompany the sad memory of those burials.

Yesterday, someone drove a car by the graves of Jeffrey James and Ulysses Parker and, in the draft from the car, oak leaves curled up and scraped across the driveway again. And you could hear the whisper. You could see families again, huddled around the graves -- one at each end of the front row of Section O. You could see the Marine honor guard and the young captain walking away, pulling off his white gloves, and lighting a cigar. You could see women step up and leave flowers on the caskets. A year is nothing. A year is too soon for the healing of a wound -- even for those of us who didn't know the young Marines or the pain their families suffered.

The Marines died in their sleep in the truck-bombing at the Beirut Airport on October 23, 1983. It was the act of a suicidal terrorist. Two hundred forty-one servicemen, mostly Marines, were killed. "How could it happen?" asked one set of politicians. "You can't prevent terrorism," answered another. On the day of the burials of Jeffrey James and Ulysses Parker, there were no politicians in sight. No president. No congressman. None of the people with the power to dispatch young Americans to the flash fires of the world. Just families.

It was like that again this past Tuesday. On the anniversary of the bombing, families gathered at Arlington National Cemetery in Virginia to remember and honor the dead Marines, their sons, brothers, fathers, and husbands. There were other ceremonies across the country. The President did not attend any of them. He went to the West Coast and gave a campaign speech. In none of those speeches did he note the anniversary of the Beirut bombing and its toll of lives.

Wednesday, the President was back at the White House, all smiles, with eighty happy medical students who were "rescued . . . from tyranny" on the island of Grenada. Only then did the President mention the dead Marines of Beirut. He "did honor them in a paragraph," according to a Washington correspondent in what must be one of the strangest arrangements of words in a single sentence by an American journalist this year. The paragraph, which amounted to twenty-eight words, was inserted into the final draft of the President's remarks at the White House.

"Let no one doubt," the President said, "that those brave men were heroes every bit as much in their peace-keeping mission as were our soldiers in their rescue mission in Grenada." That was Ronald Reagan's tribute to 241 dead Americans. It was one of the shabbiest moments of his presidency. If he believed in the mission of the brave men, if he wanted to further decry the insinuation that they "died in shame," why didn't he go to Arlington? Why didn't he console the nation during this sad anniversary? Why didn't this artful speaker find the right words for a grateful nation's remembrance of these brave men?

Reagan showed more respect for the Grenada medical students than he did for the families of those Marines. And he acted on the most cynical of political instincts: You gain more in rehashing your "victories" than in discussing your losses. All political considerations aside, the President belonged at Arlington with the families on Tuesday. It would not have been morbid, or even political. It would have been decent.

By not going, by not even mentioning the Beirut disaster on its anniversary, he belittled the deaths of those Marines. He did exactly what George Bush claimed the President's political opponents have done. The Marines didn't "die in shame" and the nation should honor their sacrifice. So, why didn't the

President muster his ceremonial powers to honor them with more than a paragraph inserted into a speech as an after thought?

Certainly the President's attitude is not the nation's attitude. The Beirut mission, and the young men who died carrying it out, were not ignored this week. Go out to Baltimore National Cemetery, to Section O, where the oak leaves are restless, and you'll see flowers on just two graves. Someone put a single purple chrysanthemum on Corporal Jeffrey James' grave. Someone put a vase of red carnations and violet chrysanthemums on Corporal Ulysses Parker's grave. And yesterday, as the leaves whispered again, there wasn't a politician in sight.

October 26, 1984

COLONEL SHRED

Oliver North, star of the very strange soap opera "The Edge of Right," arches his puppy dog brows inside the portable Magnavox on the shelf between the A-1 Steak Sauce and the plastic bottle of Steramine tablets at The Bridge Restaurant, 353 North Calvert Street. He has been here, on the shelf behind the counter, for three days now and the two waitresses, Jean Adamski and Jean Lawson, are swooning. They have found some kind of bizarre greatness in the mysterious Colonel Shred. "I was used to watching the soap operas, but this is better," says Adamski, cooling her heels after the breakfast rush hour.

The television sits below a shelf of beer mugs. Because of this, the TV antenna is angled just a degree or two above horizontal. And, because of this, the picture is a little frantic. Oliver North jitters up and down. But that is the only thing about this North that wavers. He speaks almost perfect English, as if he has given his righteous speeches a million times. There isn't an "um" or an "ah" or a "ya' know" in his language. This is part of the package that impresses the hard-working waitresses of The Bridge. "There's no doubt in anyone's mind he's done wrong," Lawson says, "but he's so *smooth* about it." And she tears into a cream-cheese sandwich.

"I could listen to him all day," says Adamski. "He don't stutter. He don't repeat himself. He just *knows* what he's saying."

"I love it. I think it's *great*," says Lawson, "He's a man of steel. I could watch him for hours and hours." And, of course, our pleasant waitress pronounces "hours and hours" in perfect Bawlmerese: "ars n'ars."

"I hope he comes out of it smelling like a rose," says Adamski. "I hope for his sake they find that eight million dollars they lost."

Inside the television, North is talking and talking. The Senate committee lets him yap all he likes. "Plain and simple," he says, "the Congress is to blame [for] the fickle, vacillating, unpredictable, on-again, off-again policy toward the Nicaraguan Democratic Resistance -- the so-called contras." And then: "I am going to walk from here with my head high and my shoulders straight because I am proud of what we accomplished."

Statements like this further impress the waitresses of The Bridge. "If you were in trouble, wouldn't you want him on your side?" Adamski asks.

A man finishes a ham-and-egg sandwich at the counter across from the TV set. "These politicians asking questions," the man pipes in, "all of a sudden they walk on water. Ain't one of them don't have their hands in some s---."

This is the way it goes in America this week. The Iran-contra/arms-for-hostages deal might have been foul but no more foul -- and no more perplexing -- than any other scandal to come down the pike since the Watergate summer of 1973. We have been beaten cynical with foul play by men in power. Now Oliver North pleads that the world is a mess and it takes strong-willed musketeers with ribbons on their breasts to figure out what's wrong and right and insert reason where insanity reigns. Here is the full-dress Rambo, sans headband

and blessed with eloquence, asking the country to let him win this time. North's plan to have the Ayatollah fund the "freedom fight" in Nicaragua was, after all, "a neat idea." Colonel Shred loves irony.

At The Bridge, three men sit at a table and watch North on a compact television.

"He has not been rattled about nothing," Jean Lawson says. "He's too cool. They can't rattle his cage."

"He was kicking a-- Monday morning," says Jean Adamski.

"I'd like to have him in my corner," says Lawson.

"I bet Hollywood's thinking about a movie about him," says Adamski.

And who would play the lead role?

"It'd have to be Martin Sheen," she says.

At some point, North refers to America's founding fathers and "a sweaty room" where great ideas were born. It is here that Jean Lawson admits that part of her admiration for Oliver North has to do with sex appeal. "I'd like to catch *him* in a sweaty room," she says.

Now George Alatzas, owner of The Bridge, comes to the counter. "What is this?" he asks, "The Ollie North Show?" Planning the day's offerings, George considers an Ollie North Special for the menu board on the rear wall of his establishment.

And what would that be?

"Kosher hot dog."

June 20, 1987

REQUIEM FOR A SURVIVOR

Where was he born? He was born in Holland. And what was his town? His town was Vilda Vank. And who was his father? His father was a tailor. And who was his wife? His wife was from a family of metal dealers in Rotterdam. And what was her name? Her name was Dinaka.

Having listened to his story on the day of the crows, having learned the truth about Dirk DeLeve, his last few friends were awed by the simplest things: his bright apartment with the Gauguin and Cezanne posters, his habit of breaking into song, his habit of greeting new tenants in his apartment building, his vigor, his stature, his dark wavy hair, his friendly manner, his love of conversation, of music, of birds, of flowers, of simple things. It was astounding that a man with Dirk DeLeve's wounds could sing welcomes to strangers and still adore the French painters. "He sounds like a man you might call charming," someone said.

"Oh, yes," a woman at the funeral answered. "That's a good word, charming."

"I would call him warm," another woman, Cecelia Bass, added. "When my sister moved into the Concord House, she was sharing a dinner table with two boring men. Then she met Dirk, and he spoke up. He was very interesting. They became very good friends." And soon Dirk DeLeve was telling his new friends the story of his life. That was two years ago. They were all sitting in the backyard of Cecelia and Leon Bass' house. As DeLeve spoke, crows squawked loudly in the trees; his friends could barely hear him. It was one of the few times he spoke of the Holocaust in the last years of his life.

"Near the end," Leon Bass said, standing by the grave, "he talked about Auschwitz. He said, 'You know, when you're in the hospital, you have plenty of time to think about things.'" The other day, when a drizzly wind whipped over a high cemetery hill in Baltimore, all that had happened in Dirk DeLeve's life came before us, came to a rest above his open grave, suspended in the mist for one last testament, one final accounting. It was time to ask questions. And to know about a man. And to touch legacy.

What happened to Dinaka? When the Nazis invaded Holland and deported the Jews, she and Dirk hid with a family in Rotterdam; but a neighbor saw the family buying extra portions of bread and turned them in. And what happened then? Dirk and Dinaka went to Theresienstadt in Czechoslovakia. And what happened then? Dinaka worked in the mica plant and Dirk went by train to Auschwitz; on the train the Nazis made the men write postcards to their wives, urging them to request transfer to Auschwitz.

Cecelia and Leon Bass never found DeLeve morbid or self-centered. He was always outgoing and enthusiastic about things. But there was something lonely about him, too; something silent and sad returned with him to his apartment at night. He could not understand why more people -- particularly those his age, he was seventy-three -- did not share his hunger for living.

He was not religious. The Holocaust destroyed his belief in God. Still, he had requested a Jewish funeral. The young rabbi, Jonathan Katz, said it was an honor to pray for the final rest of a survivor. "The test of a man is not in his theology but in his life," he said, in thick damp grass by Dirk DeLeve's grave. The rabbi found holiness in a man who reached out to others, who shared his wisdom, who sought beauty, who sought what was good.

As the grave tent smacked in the breeze, the young rabbi said Dirk DeLeve deserved sunshine for his funeral. Here was a man, after all, who had managed to emerge from the Holocaust with his humanity. "Today," Katz said, "we honor a life that sought to ennoble humanity." A life that could still sing welcomes to strangers and adore the French painters.

And so he never saw his wife again? No; they sent her to Mauthausen and she froze to death. And his brother? No. And his parents? No; only six thousand of the 150,000 Jews from Holland survived. And so he spent the rest of the war in Auschwitz? Yes; he was healthy and the Nazis sent him to work in a munitions factory; at the end of the war he weighed only sixty-nine pounds. And where was he when the Allies came? He and a friend escaped from a march and went to a farmhouse; the people there gave them eggs. He always said that when he ate those eggs he thought he had finally gone to heaven.

May 12, 1989

NATIONS UNDER STONE

BAZENVILLE, FRANCE -- All over Normandy, the old armies line up in neat rows of stone. The British are scattered at thirteen separate camps, from Bayeux to Ranville. The Americans have the high ground at Omaha Beach. The Germans are off at La Cambe and Orglandes. The Canadians have two camps of their own -- one near the coast, one to the south at Bretteville. In some towns, the Canadians share the earth with English brothers. The Polish cemetery, a severe and desolate place, is down the road near Falaise. But here, at Bazenville, off a beautiful farm road that seems to lead nowhere, old enemies are buried together. The Germans have a section of their own on the northeast side of the British cemetery. Rommel's men are a short walk from Montgomery's boys.

At first, it seems bizarre to see stones with the German names here in an old enemy's graveyard. But then, it seems the most fitting commentary of World War II or any way: German, French, British, American, Canadian, Polish . . . they've all gone into the ground, under the lush, green meadows, under neat lines of stone. The legacy of war here is written in marble and concrete: W. E. Fahrini, Canadian Scottish Regiment, 38; H. L. McKeil, the North Nova Scotia Highlanders, 33; F. E. Gibson, the Royal Artillery, 24; A. R. Ramsbottom, the York and Lancaster Regiment, 25.

Here you will find men of the Durham Light Infantry, boys of the Seventy-ninth Medium Regiment, Scottish Horse, men of the King's Royal Rifle Corps, of the Green Howards, the Royal Engineers, the South Staffordshire Regiment, and the

Royal Northumberland Fusiliers. Here are men from towns called Isleworth, Ponders End, South Chingford, and Burscough Bridge.

There is no victor in war. It's been said for a million years. Yet it is true, so very true, and here in Normandy it comes up from the ground and grabs you by the shoulders and shakes you. The war is written in stone.

The German cemetery at La Cambe is a macabre place. Five black crosses, each made of lava-like stone, stand on a bush green lawn. Name plates lie flat in the ground: Alois Maierhofer, 28; Heinrich Leise, 19; Karl Dworschak, 47; Fritz Skalla, 32; J. Rauschendorfer, 19; Willi Nordmeyer, 33; Helmut Kupetz, 22; Hermann Missal, 32; Otto Borner, 38. Then, every few steps, as you walk along the lines of flat stones, you see the words: Ein Deutcher Soldat -- a German soldier.

The Germans were a retreating army in the spring and summer of 1944, after D-Day. They had their unknowns, too; they had their mass graves. At La Cambe, a great mound rises in the middle of the cemetery, crowned with an icon of dark stone. At the foot of the mound, in German, raised letters decree: God Has The Last Word.

There is a vistors' register at every cemetery. At La Cambe, the words come out in German, French, and English: "Peace and pardon for all . . . . For all of those who enter here, stop and think. . . . No more war 'cause I'll have to fight it. . . . A wish that this will never happen again. . . . The tears of all mothers have the same taste."

World War II was the one that Americans like to call a "popular war," the one the British call "the last war." But fifty-five million people -- military and civilian, in the European, Pacific, and other theaters -- died in that popular war. The number leaves you dumbfounded. Fifty-five million is slightly more than the 1983 population of France. According to Sir Basil Liddel Hart's history of the war, the world-wide mortality count included 13.6 million Russian soldiers and 7.7 million Russian civilians; 5.3 million civilians from Poland, many of whom died in concentration camps. There were 10 million Chinese civilian deaths and 3.5 million Chinese soldiers; 1.7 million Japanese military; 380,000 Japanese civilians, a count that, of course, includes deaths from the atomic bombs. Two-hundred-ninety-five thousand Americans died in World War II.

All wars are the same; all wars end in stone. Whether you're looking into the polished black granite at the Vietnam Veterans Memorial in Washington or the white marble in the meadows of Normandy, you are reading war's epilogue.

From the small British cemetery here you cannot see houses, just pastures and cows. It is a pleasant place. A man named Gerard Veran cuts the grass every week. He keeps flowers and small shrubbery between the stones. He says it's an honor for a Frenchman to have such a job. "If someone defaced one of these stones, they would fall to my hand," Veran said. "In one town, someone defaced a grave of a Polish soldier they thought was Jewish. The town considered it such an affront they had a (rededication) ceremony the next day." The Polish cemetery near Potigny is the most severe place. Concrete, moss-flecked crosses stand in long lines across the width of the graveyard. In many cases, nameplates have fallen off or been taken from the concrete crosses. The men who are buried there -- Figarski, Miziniak, Kosinski, Bogusz, Malecki, Malinowski, Kosmowski, Kucharski, Grabowski, and 599 more -- fought with the Allies as they pushed toward the Germans at Falaise in August, 1944.

That's another thing the stones of Normandy tell you: all these men died in 1944, from the days leading up to D-Day and on D-Day and through the outbreak of the Allied forces into Europe. Most of them died in pleasant weather.

As they depart these places, visitors leave their thoughts and comments in little books in dark, cold mausoleums. At the Polish cemetery, where the roses are yet to bloom, someone wrote: "A special hello to Grandad Kaliski." A Frenchman wrote: "War is a massacre of people who don't know each other and profit for people who know each other but aren't massacred." Another wrote: "As we reach the anniversary of the D-Day invasion, we hope old hatreds will be forgotten." At the British cemetery, someone wrote: "Visiting my favorite uncle." At the Canadian cemetery at Bretteville, someone from Toronto wrote: "I'll never know my uncle but I'll never forget him."

There are white crosses and Stars of David at the American Cemetery overlooking Omaha Beach. There are 9,386 of these on a sprawling, beautifully kept lawn within a curtain of trees. When the weather turns foul, you can stand there and hear the English Channel release a homicidal roar. Yesterday, it was tranquil, nearly silent. The American burial ground has so many stones, so many names; each has a sound, a ring of the hometown boy, calling to mind a smiling face: Lawrence Bekelesky, corporal, 29th Division, Pennsylvania, June 6; Edward B. Sachs, corporal, 202d Engineers, New York, August 13; John R. Armacost, private, 9th Division, Maryland, July 10; Peter J. Nebel, sergeant, 29th Division, Maryland, July 15; Isidoro Martinez, private, 4th Armored Division, New Mexico, May 16. And more and more and more.

The American Battle Monuments Commission watches over several graveyards throughout Europe and the Pacific. At one such place, in Manila, there are 17,206 graves. Inscribed on the walls there are another 36,279 of the missing, many of them sailors, who "sleep in unknown graves."

The American cemetery at Normandy has unknowns, too. Walk among the white crosses and stars and soon appear the words: "Here Rests In Honored Glory A Comrade In Arms Known But To God." Interred here are four women, a father, and son; and, in more than thirty instances, brothers are buried side by side. It goes on and it goes on. Drive down a country road and stop for a picnic. You could have your back to a field of rye, then turn and spot a monument that seems to rise from the earth as the big Normandy sky moves with the wind. And then you look a little closer and there are stones in the ground. In the middle of the peaceful farmland you find the permanent inscriptions of war: F. H. Shank, the Black Watch; W. J. Bryant, of the Queen's Own Cameron Highlanders of Canada; A. E. Perryman, Toronto Scottish Regiment; J. E. Gillis, Calgary Highlanders; Ein Deutcher Soldat; Nieznani Zotnierze; I. Dornik; Hermann Bath; Oskar Kirchoff; Billy J. Daniel; and Charlie Summers.

All nations under stone.

June 8, 1984

SIGNIFICANT OTHERS

"You know them oddball characters you write about?" someone will ask me. "I like them columns." And the next question is, *"Where do you find these people to write about?" Well, some of them live on the street. Some have press agents. Some handle their own publicity. Some write to me. Most I just happen to encounter on the streets. Back when Phil Heisler was still managing editor of* The Evening Sun *he entitled this column "Street Talk" because "Rodricks, you write about people no one ever heard of." And, for me, that was just as well. They might have been nobodies, but that didn't mean a column or two couldn't turn them into somebodies. In my book, there are no nobodies. Just somebodies we haven't met yet.*

LITTLE SUN MAN

The gold Merry Christmas sign with the plastic holly was still in its wrapper, still price-tagged and hanging on the door of Room 314, Hotel Rochambeau, home of a prominent citizen. But the prominent citizen wasn't home. The radio in his room was on, and Dean Martin was singing "Everybody Loves Somebody" to nobody. I knocked on the door and called, "Mr. Handel."

A voice answered from down the hall, and a little man with an elfin grin pulled a plaid bathrobe about him and stepped out of the washroom where he'd just completed his morning shave. I almost didn't recognize Rudolph Handel without his sign which says "*Sun* Lies" on one side and "*Sun* Errors" on the other, and "Still Lies" some days and "More Lies" on other days.

Every day, it seems, Rudolph Handel is with one of these signs. And you usually see them together at the corner of Calvert and Centre, not in the third-floor, one-light-bulb hallway of the quaint Rochambeau. It was sort of like finding the star of the show, off guard and off Broadway, coming from his dressing room. What, Mr. Handel asked politely, was the occasion for this visit?

Well, it's like this. People are always asking about Rudolph Handel, whom they fondly call the *"Sun* Lies Man." He's a prominent citizen of the town, indeed a city landmark. So when for a couple of weeks Mr. Handel was absent from his rush-hour picket post, people noticed. He became the subject of much concern along Calvert Street. Mr. Handel suffered a stroke some years ago and people were worried he might have taken ill again.

"I'm fine," Mr. Handel says. Oh, he was in Mercy Hospital for a couple of weeks for treatments. But it was nothing serious. And, yes, he fell out of bed one night and has a swollen leg to prove it. But he's okay and when weather permits, he's back at his post. "I'm seventy-two," he says, "and on my next birthday I'll be twenty-two."

It's been a long time since Mr. Handel has spoken, for the record, to an employee of *The Baltimore Sun*. Come January, it'll be fifteen years -- 4,011 hours overall -- since Mr. Handel started his one-man protest against *The Sun* for what he calls "the lies" it printed about him in 1969. He's still seeking retractions, too. "Mr. Twigg," he says, referring to Roger Twigg, the reporter who wrote the story about Rudolph Handel that started it all. "Mr. Twigg is my man. He's my man. We're stuck together for life."

A little background: Years ago, Mr. Handel picketed "on principle" a store on West Baltimore Street. He'd purchased a TV set there and, over the next four months, it went in for repairs three times. Mr. Handel says neither the store nor the manufacturer replaced the bum set with a new one. The manufacturer sent him a "repaired set." Completely dissatisfied, Rudolph Handel picketed. Roger Twigg found this interesting and wrote about it. But Mr. Handel says the articles included "distorted facts and lies." He asked for retractions but didn't get them. The reporter stood by his story. The picket moved from Baltimore Street to Calvert Street in January, 1970.

He's been there ever since. He's retired and a bachelor and he enjoys his peaceful picket-line duty. Rush hour commuters wave and Mr. Handel smiles. He's got one of the world's finest smiles, after all.

Now, up in the hallway of the Rochambeau, Mr. Handel says he can't stand lies. Roger Twigg is a good guy, he says, but his bosses should have corrected the errors. "And they didn't," Mr. Handel says. "They're not humble. I don't care how much money, how much power you have, you have to stay humble. . . . No matter what, you've got to tell the truth. Lies hurt people and that's what I don't like to do." He's a very spry, very sincere, very genuine man who has stood by what he considers a principle for fifteen years. And you can count on one hand the number of people who make such commitments.

Right now, Mr. Handel holds up his hand and spreads four fingers. He wants to play a little game, in which the fingers represent answers to a secret question. One finger means "yes," another means "no," another means "maybe," and another means "perhaps." If you pick the right one, you win a million dollars. "Go ahead," Mr. Handel says.

I go ahead.

"Uh-oh. You didn't win a million dollars."

I laugh.

"But you're laughing," he says. "You just lost a million dollars and you're laughing. Laughter is the joy of life." There's that elfin grin again. "Laughter is your way out," Rudolph Handel says. "If you can laugh, you got it made."

December 21, 1984

SOFT SHOES

"All politics is local."-- Tip O'Neill

During the twenty years he has represented South Baltimore in the General Assembly of Maryland, it has behooved Harry "Soft Shoes" McGuirk to know things like the name of the guy who runs the silver-and-black tavern at the corner of Leo and Southport. The guy's name is John Skrzesz, which is pronounced Scratch. The tavern's down Wagner's Point in a tiny patch of rowhouses surrounded by trucks, tracks, Shell Oil, Continental Oil, American Oil, and Eastern Box. The murky Patapsco is right nearby.

On this particular day, Skrzesz comes into the street to see the senator. Out the window of his Oldsmobile, McGuirk extends a hand with a pinky ring. "John," the senator says, "how are you?"

"I just had a checkup," John says. And it goes like that. Wife of Skrzesz comes out and gives the senator a kiss. They chit-chat and Skrzesz tells the senator to have a look at the new building around the corner, a waste disposal plant. "It's a beautiful building," Skrzesz says.

Then the Oldsmobile's off and running again, through the heart of Harry McGuirk's sprawling Thirty-seventh District on the lower reach of the port. The Kingdom of Soft Shoes. Harry McGuirk, smooth as a jewelry salesman, knows his district like the back of his beefy but manicured hands. Such nook-and-cranny knowledge goes a long way. It's been good for a lot of votes over a lot of years.

That's probably why Robin Ficker, the naive first-term delegate from Montgomery County, asked McGuirk to give him a "Tour of Understanding" of the Thirty-seventh District. "Who knows this district better than Senator McGuirk?" wondered Ficker in that annoying gee-whiz style that sets him apart from his cool and reserved tour guide. "It is indeed an honor to have this distinguished legislator take me on a Tour of Understanding in this vital port district of our state," Ficker chirped.

Soft Shoes was very accommodating. So, shortly after eleven a.m. the big blue Oldsmobile pulls out of a parking lot at McGuirk's real estate office in Catonsville. The senator handles the wheel. Ficker handles the map. We go to Wilkens Avenue to look at a shopping center "with its own septic system." We run past St. Agnes Medical Center, Cardinal Gibbons High, out Caton Avenue past a Maserati dealer -- "It used to be a Sunoco station," McGuirk says -- and into a place that'll be an industrial park some glorious day. "We still have tremendous possibilities in my district," he says, and then drives us through Violetville, the old Twenty-fifth Ward and Hollinswood, past the National Casket Company, under a B & O bridge, and into Brooklyn. He points to the McCully Funeral Home. "The chairman of the Liquor Board owns that."

Now past General Refractories, up a side street, into the neighborhood where Bert Shannon was a big Little League booster. McGuirk points out baseball fields and parkland, of which he is extremely proud. Soft Shoes had something to do with getting the park. Suddenly, he stops his car and slices the air with a soft karate chop of the pinky-ringed hand. "This is the county line," he says, and at the moment the boundary appears to be somewhere on the dashboard of Harry McGuirk's Oldsmobile. Harry McGuirk knows where the lines are drawn.

Down into Curtis Bay, past St. Athanasius, Li'l Maria's carryout, onto Pennington Avenue. "People here don't like many changes," McGuirk says. "They're very critical of zoning, watch it like a hawk." The car skirts up a rise of black and brown grit strewn with bulldozer treads. "This is our famous landfill," the senator says gloomily. "It wasn't managed well and now it has a bad reputation." Back into the heartland of heavy metal, chemical clouds, eighteen-wheelers, Hess Oil, and Crown Central. And U.S. Gypsum. And Glidden. And Kennecott.

"A lot of people from Montgomery County have never seen heavy industrial operations like this," says Ficker, gee-whizzing all over the front seat of the car.

At Fort Smallwood, McGuirk says, "This is where they wanted to put the new prison," modestly leaving off the triumphant epilogue: But didn't.

Over there's Eastalco Aluminum. See it? And now the Tour of Understanding moves up Curtis Avenue along Curtis Creek past Curtis Steel. And now we're in Fairfield. "This is the area we kept screaming about the sewers," McGuirk says. In a Chessie Yard, the freighter Drake Sea eats coal. The Oldsmobile creeps along muddy roads in the Brooklyn Salvage and Waste Company's heavy-metal graveyard. Then it's out through Masonville and piles of fill.

"I can see why unemployment in your district is lower," says Ficker.

"I take a lot of heat for it. Some people can't see how that . . .," says McGuirk, pointing to a small mountain of dirt, "translates into jobs."

The car pulls into Cherry Hill, a place McGuirk calls a "community unto itself." Then we drive down by Jorgensen Steel and Waterview Avenue. "This used to be nothing but a junkyard," says McGuirk. "I think you're going to see a renaissance down here."

The car runs by the pyrolysis plant and Russell Street, stops at Park Sausage, turns, and heads into the Barre Circle homesteading area. Ficker is impressed. "Yeah, gee, this is amazing."

Next come Rash Field, Key Highway, the Beth shipyard, and the new Southern High. At the spruced-up French Quarter in Locust Point, McGuirk has a Coke with a union man named Mike. Outside, the senator points to another building and says, "That used to be Buck Glass Company." How does he remember things like that?

McGuirk is surprised at the question. "I dunno," he says, then takes me and Robin Ficker to Fort McHenry. We wrap up the Tour of Understanding with a crab cake at Gunning's in Brooklyn.

Ficker is impressed. "That's a good crab cake," he says. The senator says nothing. He goes back to the real estate office and checks his mail. Robin Ficker drives back to Montgomery County, understanding, if nothing else, why Harry McGuirk's been in the General Assembly of Maryland for twenty years.

September 4, 1981

TURKEY JOE'S WAS SOME JOINT

Johnny The Tambourine Man -- my God, he's still alive! He lives! "You call that living?" said Baseball Billie Jones.

"Everybody's been coming up to me and sayin' they thought he was dead," chimed Vince Cuffari, who, as bartender at old Turkey Joe's, knew well the Tambourine Man's merry mug. Incredible indeed, but there the twisted Tambourine Man stood, right on the Polish Home Club floor, looking his Baltimore's best, a troll who slipped through the crack in the barroom door. He wore a full-length coat of plaid material that somebody must have swiped from Shocket's. The nose was still a Bartlett pear, the grin still nearly toothless, the handshake still tiny and clammy. And the old battered tambourine was still attached to Johnny's belt.

"He looks good, don't he?" said Vince. "He's the biggest surprise of the day." The day was Saturday, the event was Turkey Joe's Reunion. It's been nearly a decade since the burly and hairy Joseph "Turkey Joe" Trabert operated his legendary Fells Point bar. With its earthy and eccentric owner as the major draw, the bar attracted guys and dolls of varying degrees of lovability. Everyone misses the scene. So they had a party, drank some beer, and remembered the old days. Everybody had stories.

A guy named Nick saw Johnny The Tambourine Man and remembered a night in Turkey Joe's. "I took a date there, and Johnny and this other guy got into a fight," Nick said. "And he knocked my date off a stool *with* a stool!"

Vince Cuffari witnessed most of this. Best job he ever had was tending bar for Turkey Joe. "It was so much fun," Vince said. "I'm not having nearly as much fun as I had back then with all those good people."

"What're you doing now?" I asked.

"Sellin' insurance."

The place was packed at twenty dollars a head -- "Potocki did the tickets!" Turkey Joe yelled -- and Chops came by and so did a guy named Skates.

"They called him Skates 'cause he skated on his check so long," said Vince. "And Monk's here, and Rat." These were all regulars at Turkey Joe's in the 1970s: Space, Augie, Captain Bobby, J. G., Lefty, and Gail Linton, a former barmaid. And don't forget that other bartender -- Karl The Clown Hater.

"There was this guy, Bernstein The Clown," Vince explained. "And Karl had to kick him out of the bar once. His way out of the door, Bernstein yells at Karl, 'Aw, you're a clown hater!'"

American Joe was there. So was his better-looking brother. "His name is Dennis," said Vince, "but everyone calls him Walter."

Jeff Knapp, the Abe Lincoln look-alike who used to be seen at the Cat's Eye Pub, had preserved a ransom note. Turkey Joe once kidnapped Knapp's dog. The ransom note arrived inside a smelly clam and demanded thirty-nine dollars for the dog's release. Instead of suspecting Turkey, Knapp suspected another local bartender, a guy named Warren. When cops confronted Warren with a ransom note, which Turkey had lettered from clipped newspaper headlines, Warren said, "That's not my handwriting."

Turkey Joe played a lot of jokes. His bar was a fun house, a zoo, a gallery of honorable vagabonds. There was always something goofy going on there. With his eclectic tastes and comic virtuosity, Turkey attracted both the erudite and the troglodyte, the kook, the cop, the prankster, the punster, the pundit, and the regular-guy. He never let them escape his embrace, either. Saturday you could see how durable his friendships are, how lucky a man he is.

Proceeds from the event, figured at two thousand dollars, went to Search Ministries, which is former Colt Joe Ehrmann's inner-city outreach program. "The only thing that ticks me off," said Turkey Joe, "is I'd like to have a piece of that two thousand."

When it was his turn, Ehrmann told the gathering he had dreamed of entering heaven. He was happy to be there but disappointed when the saints forced him to walk around handcuffed to an ugly old hag. "You are in heaven," a saint explained, "but you did a lot of bad things in your life. You must pay." With mixed feelings -- and hag on cuff -- Ehrmann went for a heavenly stroll. Suddenly, he encountered Turkey Joe Trabert. Incredibly, Turkey Joe was handcuffed to the beautiful Bo Derek. Outraged, Ehrmann demanded an explanation.

"Well, Joe," the saint said, "Bo Derek did a lot of bad things in her life." For once, the joke was on Turkey Joe. But I doubt it bothered him. All his friends were laughing, see, and that's always been the point.

March 6, 1989

BLUE BABY

She had spent her life fixing the hearts of little boys and little girls, and last night, long after all the work was done, Dr. Helen Brooke Taussig sat in a concert hall in Baltimore dressed in a blue evening gown, adorned with a luscious white orchid, and wrapped in the gratitude of a generation of healthy hearts.

She is the woman who, with the late Dr. Alfred Blalock of Johns Hopkins University, developed the intricate operation -- now named for them -- that released children from the deadly grip of pulmonary stenosis. It has become known as the "blue baby" operation. It was developed during World War II. Literally thousands of people walk the earth today because of it. Because of Blalock. Because of Taussig.

And just in case anyone forgot, Helen Taussig was summoned to the Friedberg Concert Hall of the Peabody Conservatory last night to receive a most stunning gift in tribute: Schumann, Schubert, Bach, and Beethoven from the fingers of Samuel Sanders, once a boy with a sick heart, now one of the foremost collaborative pianists of his time. She sat in the third seat of center row, a handsome and stately woman of eighty-seven years. She greeted old friends and colleagues.

Then one of her former patients played the piano on the stage and, as he played, the wonder of Helen Taussig's work seemed to engage the audience. For Samuel Sanders played beautifully. His fingers touched keys and music went into the air and into your ears, and this happened on a cold night in 1986 during a recital that might never have happened without Helen Taussig. Knowing the facts of Sanders' life -- that he had started out with a sick heart -- you became nearly as grateful as the man himself. Sanders dedicated his recital to the woman who had healed him. He kissed her. He thanked her. He called her an explorer.

In 1946, only two years after the first successful "blue baby" operation, his parents took Sanders to Johns Hopkins Hospital for the operation that would correct a heart defect that, since his birth in New York nine years earlier, had left him a weak and sickly boy. Sanders, like other "blue babies," had heart defects, causing a lack of oxygen in their blood, which gave their skin a blue pallor. In those days, pulmonary stenosis was so serious that most "blue babies" soon died or if they clung to life, they were doomed to be invalids.

"I remember her as a warm, bright, and gentle woman," Sanders said of Dr. Taussig. "And when I saw her again, it was as if I had just seen her yesterday -- a kindly, warm woman, with brightness in her eyes. It was a strange, wonderful feeling to see her again."

It was because of his medical problems that Sanders turned to music. He remembers being weak and uncoordinated and short of breath, being in special classes in school until he was thirteen, feeling a terrible lack of self-confidence among other boys. But, in the years after his operation in Baltimore, Sanders developed this dazzling skill for the piano. He performed in a young people's concert with the New York Philharmonic in 1954. He still has the letter his mother, Mollie, wrote to Dr. Taussig informing her of this great achievement.

And last night Dr. Taussig said she remembered that letter from the grateful Mrs. Sanders and how it, like all good news about all the other "blue babies" who came her way, gladdened her heart. What a tremendous feeling that must be for a doctor to heal the terribly sick, then live to see them grow up and marry and have children and, in some cases, become doctors themselves and, in at least one case, play the piano. "Medicine has its ups and downs," Helen Taussig said. "Our successes give us courage to go on."

And so one of the successes, Samuel Sanders, a man of slight build, walked onto the stage with renowned cellist Stephen Kates. They sat at center stage. They performed a work by Schumann, a work by Schubert, a Bach suite, a Beethoven sonata. Sanders leaned into the piano. You could see his long fingers reflected in the polished black wood above the keyboard.

He had performed with Itzhak Perlman, with Beverly Sills, with Yo Yo Ma. He had performed on television. He had performed six times at the White House. Now he was performing for Helen Brooke Taussig, the woman who had given him a chance to do all of this. And as the music came out into the air of the concert hall, as this wonderful music delighted an audience, you could look down to center row and see Helen Taussig's left hand, a hand of fragile strength, dance before her face in time with the piano. And you could see the high cheek bone of a smile. And you knew what she knew, what everyone knew: This music, this wonderful music of Samuel Sanders, came from the heart.

February 12, 1986

THE OLD BOYFRIEND

"I take her laundry home," Willie Myers said. "Do it all myself, too." And he doesn't mind. He prides himself on it. The old city councilman would do anything for his girl. So Willie Myers parks his compact car at the Hammonds Lane Nursing Center, and he walks the hallways, through the dining room, past the old folks in chairs, and makes a right down a hall called Maple Tree Court. Soon, he's smiling a little. And so is Margaret.

Old Willie takes off his hat, leans down, and kisses Margaret's soft cheek. She lifts her head and sees Willie's blue eyes, his strong cracked face, and his straight gray hair. They sit together in her private room and Willie plays little jokes. "Margaret," he says. "Margaret. Margaret, I'm prettier than you."

"Oh my lands," she says.

"Margaret," he says. "Margaret, my hair's prettier than yours."

"Oh well, you might think so but I don't." It goes this way every day; it's been this way for the last eight months.

They were married fifty-five years ago, and it wasn't until Margaret's health failed that Willie Myers came home to an empty house and a dog named Brutus. "That's when I get sad," Willie said, "when I go home." But he brings her doughnuts in the morning and sits with her another three hours in the afternoon.

Yesterday, he fixed himself some buckwheat cakes and sausage, put on a tie, and drove from the house on Brooklyn Avenue to the nursing home. And there was Margaret, his old friend and companion, sitting in a wheelchair and putting on a soft, sweet smile.

Willie's not about to let his girl stray from the mainstream. In fact, he courts Margaret like an old boyfriend at prom time. Back in September, they celebrated their anniversary. Willie hired a band and he bought some sheet cakes from Muhly's and they had a big party for everyone in the nursing home. "Mr. Pressman came and danced," Willie said. There's a color snapshot of Willie and Margaret at their anniversary on the TV in her room. In January, when Margaret turned seventy-five, Willie threw her a birthday party. He hired an accordion player, bought more sheet cakes and ice cream, had cold cut platters brought in. It was a big day, and Willie Myers recalls it proudly. Like each new stop sign he procured for the Sixth District, he considers the party an accomplishment.

City Councilman William J. "Willie" Myers, who will be seventy-eight next month, is to be admired for his ability to keep pace with the latest pothole, overflowing sewer, or trashy alley around Brooklyn and Curtis Bay. He's got a beeper and a telephone answering machine, the latest gadgets for his long-time job of helping constituents every day. You could say a lot of things about Willie Myers but few would be grand. He may never win the great debates, the political bosses may seldom seek his advice or consent, and he may never buck the mayor's legislation in City Council.

But his people respect Willie Myers because they've come to expect things from him that other, more self-indulgent politicians never deliver. For a man of his years, he has a lot of heart as well. So out of his schedule of constituent service, Willie makes time for Margaret. You never stray very far from a woman you've loved so long.

Years ago, Willie lived on Wheeling Street and worked for his father in the cafeteria at Maryland Drydock. Margaret Reitz lived on Riverside Avenue. And one Christmas Eve -- "I think it was 1925 or 1926, something like that" -- they met and fell in love. A year later, they were married in St. Joseph's on Lee Street. Last summer, following a streak of failing health, Margaret fell at home. She's been suffering from hardening of the arteries and other ailments of age. With much difficulty, it was decided the best thing would be the nursing home. So she's been there since July, and Willie, his sister Virginia, and Virginia's friend Mary Mannion have only good things to say about the place and the way it treats Margaret.

"But she forgets, you know," Willie says. "She forgets." That doesn't seem to stop them from celebrating, day-to-day, in small doses, their long life together. "One day I was over there, you know," he says. "And she looked up to me and said, 'You're good to me.' And I looked at her and said, 'Honey, you're good to me too . . . I'd do anything in the world for you.'"

Yesterday at noon, he kissed her and she said, "Behave yourself." Then, after lunch, Willie went back to the house on Brooklyn Avenue, said hello to Brutus, and checked for messages. In the afternoon, he went back to Margaret. There was talk about bringing her a crabcake. Margaret loves crab cakes. After fifty-five years, an old boyfriend never forgets.

March 10, 1982

IDA AND GRACE

"Oh," says Ida, "I don't know what I'd do without Grace. She's my best friend. A friend in need is a friend indeed, aren't they now?"

The voice is coming from under a big blue summer hat in a house on North Potomac Street, which is in East Baltimore. Somewhere under the hat, with the chiffon bonnet ribbon tied at the chin, is the small face of Ida Holzhaus.

Ida turned eighty-six on July 30. Her best friend, Grace Fiddeman, turned eighty-seven on July 21. They live just a few doors apart and have been friends for "oh, heaven help us, twenty-five years now." They watch out for each other. Ida can't see or hear very well, so Grace reads things to her. She tells her about the specials at the Food-A-Rama. She writes checks for Ida's bills. Grace, on the other hand, can't get around very well anymore -- "I'm a rolling stone just gathering moss and I'm sick of it" -- so Ida runs errands for her. "And she visits two or three times a day to see if I'm still navigating," says Grace. "If it wasn't for her, I would have been in the old soldier's home a long time ago."

The two women have a lot in common, starting with their friendship. But when you talk about money . . . well, that's another tale. Grace was a teacher for forty-three years; she taught elementary school at PS 42 and PS 83. She quit in 1959 to take care of her aging mother. She's been home ever since. She collects Social Security and a "very generous" pension from the state.

But Ida is different. Ida never married and she never had a job. She was born with eye trouble. All her life, she's had nothing more than twenty-five-degree peripheral vision in one eye, no vision in the other. She lived with her mother, father, two brothers, and a sister. She cooked and cleaned the house. Then the sister married and moved away. Her parents died years ago. Her older brother, Joseph, died in 1948; her other brother, Bernard, died about eight years ago.

Until his death, Bernard had received a pension from his union. When he died, Ida Holzhaus was in her late seventies and she was left with about seven thousand dollars from her brother's life insurance. Because she never held a job, she never contributed to Social Security, so she doesn't collect it. She lives off the savings and, according to Grace, it's dwindled down to about four thousand dollars now.

"I'm a good manager," Ida says proudly. "I buy groceries when it's on special. I go to the bank every couple of months and take out some money. . . . The fuel bill is the worst. The last one was a hundred-and-something dollars. In the winter, I go to bed early and cut the oil off. I get in bed and cover up." She doesn't receive food stamps or Medicaid. "I don't go to the doctor," Ida says.

A few years ago, Grace took Ida down to the old Social Security office on North Calvert. Ida applied for Supplemental Security Income (SSI), a federal program for old, disabled, and blind people who have limited assets. The old folks call it the Gold Check. "That Gold Check is what it was," says Ida. "We went down every time they advertised it. The girl there said she thinks I'm entitled to some, but not the full amount."

"We went up there with a certificate from Ida's doctor that said she was legally blind," says Grace. "We took her bank book up there and showed the girl what Ida had. She had no means of income other than the interest from her savings. But the girl said that her blindness counted in her favor."

Still, Ida got nothing. To be eligible for SSI in America, a person can have no more than fifteen hundred dollars in assets. (One's house doesn't count.) Because she had anywhere from $3,500 to $4,000 in savings, Ida was rejected. Maybe if she lied, she could get help from Washington. "You don't rise to the top by telling the truth," says Grace.

"I don't want welfare," says Ida. "I'd rather have that Gold Check, a little something to get by. I would like them to give me a little allowance. But I can't make them, can I?"

"You could if you were a congressman," says Grace. "They

take out what they want and see what's left for the rest of the country."

So life goes on. So Ida walks three long city blocks to save forty cents on a gallon of milk. So she shuffles through the Food-A-Rama looking for the coffee that's on sale. So she goes to bed early to save on her fuel bill. So she eats a TV dinner, and it's a treat. So she avoids going to the doctor. So she goes to the bank and draws from her savings. And, through all of this, she doesn't complain. She's very proud of herself. "I'm fortunate," she says. "I'm getting along very good. I've had bad eyes all my life, but I'm getting along. I did very well. I'm never lonesome. I come here and see Grace. A true friend is worth all the money you can have, isn't she?"

August 15, 1983

BILLY BOY

"You know what he likes?" Mary Langston said in the living room of the rowhouse on South Collington Avenue. "You know what kind of sandwich I make for him every day? Peanut butter and jelly. Ain't that right, Bill?" Ten feet away, Mary Langston's son lifted his head and cracked a smile. His neck stretched and his head floated back until it rested across the back of the wheelchair. Billy gently stroked the whiskers on his chin with the curled fingers of his right hand. The smile was wide and sweet.

"That's what he takes for lunch to the day care every day," Mary Langston added. "Peanut butter and jelly. I tried making him other sandwiches. Ham and cheese. Tuna fish. But I'd get these notes from the people at the day care: 'Billy prefers peanut butter and jelly.' Right, Bill?" This time you could detect slight embarrassment in Billy's smile, for mother was getting personal. She was reciting details from Billy's life: what he likes to eat, what he likes to watch on television, where he likes to go for outings. Other women can proudly recite the accomplishments of their sons and daughters: the schools they attended, the careers they've made. But when it comes to Billy, Mary Langston, who is fifty-three years old, must content herself with pride in small things.

"See, he's taking his shirt off now," Mary said. And in the wheelchair, her eighty-nine-pound son slowly pulled a red-and-blue striped jersey over his head. "I put out his clothes every morning, and he dresses hisself. And he does NOT put them on wrong. He can slip right into some shoes. But if he wears shoes with laces, I got to tie them for him. And I have to button his shirts and fix his pants. But that's all."

Thirty years have gone by since Mary Langston, twenty-three years old at the time, went to Maryland General Hospital to deliver her third child. The damage to Billy's brain occurred during birth. "The umbilical cord was wrapped around his neck twice," Mary said. "He had a cerebral hemorrhage. He was in the hospital sixteen days. I remember that they had given him some kind of drug and I had to help him suck to get his formula from the bottle, he was so drugged up. . . . I remember all the doctors telling me he had cerebral palsy and that he'd never talk, he'd never walk, he'd never even be able to sit up. But I didn't listen because nobody knows. Only the good Lord really knows. It hurt, you know. I felt bad for a long time. But I had two other kids and they were healthy, and I had two more kids after Billy."

So she was a young mother with full hands, and holding part-time jobs to make ends meet. She placed Billy in Rosewood Center when he was twelve. He stayed there a few years and, after that, in a residential facility in East Baltimore.

"They taught him how to dress hisself and how to use one of those communications boards. He can hear what you say. He comprehends. He just can't answer you." But he can smile.

Billy came home about ten years ago, after, as Mary said, "I got the other kids raised up." Mary's second husband died two years ago. So now she and Billy share a life in the very modest rowhouse on South Collington. They live on roughly five hundred dollars a month, including food stamps.

"For years I carried him up the front steps into the house. And I carried him up to the second floor to his room, so I could give him a bath. I used to carry him on my back, with his arms over my shoulders and his legs around my waist. Sometimes, I'd put him over my shoulder and carry him up. He can't go up the stairs unless someone holds him up. When he comes down the stairs, his head goes from side to side."

And the staircase is only twenty-eight inches wide. For all these years, Mary Langston carried her son up and down the stairs.

"Carried him by myself," she said. "I stopped about two years ago. I can't do it any more. I like to take him up there to give him a bath. So now I catch whoever comes by, my daughter or whoever happens to be here, to help take him up and give him a bath."

United Cerebral Palsy has pledged enough money to cover the cost of materials for a wooden ramp down the front steps to the sidewalk. That will help. "But I'd like to get a chair lift to take him to the second floor," Mary said. "I called around. They cost about $2,500. . . . To rent, they cost about two hundred dollars a month, and you know, I can't afford that." So Billy sleeps on a single bed in what used to be the dining area of the first floor.

"He backs his chair up to the bed every night and gets right in. Don't you, Bill?" And mother laughed. And son smiled.

March 18, 1988

THE PIANO MAN

A guy gets piano in his fingers and he never can beat the urge to play. Ain't it so? He could walk away for a decade, take up real estate as a career or bourbon as a vice, but never get away from the piano. Not after he's played a crowd, not after they've filled his cup with nickels.

It's the delicious addiction of performance: Please 'em once and you want to please 'em again. Even when the music gets old, even when the applause turns polite and the boozers begin to snore, there's always something there. Always the piano and the man and what the two make together. It's an eternal friendship. The piano's always a pal. With Melvin, I had the distinct impression that the man actually longed for a piano, needed a hit or two.

I met Melvin in a windy winter freeze and even then, when it was unwise to stand on Calvert Street too long, all he could talk about was the piano. "Ever been to the Peabody Book Shop?" he said. "I used to play the piano in there. I was a musician. Oh, pretty good, yeah, pretty good. Rose hired me."

Melvin played where a gang of musicians played. The late Rose Hayes, proprietor of the famous book shop and beer stube, brought them to the Peabody to please the regular crowd. Eddie Mitnick and his wife played there. So did the magician, the Great Dantini, a guitarist named Dick Phillips, and a zither player named Paul Gunther. Melvin, whose last name is beyond the reach of memory, dropped by now and then to bang the keys in the upstairs bar.

But by the time I met him on the street that winter day, appearances told me, as they would have told anyone, that many, many months had passed since Melvin had a paying job at the keys. His clothes were well-worn, ragged really. He needed a shave and a haircut, though the top of his head was balding and sunburned from too many days on the street. In his right hand he clutched the handle of a stainless steel cart full of aluminum cans. I guess Melvin was in his late forties; he looked older. The woman with him was older still, a small bird with frayed, gray hair. She wore a dingy tan wool coat festooned with buttons, one of them a laminated photograph of her pet, I think a dog, though it might have been a cat. I can't remember which. She talked at length about this pet the way Melvin talked at length about his piano days. Her name was Anita.

She and Melvin lived together, traveled the streets together, collected cans together. Each morning they stepped out of a rowhouse in Fells Point and walked all the way to Mount Vernon, collecting cans in the alleys and gutters. "We're doing this to get something extra to get by," Melvin explained. "She gets a Social Security check each month but I got nothin'."

They traveled Calvert Street, Madison Street, Monument Street, St. Paul. By noon each day, they sat to rest in a small park on a Calvert Street corner. They hit the soup kitchens and the day shelters before heading back to Fells Point for the night.

I hadn't seen Melvin or Anita in months. The Peabody Book Shop remains closed, so that leaves one fewer place for Melvin to find work -- if, in fact, he looks for it. But no matter what problems clutter Melvin's life, he apparently still has piano in his fingers, still can't beat the urge to play.

This past Sunday, he and Anita wandered up Centre Street and into festivities marking the reopening of the Walters Art Gallery. It was a splendid Baltimore day, and hundreds of gallery patrons took brunch under a three-hundred-foot tent in the middle of Centre Street. Into the splendor walked Anita and Melvin -- she in her pink curlers and trench coat, he in a ragged green sweater. Melvin, the old piano man, had spotted an unattended Yamaha baby grand left from a large dinner the night before.

"May I play the piano?" Melvin asked. At this moment he stood before Claudia Bismark, director of special events for the Walters. Claudia listened, as so many others have listened, to Melvin tell of his piano days, of his gigs at the Peabody. She heard the old longing in his voice.

"May I hire you?" Claudia asked. Melvin smiled. Then he sat at the bench. Anita sat beside him. And Melvin, the old piano man, played and played, a little Gershwin, a little rag, a little jazz, a little of this, a little of that. A crowd gathered about the piano. An elderly woman stood and requested "Bill Bailey." Melvin accompanied her beautifully. The crowd applauded. Melvin smiled. He played for two hours, and then it was time to go again, to leave the piano that never left him.

May 18, 1988

A LIVELY SMILE TO STAND ON

What a pretty day it is in Pigtown, and here comes Hunky Sauerhoff, right down to the corner near Sid's Tavern, right on time for our appointment. Hunky called Monday and said come over and meet "Baltimore's most endurable one-legged walker." Hunky, a proud native son, is always promoting Pigtown phenomena, and today the phenomenon is the one-legged Mr. Joseph Moyer of 1120 West Cross Street.

As we walk, the bright sun hurts Hunky's eyes. "I had a few drinks last night," he says. "I turned right into a monkey. All I need is a monkey mask. Boy, I tell ya, I turned right into a monkey." Hunky is also wearing a week-old beard. I ask how often he shaves.

"Whenever I feel like it," he says. "I take pliers and break the plastic off them little Bic razors. That's what I use. I probably get 190 shaves on one blade. But it's probably dangerous for retarded people to do that; they might cut theirselves."

Today, not even a hairy hangover will keep us from visiting One-Legged Moyer. "He's amazing," Hunky says. "He lays cinder block, puts up paneling, and everything. And he'll beat me out in a hundred-yard dash any day, brother." We are welcomed into the Moyer home, and here is the man of the house sitting in a wheelchair in the middle of the front room. The stump of his right leg is the first thing that catches my eye. The smile is the second thing. Mr. Joseph Moyer has the grin of a leprechaun, charming and clean and full of energy. He has a laugh that bounces off the ceiling.

"That laugh's known all over Baltimore," Mr. Moyer says. Let it be clear that what we have here is not some sad tale of an old man who lost his leg and lives a life of hobbling desperation. Nothing like that. Mr. Moyer, who is seventy-two, does not want sympathy. He comes across as a tough and happy old boy with a streak of independence two blocks long. You should see that smile of his.

Right now, Mr. Moyer awaits a phone call from "a relation in the family" who wants him to install a "spicket" in a shower. And he just finished laying a plywood floor in a house. Mr. Moyer is a Pigtown handyman. Always has been. The amputation of his right leg nine years ago didn't slow him down a step. He didn't even cry about it. "Of course not," Mr. Moyer says indignantly. "Christ, babies do that. You gotta be strong. I'm an Irishman." He was born in Pigtown, the youngest of fifteen children. He grew up around Ostend and Ridgely, where the Top Hat nightclub was. One of the boys from that old neighborhood was Hacky Hoffman.

"He weighed 480 pounds," Hunky says of Hacky.

"More like seven hundred," Mr. Moyer declares. "When he died, they had to take out the front window to get him out of the house. . . . There's a picture somewhere of Hacky on a little scooter." These are the tales of which Pigtown folklore is made. So are the ones about how Joe Moyer came to be One-Legged Moyer and how he managed to live his life on one foot.

"I was a plumber for sixty years," he says, and that includes several years as a laborer. "We would lay a sewage pipe from a house to the street. Sometimes you had to go down three or four feet or sometimes five feet. I was in four cave-ins. I was covered in a ditch with a big rock pressing against my leg."

Later on, those old ditch-digger injuries caught up with him. The circulation in his right leg went bad and it was amputated when Mr. Moyer was sixty-three. But the day he came home from the hospital, he finished installing a new ceiling in his house. "Feel that arm," he says, and he flexes and I feel the muscle in his left arm and it is hard as oak. Now Mr. Moyer wants to show how he installs a ceiling. He hoists himself, puts his surviving foot on the wheelchair, and stands, one-legged, in the middle of the room. "I dance, too," Mr. Moyer says.

"You should see him dance," Hunky says. "Hey, Joe, when were you supposed to die?"

"Oh, I was just a baby. That was the big flu, what did they call it? Diphtheria. It was going around."

"The doctor said he was supposed to die," Hunky adds.

"They wanted to put braces on my legs," Mr. Moyer says. "But they didn't. I never had braces." And he hardly ever wears the artificial leg which, at this moment, is leaning against the TV set in Mr. Moyer's living room. "I do all right," he says modestly.

"He walks everywhere," Hunky says, "I seen him out Route 40. Way out by East Baltimore. Seven days a week, Joe's walking somewhere, walking way out, way out somewhere." And he always walks with forearm crutches. Some days he walks to the Inner Harbor.

"What do you do there?" I ask.

"Talk to the girls," he says, and the grin explodes and the laugh goes up to the ceiling. You should hear the laugh of One-Legged Moyer. You should see his smile. They make you glad to be alive on the pretty day in Pigtown.

March 27, 1985

THE BEAUTY OF HILDA

Hilda Morris was a waitress, but in the kind assessment of a friend, not a very good one. She was a small finch of a woman, slow and ungraceful, something odd to look at. She appeared a lot older than her forty-six years. With her thick eyeglasses, round nose, square jaw, and funny teeth, her looks were those for whom the word homely is reserved.

When her photograph was presented across a table the other afternoon, the beauty of this little woman -- and there was, of course, something exquisitely beautiful about Hilda Morris -- escaped the eye. Her face was the ordinary face that waits at bus stops, that disappears easily in crowds, that is seen but not remembered -- or is remembered only because it becomes familiar.

At Lum's in Randallstown, where Hilda waited tables, she became familiar to customers, some because they wished to avoid her, others because they liked her. There might have been a bit of pity in the five dollar tips two young men regularly gave her. She made up for her slow, awkward manner by working hard, by staying late to help Shirley Collins, the night manager. She was always willing to come in when Shirley needed an extra hand. Hilda was a quiet woman who never said much about her past. At times, however, she confided in Shirley.

"She said she was married once," Shirley said. "She had two children but her husband took the children and went off when the children were young. I think she spent many years alone. She had a little dog, Pepper, a Lhasa-cross."

And Hilda had one close friend in the world, a woman in her mid-fifties named Jean Etchinson. "Hilda had lived downtown," Shirley recalled. "I think she worked in a carry-out somewhere. She lived with Jean, and the two of them moved to the county here in 1986, or early '87.

"For a long time, I never met Jean, but I spoke with her on the phone. She sounded like an educated woman with a good vocabulary, stable and even a little stern. She was very protective of Hilda. I had the impression that they were two lonely people, and that Jean was taking care of Hilda."

There was something mysterious about Jean, and it intrigued Shirley Collins. "Hilda said Jean was a nurse of some kind. She visited people in their homes, usually elderly people who had just come out of the hospital. But she didn't always work steadily. Hilda always worked and, I think, handled all the money, what little bit there was."

It wasn't until last fall, when doctors found cancer in Hilda, that Shirley met Jean. "I went to the house they rented together," she said. "I went over there to tell Jean that she had to find a job now because Hilda couldn't support them any more. . . . Jean was a tall, thin woman with reddish-auburn hair in a page-boy cut. She was very plain. . . . She went in the bedroom and closed the door.

"That was when Hilda told me that she and Jean weren't really sisters; she had told me that once. She said, 'We're *like* sisters.' She told me that when she was living downtown in '85, she was walking her dog through a park, and she saw this lady. She was living in the park. She was a bag lady. Hilda told Jean that she had a house, that she could come home with her. . . . Hilda was very innocent; she didn't see any bad out there.

"I realized right then," Shirley added, "that it hadn't been Jean caring for Hilda, but the other way around. Hilda had done a lot for Jean that I didn't know about." That no one knew about.

In the park that day in 1985, Hilda Morris had taken into her life a woman who, like herself, had no one and needed someone. The quiet little waitress, who lacked so many skills, had offered heart and home to a very troubled stranger, which is evidence of beauty unseen in a photograph. Hilda saw in Jean a way to end the loneliness in her life.

Jean must have felt the same way, perhaps even more so. Last fall, when it was clear that her friend was going to die, Jean left Hilda before Hilda could leave her. She walked off into the woods during an extremely cold weekend. She died from exposure. The police recovered the body. Shirley Collins identified it. Hilda was shattered.

"I guess," said Shirley, "that Jean was just afraid of being left alone again."

Hilda fought on. She spent the next eight months enduring the cancer, making trips to the hospital without complaint. She moved in with Shirley Collins on June eleventh. She died a few days later.

"To the end," Shirley said, "Hilda was very courageous." To the end very beautiful.

June 27, 1988

GIFT FROM A STRANGER

The detail is hardly worth mentioning and, besides, it probably had nothing to do with the gift from the mystery lady in the raincoat. But the hole in Nick's pants was there; it was definitely there. And any flatfoot worth his Florsheims would consider it a factor.

After all, boys will be boys. Given time and kiddie tectonics, they will crack holes in a pair of khakis. That was Nick. In the winter, his green pants sprouted a smile the size of a dollar at the right knee. His mother patched the hole with blue material and forgot about it. Two Sundays ago, Nick wore the pants to church. He went with his mother, Gina DeLeonardis. Ms. DeLeonardis, a young working parent, has the honor of being mother to this four-and-a-half-year-old future matinee idol named Nick.

Nick is a short stack of puppy-dog boy with a cap of curly brown hair and a puddin' face. He looks like one of those kids who play soccer in the narrow streets of Italian movies, then scurry out of the way when a Fiat comes screeching through. Cute? Nick's the kid for whom they invented the word. So it is not surprising that people come up to his mother and make kind comments about her little boy. In fact, she's used to it. Especially in church. Gina and Nick attend St. John's Catholic Church in Hydes, northeastern Baltimore County.

On the day in question, Nick was very good. He did not tease his mother's tumbling brown locks, did not stand on the pew, did not complain about the length of the sermon. He was quite the young gentleman and, at some point during mass, he caught the mystery lady's eye. The mystery lady will be described as grandmotherly for that is what Gina DeLeonardis remembers of her. That, and her dark raincoat.

The lady sat across the middle aisle and to the rear by four pews. She noticed Nick and seemed to appreciate him as a cute kid. And when Gina turned and caught her eye, the lady smiled. Gina smiled back. But that was all -- a brief exchange that takes place when eyes intersect in crowded churches. And that day, St. John's was crowded; the church seemed to swell even more when mass ended and the parishioners started to leave.

Gina held Nick's hand as they made their way through the crowd. And now the little old lady in the dark raincoat made a move. Here she was, with the grandma face, looking up into Gina's eyes and smiling again. Here she was, speaking words: "You've got such a precious little boy . . ." And the old lady pushed her hand into Gina's. "Here . . ." Flesh against flesh, with small paper in between. "Buy him something for me."

Just like that, and nothing more and nothing less, without another word, the old lady in the raincoat vanished into the crowd. Vanished so quickly and smoothly and softly that her face faded from Gina's mind. Just like that. "The fairy grandmother disappeared," Gina said.

Now Nick was announcing that he had to visit a bathroom. Gina's mind was spinning and sure, Nick, OK, let's go downstairs to the boys' room. She did not look at the paper in her hand. Did not bring it up to her face. Did not even open it. In fact, she paused at a charity basket and considered dropping the paper in. "But no. If she wanted that, she would have done it herself," Gina thought. So Nick descended the stairs. And Gina stood on the stairs, the paper in her hand. Then Gina brought the paper up. And she unfolded it. And she expected to see a dollar bill or maybe a five dollar bill but what she saw was a hundred dollar bill. And this left Gina DeLeonardis dazed.

She told Nick, and Nick thought it was nice. She told the priest and the priest said well, if the money was intended for Nick, then the old lady gave it to the right person. This did not settle Gina's mind. But something else did, and you don't have to be a detective to figure it out.

The perfect gift comes with no strings; it's given for the pure pleasure of giving. Maybe the patch in Nick's pants had something to do with it. Maybe not. An old generous woman in a dark raincoat wanted to give something to a little boy she didn't know. "It lit up everything," Gina said. "And I'm one of the biggest cynics I know. But you know what? Everyone I've told the story to believes it. And that means something too."

Last Sunday, at the same mass, Gina gawked but was unable to find Nick's mystery benefactress. Maybe it's better like that. So, in the meantime, Gina wants to say thanks, whoever you are. She bought Nick a savings bond and a new Easter suit and he's thrilled. Especially about the suit. He likes the suit a lot.

March 24, 1982

CHRISTMAS CAROLS

I get inspired -- read that "cornball" -- around Christmas. But then, none but a curmudgeon can avoid it. The season brings the sentimental out of the toughest of man and woman. Me, I'm a total wimp for a good Christmas story. So I try to treat readers to one or two each year. That's the great thing about a column -- you can use it to send little gifts to your friends. So come Christmas, I let it bleed. I want peace, love, and charity -- even if it only lasts a day or so.

A CHRISTMAS WISH OR TWO

I want Christmas the way Norman Rockwell painted it. I want Bing Crosby on the hi-fi, Nat King Cole on the radio, the old Scrooge movie on TV, mother wrapping gifts in the basement, and father out in the woods freezing his rear and cutting down Large Louie's best scotch pine. Pardon the corn, friends. But it's been a rough year. So let's go for it.

Let's have every homeowner in the neighborhood put candles in the windows and string white lights on the shrubs all up and down the street. I want snow. Not too much. Just enough to make the world look like a scene from Gorky Park.

I want kids on the sidewalks singing carols. They should have thick mufflers around their throats and large stupid-looking winter hats. Angels with dirty faces. Let's make their cheeks red too, give them runny noses. And then, let's have some nice old lady send out hot chocolate to thank them for the song.

Let's have every choir in every church suddenly sound like the Vienna Boys Choir. I want to hear Freddie Lombardi singing Ave Maria up in the choir loft. The churches should be bright and alive at midnight, with the people in their best clothes and the preacher saying nice things about the spirit of the season. He should *boom* about the spirit of the season! And I don't want to hear a single priest criticize anyone for showing up just at Christmas and avoiding church the rest of the year. Let's have none of that.

Empty all the hospitals. Send all the kids home. Clear out the nursing homes. If we can't manage that, then let's have caravans of cheerful people visiting everyone in an institution. I want to see Aunt Sadie, a nurse in the veterans' hospital, wheeling the invalids out into the hall to sing and have some hot cider. And I want families and friends to visit those guys. No one should be alone this weekend. That's a tall order. But, hell, if you can't wish these things at Christmas, when can you?

I want all single parents to bury their misery in the joy of being with their kids. I want all divorced fathers to be with friends if they can't be with their kids. I want people like Sue and Dick, both divorced, to help other single parents cope with the feeling of being left out at Christmas. They're having an ecumenical worship service at Towson United Methodist tomorrow night. I don't want anyone left out this time.

There should be no desolate-looking old men standing in subways or doorways on Christmas Eve. No man or woman should have to pick through the dumpsters of a city for a Christmas meal. I want every door of every house to open for travelers and out-of-towners. No one should have Christmas dinner in a Howard Johnson's. I want people baking cookies. I want them hustling around the malls, doing last-minute shopping, and bumping into old friends.

I want young men and women getting engaged in the glow of Christmas trees. I want old folks sitting by the fire and reminiscing about how they never had much but always managed to give the children a Christmas. That's always nice. I want people with comfortable, healthy lives to consider how lucky they are. I want people feeling good about their families, their friends, their town.

I want the dying to stop. I want the killing to cease. I want the Marines home and the battleships in drydock.

I want soldiers hugging their girlfriends. So let's have one last round at Dypsky's and be gone. Let's keep the drunks from killing themselves and others. Let's close the emergency rooms with the hope they won't be needed. Send all the cops and nurses and doctors home for the night.

I want to stop all the yelling and punching in families, and I want people who haven't spoken to each other for a while to realize that life is too short and that it's Christmas. I want them to kiss and make up.

Somewhere in the night, I want old friends to think of each other. Maybe they're apart now. Maybe they've gone off and married and started families. But I still want them to think of each other, their youth, the years, and the fun they had together.

Think of the happiest Christmas you ever had. Then look around, here in 1983, and let the memories come. Because, whenever times are tough -- and they are always tough -- memories carry the day. Young people should be nice to old people. Old people should tell young people about the great ethnic Christmas traditions. I want to hear some stories this Christmas. I want to be there when the kids come down the stairs and see the tree.

I want them to have the memory of Christmas so that in later years they'll know how lucky they were. I want all the whining and complaining to stop. I want people to be grateful for what they have and I want them to share it with others. And, like everyone, I want the spirit to live forever.

I'm hopeless, I know. But that's what I want for Christmas.

December 23, 1983

CHRISTMAS ROSE

The doctor told my mother to put me into a room, to pull the shades, draw the drapes, and close the door. Feed the boy medicine. She followed orders, leaving me in the dark quarantine in the days leading up to Christmas. I had measles, and darkness was said to help keep a measled kid from hurting his eyes. During the day, the light in the room was orange-brown. At night, it was pitch black. From the window, a seven-year-old boy could hear the voices of other kids, coming from school, playing in snow. In the bedroom, an old radiator hissed; the rest of the house was silent. And, worst of all, it was Christmas.

Christmas, my mother said, was always the best time. Even when I was seven and sick and the world was dark; even when my father's business burned to the ground and he went to the hospital. Christmases are a medley of groggy memories now.

But one or two of them keep coming back because they were entwined in darkness, and because my mother tried to make them glow. She always tried, especially after the fire. It destroyed my father's foundry, his business for fifteen years. One night in autumn, something went wrong with the propane tank, and that was the end of it. A little while later, he went to a hospital with emphysema -- thirty years of foundry dust and cigarettes choking his lungs. He was away for a long time. Too long. And so Rose Rodricks had no choice; she took a job in an electronic components plant.

And me, I remember that Christmas of a dark bedroom and measles and feeling sorry for myself. I already had been beaten up by consecutive jabs of tonsilitis, chicken pox, and mumps. I missed a month of the second grade. "You had it good," everyone says now. I spent the Christmas season in a dark room, with no visitors except my mother. When my older brother came home from college, he just stuck his head into the bedroom and said hello. So it was only my mother, each day with pills and juice and food and school work the teacher brought to the house.

For the first time that I could remember, there was no magic in the days before Christmas. No music. No laughter. All families have days like that. And I started to worry, there, in the dark. My mother, who always had been the source of Christmas spirit, didn't ask what we wanted. She didn't ask me, and she didn't ask my younger brother. So, when you are little and sick and there is no laughter in a house, you worry. You lie there, in the dark, and listen to sounds coming through the walls, hoping for laughter.

Little kids get hints; they know when things are wrong, and in those days it was very easy to forget that Christmas should always be the best time. "When we were little, all we ever got was an orange in the stocking." She said that every Christmas, but in the bad years she said it more often. Like every day. And after a while, I sort of got the message and rolled back into the darkness.

Christmas Eve arrived, and my mother came home and, after supper, I think she went out somewhere with my older brother. I think I heard them leaving through the kitchen door. They were gone a very long time. In fact, I don't remember hearing their return. And I had stayed up, waiting for them, listening for sounds in the house. But there were none.

Then, at last, I must have fallen asleep because the next thing I remember is the door to the bedroom opening. She was there again, and she whispered and took my hand. Now, for the first time in two weeks, I was out of the black bedroom. We were walking through the kitchen. I felt her robe and held her hand. We walked into the dining room, then the living room and, through the windows, I could see that it was still dark outside. Still very early. And there was not a sound in the house. Everyone still sleeping, except her and me.

When we were, finally, in the living room, she said, "Now stand there." She went over and stuck a plug into the wall and suddenly, like a comet from the night sky, a Christmas tree appeared, full and glowing. It glowed so wildly it hurt my eyes, which were tender. The tall, gaunt tree gave light to a season of darkness. I put my hands to my face, then slowly pulled them away. She leaned down and flicked a switch, and a train started to move. The train set had no straight sections of track. There were only bends in the track, so that it made a circle, and I looked down and watched the yellow engine and a green cattle car move around the track. It made a loud scratching noise, and it was the only sound.

Soon, I was back in the darkness, in the bedroom, and my brothers and my sister and grandmother were awake now. I could hear them through the walls. I could hear laughter through the walls, and my mother's voice. In that house, that season, anyone who laughed owed it to her.

December 24, 1982

LIGHT FOR SERGIO

Walking through the holiday traffic in the sprawling parking lot of the big American shopping mall, Sergio Rossi looked up and rediscovered light. There it was, gleaming in the night, the first letter in the first sign Sergio Rossi had been able to read in 14 years:

J.

And then another letter:

C.

And another:

P.

And then E and N and N and E and Y.

"Posso legere," Sergio Rossi said, quietly astonished. "I can read." The three people with him, who were guiding Sergio across the parking lot, stopped and gazed at the beacon that had awakened the nerves in his left eye. The first thing the blind man from Italy could read was a large brilliant sign on the exterior wall of the big American shopping center. Fourteen and a half years after the explosion that blinded him, Sergio Rossi's day of light had come in the night, in the darkness, when he said, "J. C. Penney."

There was a time, of course, when Sergio would have taken such a spectacle for granted -- as we with the gift of sight do every day of our lives. Back in 1970, he was twenty-three years old, a self-employed contractor in a small village called Capolona in Arezzo, Tuscany. One day in June of that year, Sergio was twenty-four feet into the earth, digging a well. When he hit stone, he decided to blast his way through, for the vein of water was not far away. He packed powder and set a charge, but the charge didn't work. So there was Sergio, working a three-foot rod around the hole in which he had placed the explosive powder, trying to clean it out so he could set a new charge. There was a spark. There was a flash. His older brother, Graziano Rossi, says it was more like an explosion. Sergio lost his right eye completely. His left eye was full of debris. His face was full of blood. His days as a digger of wells were over. He could see slices of light through the left eye for a while but, a few months later, when an infection set in and a doctor tried to treat it, the slight vision that remained in the left eye disappeared.

It was about eight years before Sergio went back to work. He found a job as a telephone operator for a bank. Never, he says, did he lose the hope of seeing again, of waking up in a day of light. He prayed to Santa Lucia, the patron saint of vision. He underwent a dozen operations. He visited a faith healer named Mama Lucia, who told him his future included a day of light, and that he would find the light in America. In 1983, an Italian doctor told him of an American specialist, an eye surgeon from Baltimore, who might be able to help him. Sergio just had to be patient. Someday he would get a phone call.

The call came last September, as eye surgeons from around the world convened in Rome. Sergio went there and, for twenty-three hours over two days, doctors from Germany, Japan, and Spain examined his left eye. They all agreed that Walter Stark, from the Wilmer Eye Institute at Johns Hopkins Hospital, was the man for the job. He was probably best suited to perform a cornea transplant on Sergio's left eye and handle the tricky complications that might result.

Go to America, Sergio was told. They had advanced techniques for tissue-matching and microsurgery there. The world's leading eye bank is in Baltimore and there's a supply of "good donor material," as the doctors say. This, of course, would require money, about seven thousand dollars for the trip and operation. Sergio's friends and co-workers at the bank pitched in. They raised fourteen thousand dollars. And by early December, Sergio and Graziano were on a plane for America.

The transplant took place at Hopkins on December thirteenth, which happens to be the Feast of Santa Lucia on the Roman Catholic calendar. Stark cut a donated cornea to fit Sergio's left eye and, working through a microscope, sewed it into place. The first few days after surgery were mostly a blur to Sergio, but he could see slices of light again. As blood deposits in his eye cleared up, more light filtered through his new cornea.

One week after surgery, as he walked across the parking lot of the big shopping mall near Baltimore, J. C. Penney appeared from the darkness. And there were more lights in the mall, and he could see cars and street lights and Christmas decorations and smiles on the faces of strangers. Sergio Rossi was quietly astonished.

On New Year's Eve, in a rowhouse in Baltimore's Little Italy, he was shooting pool.

January 2, 1985

LITTLE EDDIE'S BIG NIGHT

Though it was probably unfair and though he tried hard to prove otherwise, Little Edward Hennessey had a reputation as a sissy. This was about twenty years ago, I guess, when he was about eight and lived a few doors down the street. Little Edward grew up with future dentists and second-story men; it was a typical American neighborhood, with some tough guys and some nellies, but most of the kids just something in-between.

Most kids considered him a sissy. Sissies got shining report cards and easily won the affection of teachers. Little Edward was not very bright. In school, he was pretty dense, with his mind usually up in the clouds when the teacher called on him. On the street, he was also slow. His major stupidity was trying to be like the other kids.

At the age of seven, he was dared to bust the watermelons in Pasquale Viola's garden. But when he tried this, Little Edward found himself being chased by a dog with a mouth the size of a parking garage. When Little Edward, who was chubby, tried to play football with the other kids, he was always picked last, and the results were always the same: His mother called him home at halftime. I can still hear her -- "EeeeedddddWARD, home now, this instant!" After a while, Little Edward spent most of his time indoors, either reading books or practicing the saxophone. He loved music, and one Christmas we learned how great that love was, and we finally discovered that he was no sissy at all. In fact, he was probably the bravest kid among us.

One of the things that contributed to Little Edward's reputation as a nellie was his unwillingness to give up on Santa Claus. He tried to be very cool when the older boys said, "Ah, there ain't no Santa Claus. Your mother buys all the presents." So at the age of eight, Little Edward finally popped the question while his mother was ironing shirts in the kitchen.

"Santa Claus visits the house of everyone who believes in him," she said. "Only the kids who don't believe get gifts from their parents. I still believe. And your father still believes." And after that, he still believed, though the local youth continued to give him a hard time. His chubby face broke into a weird little grin when one of the older kids told him Santa Claus was a fake. Soon, Little Edward went about his business and kept away from the other kids; he had learned the dangers of trying to be like them.

That Christmas came during a particularly snowy season, and we hardly ever saw Little Edward outdoors. We didn't even think about him. We'd be out building snow forts and throwing snowballs at public works trucks. But Little Edward would be indoors, listening to a Mitch Miller sing-along Christmas album. We all learned this after the fact.

During the days leading up to Christmas, he played the Mitch Miller album over and over on his father's hi-fi. The lyrics to the songs came with the album. And one day, Little Edward had a brainstorm. He would copy all the lyrics on separate sheets of paper and hand them out to other kids, and we'd all go caroling on Christmas Eve. He must have picked up this idea from some old Bing Crosby movie. Whatever, Little Edward was inspired. So for two days, he copied the lyrics to about ten different Christmas carols on large sheets of blue paper. Then, on the day before Christmas Eve, when we all got out of school, he came from his house with the papers in his hands.

"How 'bout we all sing Christmas songs tomorrow night?" Little Edward said. Immediately, the gang broke into laughter. There must have been seven or eight kids laughing at him at once. Then the laughing stopped, and someone called him a sissy again. I can't remember if I threw snowballs at him, but I know I stood there and watched it -- with the blue papers flying into the snow -- and I've felt lousy about it ever since. To this day, I feel like I missed something by being among those who avoided Little Edward.

Because, that Christmas Eve, after dinner, we heard a muffled voice coming from outside. We went to the frosted windows. Someone flicked on the porch light. And there -- standing on the snowy sidewalk, the blue papers in his hands, a scarf around his neck, and a red stocking hat on his large head -- was Little Edward. And he was singing as loud as he could, in a funny crackling voice. And he was alone.

He sang two songs, "Jingle Bells" and "I Saw Mommy Kissing Santa Claus." Then he moved on to the next house, the Rings, where there were large flood lights, and he sang two more songs. And on and on, down the street. I remember older people standing in the front doors of the houses, applauding, and saying, "Very good, Edward," and sending cookies and hot chocolate out to him. And there was a great smile on his face. No one in that neighborhood has ever forgotten that night, especially, I'm sure, Little Edward himself. He was king of the street. Standing out there, alone, with nothing but a voice, the spirit of the season, and blue paper with lyrics, took a lot of nerve. More nerve than any other kid in the neighborhood had.

December 20, 1982

A CHAIR FOR JASON

The boys strung red, white, and blue pennants over the front of the Fort McHenry American Legion Post, 506 East Fort Avenue, and someone made a sign that said, "Today is Jason's Day," a very important day indeed. The boys had been waiting all year for this. This was the day Jason Stigler, a Tiny Tim of our times, got his wheels.

So as the hour approached, there was much merriment and handshaking like crazy at Post 133. The American Legion boys were out on the sidewalk in their overseas caps -- Carlton Howard and Eddie Floyd, Uncle Jessi Curtis, Joe Nuth, Ray Pollack, and Phil Prestianni, Jay Ruffini, Richard League, Tom Ridgley, and Greg Carson. They had a couple from Boumi Temple dressed as clowns and a guy decked out like Uncle Sam. They were all waiting for Jason.

The bar was packed and noisy and when Brooks Robinson walked in, there was a great movement of bodies and hands and pats on the back. The three city councilmen from the Sixth District -- Joe DiBlasi, Willie Myers, and Tim Murphy -- were facing the door, their backs to the bar. Someone even brought a proclamation from the mayor's office. A big day indeed.

Just after one p.m. a guy said, "There's Jason. There's the boy now." All heads turned toward the front door and in walked Uncle Jessi Curtis with a bundle in his arms. The bundle had soft sandy hair, neatly parted, and eyes like chestnuts. People with tender hearts should not look at bundles like this. Jason Stigler's small legs hung down from under Uncle Jessi's arms and you could see the white socks and the steel braces that went from his shoes up into his pants. His mother, Cindy Stigler, had dressed her son in a brown corduroy sport coat and brown flannel pants, a dress shirt with a button-down collar, and one of those clip-on ties that look splendid on little boys. In all the hugging, the tie had started to come off Jason's collar, so Uncle Jessi tucked it back into place.

There are things you should know about Jason Stigler before we go upstairs for the ceremony. He was born with spina bifida, a terrible birth defect in which the spinal column fails to close. For parents, the cost of raising a child with spina bifida is fantastic. Jason has had five operations. His braces cost two thousand dollars. He can get along slowly with a walker, but what he really needed was a wheelchair. Jason's mother and father are divorced. Cindy Stigler is a twenty-eight-year-old nurse. She and Jason live in an apartment in Arbutus. A bit more than a year ago, Cindy Stigler, whose ex-husband is a veteran, had inquired about federal benefits for her boy. But there were none. Sometime after that, word got around that an Arbutus woman was looking for a wheelchair for her son. It's unclear how this whole thing started but, for the last year, the American Legion has been raising money for a boy named Jason.

"Two dances and raffles and donations," Bob Davis said. "That's how we raised the money for the wheelchair." Why, you might ask, does it take a year of fund-raising by the American Legion to put a five-year-old boy in a wheelchair? The government spends millions in tax dollars to send two-thousand-pound shells flying into the mountains of Syria but Cindy Stigler couldn't get some help from her government for a wheelchair.

"I make too much money," is what Cindy Stigler, a single parent, says she was told. Maybe that was all beside the point now because the ceremony was starting and they sat Jason Stigler down in a chair next to Brooks Robinson. Brooks said hello. Jason said, "Who are you?" When Santa Claus came into the room it was as if Jason had been hit with a bolt of electricity. His hands started flapping and he said, "Ma, ma, ma, ma, Santa Claus!" There were a few speeches. The American Legion boys congratulated each other and Brooks stood and said it was a fine thing to have done for little Jason, a small lad who makes big people stop and count their blessings.

Then it was time for the chair, so they pushed it into the room and that was the first time Jason Stigler cried in all the excitement and camera flashes of the day. Uncle Jessi picked him up and placed him in the chair and he tried to say something but he couldn't. Jessi Curtis' face was dripping with tears. Jason's pretty grandmother, Helen Hipsley, put a tissue to her face. The whole room was quiet now and there's not much you can say about a scene like that. If there was a dry eye in the place, I didn't see it. Jason's chair is a Catalina stainless with blue padding. Ken Nycum, from Post 187, said it cost $1,292. The boy took to it right away, put his hands on the wheels, and started rolling. "Hey that's good," Brooks told him. "That's pretty good."

Joe Sefa, who was running the ceremony, asked if anyone else had anything to say, and there was silence. People started getting up to leave. Jason had a word with Santa Claus, told him what he wanted for Christmas. Then he played with some toys "one of these guys gave me" and he wheeled himself across the room in the new chair. "Know what?" Jason said. "I wanna have a race with my Hot Wheels buggy."

His therapist, Cindy Potter, arrived late and she bent down to Jason and said, "Do you remember who I am?" Jason paused, then reached out from the wheelchair with his left hand, pulled on Cindy Potter's chin, and puckered his lips. He was a very grateful lad.

December 19, 1983

THE MAN WHO HAD EVERYTHING

There came a time when Jack and Dorothy had, you might say, everything. Well, maybe no man, no woman, ever has everything, but with enough money in a money-conscious, go-for-it world, you can come pretty close.

It's a matter of the mind and of the heart. Everyone measures success differently. One man's poverty is another's prosperity. By the end of 1982, Jack and Dorothy had reached, you might say, the peak of personal wealth. They had everything. At least, that's how Dorothy came to see it.

As Christmas approached, her conscience started to itch. Every year at this time, Dorothy sat in her splendid home in Guilford and tried to dream up the perfect gift for her husband and got depressed. One year, she gave Jack a sauna. Each year she tried to outdo herself. After a while, it all seemed pointless. If there was such a thing as the Christmas spirit, it didn't present itself in any of the material things Dorothy considered giving Jack. Finally, she developed a plan. She wanted to find some needy kids and bring Christmas to them. She wanted to set the whole thing up and surprise Jack with the Christmas Eve assignment of delivering the goods.

Dorothy's conscience was itching again. Something told her this was the way to celebrate Christmas, the way to say thank-you for the big house, a great husband, two healthy daughters, and all the other blessings in her life. So she called a nun in South Baltimore, Sister Mary Patricia, principal of the school at St. Mary, Star of the Sea Church. Was there, Dorothy asked, some family down there that needed help?

In December 1982 the recession had set in for the winter, the unemployment rosters were long, people were out in the cold, standing in line for blocks of American cheese. Somewhere in South Baltimore, a man was out of work, and he had a wife, and they had eight children. Sister Mary Patricia gave Dorothy the address, the names of all the children, their ages, their clothing and shoe sizes. The kids wanted tennis shoes; that was all they had asked for.

Well, in a week or so, Dorothy had personally boosted retail sales in Baltimore department stores. She bought eight pairs of Nikes. She bought clothes for each of the children and something for their parents. Dorothy got her daughters involved in the project. They went into a closet and pulled out games they had never played with. "And that made me even more depressed," Dorothy says now. "Here were games we'd given the girls and they hadn't even taken the cellophane wrappers off. We'd spoiled them. Of course, we're all a little spoiled."

Christmas Eve came and, while Jack was at work, Dorothy and her daughters wrapped all the gifts. They filled the living room of the big house with packages. To top it all off, Dorothy wrote Jack a note explaining why his living room was filled with Christmas presents for two strangers and their eight children. He came home from the office and, when he saw all the gifts, Jack said, "What's this? We don't need all this. This is ridiculous." Then he read the note from Dorothy. It said that his Christmas gift for 1982 was Christmas for a family of needy strangers. Dorothy was giving him a family to share his blessings with. The note told him where to make the delivery.

When he finished crying, Jack changed his clothes, then he and his friend Bobby loaded a station wagon with the gifts and donned Santa caps. It was ten p.m. when they left Guilford and drove to South Baltimore. Jack went to the front door of the rowhouse and said, "I'm making a delivery for Sister Mary Pat." Then he started unloading the gifts. All the kids were in bed. Their parents stood in the cold house and watched and didn't say a word.

There were no rugs on the floor of the living room. There were eight small gifts under a tiny Christmas tree. Stockings with a few pieces of candy were hanging on the mantel. And Jack and Bobby kept coming through the front door with gifts, filling the room with gifts, filling the night, you might say, with the magic of Christmas.

December 17, 1984

POSTFACE

by

Alexander Clunas

Dr. Clunas is an assistant professor of writing at Loyola College in Maryland where he teaches courses in writing about travel and neighborhoods.

As the cliche has it, Baltimore is a city of neighborhoods. If you look at one of those Planning Department maps, you see a crazed proliferation of boundaries created by politics, class, industry, race, topography, immigration. Every big city breaks up into villages, because the modern city is too big to function as an organic and personal unit: Greenwich Village, Oak Park, Kensington, Passy. These villages belong to metropolises, and their inhabitants call themselves New Yorkers, Chicagoans, Londoners, Parisians, thus achieving a kind of double loyalty, to the political entity of the City, on the one hand, and to the more intimate locality, on the other. Despite the distress of many of its neighborhoods, Baltimore often manages the trick.

But, political and geographical boundaries don't always mean much in themselves. I can move tomorrow to Greenwich or Charles Village. This doesn't mean that I belong to a community. The important thing about Baltimore is that, despite the depredations of the flight to the suburbs and often uneven development, it clings in its neighborhoods to a sense of community. In fact, its very failures in development (beyond the Holy Shrine of the Inner Harbor of St. Rouse) may have contributed to the livability of its neighborhoods; it may have benefited, as well as suffered, from being the hole in the County doughnut. To say this is not to underplay at all the social-economic miseries of many city areas and the impoverishment of its communal resources.

The word community is a difficult one. The Latin original *(communitatem)* could be used pretty neutrally to refer to the "common people" or the folk who inhabited a certain district or neighborhood. Later on, it came to mean those individuals who had a community of "interests" or "beliefs" or "goods." In other words, the term shifted from being a cold description of the taxpayers or residents of such and such an area to describing a quality of *relationship*, the way persons dealt with each other.

Dan Rodricks came from the Commonwealth of Massachusetts to Baltimore in 1976, and he writes about people in the context of this latter quality of relationship, though often about individuals for whom community has failed. The best pieces in this collection of this columns about Baltimoreans speak about the successes and failures of our community in stories. There is the narrative of the ten-hour marathon attempt to save "Margaret," a lady of the streets brought to the emergency ward suffering from hypothermia and a heart attack. There is the intensely dramatic story of a professional fireman who struggled for, and won, his life in a dockside blaze. There is the sketch of a young boy casually tormenting a pigeon in his back yard, both of them -- boy and pigeon -- prisoners. Rodricks has also some success in following back to their beginnings those bitter tales which only end in our courtrooms. In thus telling the stories of our lives and deaths, he reminds us of our broader connections to others.

Some might say that these pieces are ephemeral, that they are brief reports on the passing pageant of the City, and that they have no significance for the task of understanding and improving Baltimore. This would be a false impression. It is in the moment and in stories that we can get a handle on reality, not in the "blue ribbon" reports and the social scientists' analyses, though these too have their place. For instance, I think I first decided to move to Baltimore at a very specific moment. I was commuting at the time from Annapolis. I came in on 292, over that rise that lets you hit the Bumps at sixty, down to Russell Street, at six-thirty a.m. with Hopkins radio playing Wagner, and the sky over downtown a smoky lilac, as I roller-coasted in. That was just a moment, soon past, and not much as epiphanies go. But, it was actual, luminous, and it had nothing to do with house prices, amenity-indexes, or the like. In fact, the sky was probably that lovely color from extensive air pollution.

Many of Dan Rodricks' columns describe instants of illumination like that. I would call these efforts sketches. They come out of what he saw, just walking through a neighborhood or standing on the corner looking, looking closely. The others, the majority, could be called stories, because they have an element of plot about them -- the plot of a dramatic event or of a life. They are seldom "success stories." In fact, they concentrate most on the people who have missed out on prosperity. While we gape at the millions made by those young futures hustlers on the Chicago Exchange, Rodricks reminds us that Americans die on the streets from hypothermia and surrender their lives to political whim like the temporary occupation of Lebanon. To the victims of the Reagan years he gives a local habitation and a name.

In both the sketches and the stories, Rodricks is the inheritor of a tradition in newspaper reporting, and indeed in American letters as a whole. Shelley Fishkin, in her book about that long list of American writers who started out as newspapermen, quotes Philip Rahv: "'[T]he basic theme and unifying principle' of American writing since Whitman was 'the urge toward immersion in experience.'" Twain, Dreiser, London, Crane, Dos Passos, Hemingway, were all at one time in their careers feature journalists, capturing the passing scene and telling the particular story. Stephen Crane, for instance, thought that some of his best work was contained in his short sketches of New York life in the 1890s, all of them done for an assortment of newspapers. Sometimes wryly voiced, sometimes bursting with compassion and anger, Crane's articles derive their strength from coming face to face with actuality, the immersion in experience. Here is part of Crane's description of the electric chair at Sing Sing:

The walls and ceiling were of polished wood and the atmosphere was weighted heavily with an odor of fresh varnish. . . The chair, too, was formed of polished wood. It might have been donated from the office of some generous banker.

A long, curved pipe swung from behind a partition and at the end of it there hung a wire almost as thick as a cigar. Some straps, formidably broad and thick, were thrown carelessly over the arms of the chair.

It is the focus on the detail that carries the emotional kick of this kind of reporting. Here is Rodricks, describing an eight-year-old boy who, the day before, had been arrested in possession of fourteen bags of cocaine.

The little boy grabbed the little pigeon and crumpled it in his hands as if the bird were a wad of black-and-white paper. Then the boy threw open his hands. The pigeon's wings unfurled, flapped, and made that familiar smacking sound. The bird flew limply, just above the concrete, into a cage beneath the rickety rear porch of the house.

In such passages, Rodricks' antennae are scanning the actual and bringing it home.

This does not mean that there is no sweat in making these pieces. Some of them, as I have said, look very immediate, like journal entries. But the bulk of the stories have solid journalistic legwork behind them. He has sought out and interviewed the kitchen worker at Our Daily Bread, and the second cousin of the victim, and the doctor who trained the intern who stopped the hemorrhage. He has checked his facts.

It's just that the facts can be as dead as fish on a marble slab, and journalists like Rodricks have the remit to go beyond the reportorial basics to try to affect their readers. We have seen the spread in recent years of what Jon Franklin calls "the non-fiction short story." In this *genre* the reporter works with many of the devices of the fiction short story (pacing devices, developed and consistent point of view, foreshadowing) in the interest of telling a true, verifiable story which nonetheless immerses the reader in experience. He or she tries to achieve intensity as well as accuracy.

The most intensely dramatic story in this collection, and the one which most closely approaches the narrative economy of a well-made short story, is "Fireman in the Water!" The story, although it is in the third person, indirectly recreates the point of view of the fireman, Don Schafer, only occasionally looping out for a short paragraph to explain the background or to give Schafer's own subsequent thoughts. It is well paced, closely focused on details, and exciting. Its themes are as old as stories: a life or death struggle against fire and water. And, unlike many of the tales in the book, it has a satisfactory resolution, as well as a hero. I invite you to re-read this piece and imagine the same incident being recounted in the accents and sequence of hard news reporting, and then to consider the advantages to human interest of short story technique as applied to events like this.

Most of the rest of the stories are sadder than that one, and Rodricks obviously feels that it is not possible to speak with quite the same warmth as Mencken did in 1913 of "[t]he indubitable charm of the old town." But, then, Mencken was a lover, and lovers are allowed to exaggerate the charms of the one they love. (As another, later, William Donald Schaefer, is apt to do.) In effect, the task of a writer reporting on

Baltimore must include resisting the rhetoric of those who see their primary job as marketing the City. As a consequence, *Mencken Doesn't Live Here Anymore* devotes a lot of attention to the underlife of Baltimore: to the dispossessed, the marginal, the ill, the transient, the victims of violence and of institutional indifference, as well as to those clinging to some kind of life through the blows of the Reagan years. It is also about those who try to help the people on the edge of community and beyond it.

If we take Dan Rodricks' stories to heart (and that organ is where most of them are aimed, unabashedly) then our chances of creating a real community, not just a more extensive tax-base, may be increased.